Red Diapers

Red Diapers

Growing Up in the Communist Left

Edited by

Judy Kaplan and Linn Shapiro

University of Illinois Press

Urbana and Chicago

The excerpt from Carl Bernstein's *Loyalties: A Son's Memoir* is
reprinted by permission of Carl Bernstein.
The excerpt from Kim Chernin's *In My Mother's House*, © 1983
by Kim Chernin, is reprinted by permission of Kim Chernin and
Ticknor & Fields/Houghton Mifflin Company. All rights reserved.
The excerpt from Mark Lapin's *Pledge of Allegiance* is reprinted by
permission of Mark Lapin. All rights reserved. © 1991 Mark Lapin.

Manufactured in the United States of America

1   2   3   4   5   C   P   5   4   3   2

This book is printed on acid-free paper.

Library of Congress Cataloging-in-Publication Data
Red diapers : growing up in the communist left / edited by Judy
Kaplan and Linn Shapiro.
p.   cm.
Includes bibliographical references (p.   ).
ISBN 0-252-02161-4 (acid-free paper)
ISBN 0-252-06725-8 (pbk. : acid-free paper)
1. Communism—United States—History—20th century—Sources.
2. Children and politics—History—20th century—Sources.
I. Kaplan, Judy, 1949–   . II. Shapiro, Linn.
HX83.R44   1998
335.4′092′273—ddc21
[B] 98-8905
CIP

For Joshua Phillip Kramer, in memory of his great-grandparents
Helen Schultz Chasman, Louis Chasman, Edith Zeitlin Kaplan,
and Nathan Kaplan;

and in memory of Barbara Flynn (1946–1973)

—Judy Kaplan

In memory of Esta Armstrong (1927–1995),
red diaper baby and organizer until her last breath;

and of Sophie Saroff (1896–1995),
mainstay of Camps Unity, Calumet, and Webatuck,
who nurtured generations of red diaper babies
with much more than food

—Linn Shapiro

Contents

Part 2: Political Trauma as Personal History

Part 3: Claiming Our Heritage

Acknowledgments

For their invaluable contributions to this book, our thanks to:

Stephanie Allan, Albert Vetere Lannon, Fred Solowey, Amy Swerdlow, and Marianne Ware for permission to use personal memorabilia and photographs; Beth Perry, for hours of work in preparing the manuscript; Susan Protter, for her professional insights and support; the staff of the Tamiment Institute Library, whose expertise has greatly enriched our understanding of U.S. Left history; the Somerville Community Computing Center, Somerville, Massachusetts, and the dedicated volunteers who provided technical assistance and ongoing support: Adam Glick, Nancy Havelka, Chris Lee, Patti Lee, Joe Marletta, Rob Miller, and Bosco So.

Introduction

Judy Kaplan and Linn Shapiro

The first red diaper babies were the children of Karl and Jenny Marx. Of the Marxes' seven children, only three survived to adulthood. Poverty, recurrent illness, and the strains of exile plagued the Marxes' London home. Yet family life was often remarkably ordinary. Eleanor, the youngest, rode on her father's shoulders, doodled on his correspondence, and demanded that her parents read fairy tales to her over and over again. "And woe to us," wrote Jenny Marx, "if we leave out a syllable from the story of Rumpelstilzchen or King Drosselbart or Snow Maiden."[1]

All three daughters supported their father's work. Jenny, the eldest, served as Marx's secretary and worked with the Fenians as they attempted to end British control of Ireland. She married an exiled member of the Paris Commune who was active in Marx's International Workingmen's Association, known as the First International. Together they eked out a meager living as teachers. Jenny Marx Longuet died, probably of bladder cancer, a month before her thirty-ninth birthday.

Laura retranslated *The Communist Manifesto* into French to improve on an inferior effort. She, too, married a man active in the First International. Marx disapproved—not of his son-in-law's politics but of his mixed French, Cuban, Dominican, and Caribbean Indian parentage. Ill health, poverty, and the early death of three children scarred the married life of Paul and Laura Lafargue. In 1911, approaching old age, without resources and not wishing to be a burden to the socialist movement, at Paul's initiative the couple jointly committed suicide by cyanide injection.

Of his youngest daughter, Marx said "Tussy [Eleanor] *is* me."[2] Six-year-old Eleanor wrote Abraham Lincoln with advice on how to conduct the Civil War. At age eight, she analyzed the Danish-Prussian conflict over Schleswig and Holstein and sided with the Poles—"those brave little fellows"—in their uprising against czarist Russia.[3] As a young adult, Eleanor considered a career in the theater and performed occasionally, but she instead became a full-time political activist—a founder of the Second International and a well-known speaker, writer, and union organizer. Eleanor's fact-checking and editing made possible the posthumous publication of many of her father's classic works, including *Wages, Price, and Profit* and the first volume of the English version of *Capital*.

Toward the close of the century, Eleanor Marx became discouraged by her inability to influence the direction of the British working-class movement as it veered from Marxism toward social democracy. Estranged from Friedrich Engels, who had provided emotional, intellectual, and financial support throughout her life, and learning that her longtime companion had married another woman, forty-three-year-old Eleanor Marx committed suicide.

Few red diaper babies have encountered the hardships faced by the Marx daughters, but we all have had to choose the degree to which we will become our parents' children, the extent to which we will accept or reject our political legacy. How we understand and evaluate our childhoods, our political inheritance, and our place in the history of this country is the subject of this anthology.

Between 1919, when the Communist Party of the United States of America (CP) was founded as an offshoot of the Socialist Party, and 1956, when Soviet leader Nikita Khrushchev repudiated the abuses of the Stalin decades, hundreds of thousands of people joined and left the CP.[4] Thousands more never became "card-carrying communists" but oriented their political and social lives around the Party, participating in CP-led organizations or in coalitions in which Party members played important roles.

In this anthology, we define red diaper babies as children of CP members, children of former CP members, and children whose parents never became members of the CP but were involved in political, cultural, or educational activities led or supported by the Party. (Both of us fit this definition.)

Not included are children of parents who were members of or close to the Socialist Party (SP) or the Socialist Workers Party (SWP)—the other major left-wing political parties in the United States from the 1920s through the 1950s. Although certain childhood experiences were shared (for example, the image of the FBI agent at the door is part of the collective memory of children throughout the U.S. Left), life differed in crucial ways for children of the CP and non-CP Lefts.[5] A woman who grew up in an SWP family in Los Angeles explained one distinction: "For me, not only was there the image of the FBI and capitalism but there were these dreaded Stalinists that were after you."[6] In contrast, children of communists generally viewed "Trotskyites," as those in the CP milieu called members of the SWP, with scorn and disdain. Perhaps this resulted from numerical superiority—although never large, the CP was the largest political party of the American Left from the mid-1920s until its demise as an effective force in the late 1950s. Perhaps the difference was also a function of the ability of Communists to assert the authority if not the prestige of Soviet state power.

The phrase "red diaper baby" originated in the 1920s, coined by CP activists to criticize comrades who relied on birthright rather than their own efforts to move up in the Party's ranks. The expression remained primarily a term of derision within the Left until the mid-1960s, when the John Birch Society attempted to quell political activism at the University of California at Berkeley by publishing the names of red diaper babies on campus. The effort at intimidation backfired; students found each other through the list, which helped their organizing efforts immeasurably. Since the 1970s, fictionalized accounts of red diaper life have appeared in novels and films and the term has begun to gain mainstream acceptance.

The red diaper story in the United States begins in the late nineteenth century with the children of native-born and immigrant radicals. Among the earliest red diaper babies were the children of Ella Reeve Bloor (1862–1951). "Mother Bloor," descendant of Revolutionary and Civil War veterans and antislavery activists, began a lifetime of left-wing dissent as a champion of women's suffrage. She later became a member of the SP and in 1919 sided with that party's Left wing, which would eventually form the CP. Of the six Bloor children who survived to adulthood, two (Carl Bloor and Harold Ware) became well known CP activists; the others—a nurse, a violinist, a commercial artist, and an English professor—remained uninvolved with left-wing politics but supportive of their mother and her unconventional lifestyle. Bloor attributed family solidarity to her practice of always informing the children "what I was doing and why."[7]

Also among the first red diaper generation were the children of immigrants who had been active in European revolutionary movements. Peggy Dennis, whose childhood memoir is the first story in this anthology, was born in 1909

FOR A FREE, HAPPY AND PROSPEROUS AMERICA

| ☭ | **VOTE COMMUNIST** | X |

Courtesy Linn Shapiro.

to parents who had been revolutionaries in czarist Russia—her mother active in an illegal organization that supported Lenin, her father in an opposing group. By the time of Dennis's birth, her parents had claimed this country as their home and its revolution as their task. Peggy Dennis became a full-time CP activist; her husband Eugene Dennis was a long-time Party leader who served as General Secretary from 1946 to 1959. Their son, Eugene Dennis, Jr., is also represented in this anthology.

Succeeding generations of red diaper babies include those who came of age during the Depression and the mass movements of the 1930s and 1940s, during the so-called silent 1950s, and during the social and political rebellions of the 1960s and early 1970s. The youngest red diaper babies are the children of those Sixties activists who chose to join the CP instead of the New Left. This multigenerational cohort is a finite one. There will be further generations of leftist children in this country, but, for the foreseeable future, they will not be able to define their political identity in relation to a powerful international communist movement.

★

Red Diapers: Growing Up in the Communist Left is organized into three thematic sections; within sections, articles appear chronologically.

"Family Albums" highlights the daily lives of red diaper babies, exploring the intricacies of parent-child relationships, the role of alternative cultural and educational institutions, and the effects of class, race, religion, and geography on left-wing children's lives. The section opens with Peggy Dennis's recollections of the Los Angeles Jewish Left during the 1920s and then spans a cross-section of cultural and ethnic backgrounds, generations, and locations— from Hollywood to a Finnish enclave in the upper Midwest to Birmingham, Alabama.

"Political Trauma as Personal History" documents the impact of political persecution on red diaper children. The archetypal event, which continues to provoke controversy and heated emotions over forty years later, is the execution of Ethel and Julius Rosenberg. Several articles in this section demonstrate the pervasive, almost devastating, impact of the Rosenbergs' arrest, imprisonment, and death on left-wing children and adolescents. In dramatic contrast, Robert Meeropol, the Rosenbergs' younger son, writes not of trauma but of the supportive left-wing community that sheltered him and his brother until as adults they decided to reclaim their parentage. The effects of parents being called to testify before congressional committees, serving time in jail, being blacklisted from employment, or going "underground" are among the other issues addressed in this section.

"Claiming Our Heritage" examines varied ways in which red diaper babies have come to terms with a left-wing political legacy. Contributors discuss work and career choices, degree of political involvement, and the politics of personal relationships. These articles demonstrate that as adults red diaper babies have made a range of political choices, some embracing their parents' politics and remaining within the CP milieu, some reinterpreting the heritage into their own styles of activism, and others distancing themselves from any political involvement.

Among the contributors to this anthology are the children of well-known figures on the American Left, including the son of blacklisted screenwriter John Howard Lawson, the daughter of historian Herbert Aptheker, and the daughter of civil rights and labor activists Louise Thompson Patterson and William L. Patterson. Most, however, are the descendants of rank-and-file communists whose unheralded contributions altered the landscape of this country in ways historians have only begun to document. Yet despite its breadth—with authors ranging in age from their early twenties to their mid-eighties describing life in communities across the nation—this collection is not an exhaustive portrayal of red diaper demography. The experiences of the children of Mexican Americans, Japanese Americans, and other immigrant groups that helped give the CP its vitality remain to be told. Additionally, only a few African American families are represented here. Even in this post–Cold War era, there may still be validity to the statement attributed to labor and civil rights leader A. Philip Randolph: It is hard enough to be Black in the United States without being Black and Red.

Only J. Edgar Hoover, with his view of communism as a "monolithic unity,"[8] would be surprised at the variety of parenting styles described in this anthology. Some authors recall their parents as warm and supportive; others depict families in which deviant politics exacerbated parental dysfunction. Still others describe growing up with parents who were loving yet oblivious to the challenges, even traumas, their children faced.

The FBI director's demonic notions aside, the CP had no "line" on how to inculcate communist values and behaviors. On occasion, Party publications offered suggestions on proper child rearing. A newspaper article entitled "Children's Camp" (1935) urged parents to demand urban summer programs for youngsters. "How to Bring Up Communist Children" (1946) asserted that the path to good parenting lay in being a good communist. "The Youth" (1956) defied postwar experts in arguing that working mothers did not cause juvenile delinquency. Book reviews in the Party paper alerted parents to racist or anti-Semitic tracts used in public schools and suggested alternatives, along with pointers on how to organize to rid schools and libraries of such

materials. Left-wing youth organizations, schools, and summer camps provided additional support to parents who wanted to raise children to see the
world through anticapitalist eyes.

In her autobiography, Elizabeth Gurley Flynn, the CP's most prominent
female leader, herself the daughter of socialists, discussed her approach to child
rearing. Like Mother Bloor, she believed that parents should be open about
their political activities. Despite the "modern" convenience of baby-sitters,
Gurley Flynn urged that children be taken to meetings, although selectively.
"A big rally where there are many people and great enthusiasm," she argued,
"gives a child a sense of belonging, a feeling of identification with others, that
'we are many,' and that their parents do not have queer ideas and are not
alone." Writing at the height of the Cold War, Gurley Flynn derided the attempts of some CP parents to shield children from knowledge of repression
or other painful realities. She considered such protective behaviors "an excuse to divorce children from all progressive ideas and to deprive them of all
antidotes to the daily poison poured into them." Nor did she approve of the
increasingly popular laissez-faire approach to raising children. "More likely
to develop egocentric reactionaries than defenders of peace and democracy,"
she asserted.[9]

Because there is no prototypical red diaper experience, we as editors have
chosen to respect heterogeneity rather than flatten complexity or round off
harsh edges. By selecting and ordering an anthology's contents, composing
an introduction, and commenting on individual articles, editors help readers
to recognize themes, patterns, continuities and discontinuities. Yet, suggesting
essential meanings is risky. We do not subscribe to the tendency in current
scholarship that insists on the impossibility of discerning truth in written texts.
But even more problematic than denying that historical reality can be found
in these memoirs would be aggressively or dogmatically attributing meaning
to them. The articles in this book represent raw data, most of which are being made publicly available for the first time. We as compilers and editors do
not want to overinterpret, to make mechanistic comparisons, to create arbi-
trary categories into which these experiences can be pigeonholed.

In most cases, the first-person narratives in this volume were written decades after the events they describe. Although presented as factual statements
of past events, they are better understood as reflections produced by what
historian David Thelen has called "memory as a subjective process of active
construction."[10] Historical memory is one of many forms of evidence from
which the past can be re-created; like all other sources of data, memories must
be evaluated critically. What psychological or political reasons might a red
diaper baby have for presenting events positively or negatively, for claiming

to embrace or reject the family political line, for minimizing some events while exaggerating the impact of others? To what extent are authors' descriptions of long-past events influenced by subsequent changes in their life circumstances? Oral historians have established that people tend to forget material that is of limited interest or significance to them; to distort unpleasant events; to condense, reorder, or reconfigure connections between incidents. Coherence or inevitability may be imputed to situations that lacked either or both. Gender, age, class, ethnicity, occupation, even family dynamics influence how people remember their own pasts, just as these factors influence the writing of standard histories.

Meaning and truth are rarely self-evident, and they are in a continual process of being formed and re-formed (or reformed). What "really" happened in the incidents recounted in this book may be very different from the narrators' recorded depictions of them. Family members and friends reading of experiences in which they participated may roar in outrage or, sensing the emotional truth between the lines, may experience a small eureka of delayed understanding. Each of these stories is—as are all historical accounts—unreliable, untrue, and yet each illuminates a bit of the past. People create their lives in accordance with what they think they know. For better and worse, it is on the truth as we recall it, partially remembered and partially constructed, that we base our sense of self and our life choices.

Despite the limitations of historical memory, these accounts are more than literary home movies, intelligible and of interest only to those who grew up in the CP world or who would glorify or vilify the American Left. Red diaper babies' stories shed light on a range of interconnected historical, sociological, and psychological issues critical to an understanding of twentieth-century U.S. history. Among them:

How are political values transmitted across generations? The articles in this volume illustrate the ways in which political values are conveyed by family, extended family, peers, and formal and informal institutions. Significantly, the authors describe the operation of informal processes—listening to adult dinner conversation, playing on the stairs at Party headquarters, marching in demonstrations—more often than formal lessons on "correct" behavior and thought. Many red diaper babies absorbed left-wing values and ideology by "osmosis." Looking back, some wish that their parents had taken the time to systematically transmit political values. Others, in contrast, resent what they perceive as early indoctrination.

Among the parents who avoided overt instruction were those who did so, with varying degrees of self-awareness, to allow children freedom to assimilate and integrate rather than merely imitate adult political beliefs. Some parents, motivated by fear, wanted to protect their children by not burdening them with potentially harmful knowledge. Some may have worried that if they pushed too hard in one political direction their children might turn against them and what they stood for. Often, parents held back information by a process that was itself laden with fear, confusion, and secrecy. Picking up on the emotion without the content, their children felt anything but protected.

What role have political subcultures played in sustaining dissident movements? Historians have described the role that "movement cultures"[11]—values, beliefs, customs, and networks of alternative institutions—have played in the development and maintenance of social movements, from the Populists of the late nineteenth century to the Civil Rights Movement of the 1960s. Aspects of a movement culture can be life-sustaining. The inspirational and healing force of songs rooted in the African American religious tradition helped civil rights workers persevere despite the terror to which they were subjected. Similarly, many red diaper babies recall how an all-encompassing belief system as well as a range of social, cultural, and educational institutions fortified them against the strains of daily life.

Ironically, the subculture that nurtured the children of communists, helping us feel part of a larger whole and proud of our identity, failed to sustain the political movement that was central to our parents' lives. While many red diaper babies have been involved in left-wing political activities, few have become active Party members.

What role have children of communists played in this country's radical social and political movements? Thoughtful researchers as well as those looking for evidence of a communist conspiracy have noted the presence—although never the dominance—of red diaper babies in the civil rights, antiwar, women's, and other social justice movements of the 1960s and 1970s. In his analysis of the process by which student activists became politicized, psychologist Kenneth Keniston found three red diaper babies among the fourteen leaders of the 1967 Vietnam Summer organizing project. Keniston also referred to a body of research documenting that many members of the New Left came from "families with unusually liberal or left-wing political values."[12] Similarly, historian Kathleen Weigand has described red diaper babies as both participants and leaders in the women's liberation movement of the late 1960s and 1970s.[13]

Carrying on the "family business,"[14] many of us have enthusiastically added our voices to the long tradition of indigenous American radicalism, functioning as a hereditary Left and linking generations of activists. Others have maintained a distant and uneasy relationship with the radical tradition. Some red diaper babies, especially among those who were teenagers at the height of the McCarthy terror, have shied away from left-wing politics. Some, concerned that their political parentage would be used to discredit social movements, have avoided the public scrutiny that comes with leadership and prefer less visible roles.

Those who participate in radical social movements bring with them a variety of skills, from techniques of political analysis to leaflet writing and envelope stuffing. During the Sixties, many of the red diaper babies who joined the New Left offered a competing point of view to the belief that revolution was around the corner and that college students would make it happen. Radical change, we had been taught, results from painstaking organizing, often requiring a lifetime commitment, among the working masses.

The contributors to this book look back on their childhoods with varying mixtures of nostalgia, pride, confusion, anger, and pain. Some red diaper babies identify the major issues in their childhoods as fear and secrecy. Others refer to a sense of purpose and a feeling of community. The articles in this anthology point to variables that may account for differences in subjective experience: quality of parenting; strength of political community; extent of external repression; gender, generational, and geographic differences; even birth order. Yet several common themes run through the lives of red diaper babies, whether raised in the manufacturing cities of the U.S. heartland, on chicken farms in southern New Jersey, or in the Red Belt of the Bronx (where the Socialist Party was considered the extreme right wing). Among these themes are: (1) the centrality of left-wing politics to everyday life, (2) an oppositional identity, (3) a heightened historical awareness, (4) a feeling of connection to an international community of people working for social change, and (5) a belief that one person's actions can make a difference and that by working together people can radically change society.

To the majority of Americans, politics bear virtually no relationship to daily life. It may be difficult for those outside the CP world to believe how completely national and international events permeated the lives of even very young children—influencing what we read, spoke, wore, ate, and, of course, thought. Everyday choices—to say People's Republic of China when classmates said Red China or to refuse to drink Coca-Cola because of the company's alleged support of segregationist White Citizens Councils—took on political ramifications of overarching importance. For those in the CP milieu, the personal has always been political.

The goal of changing American society by ending capitalism is the basis of the oppositional identity shared by red diaper babies. Embracing our heritage, choosing to be like our parents, requires that we reject some of society's most deeply held values. And while it is becoming increasingly inappropriate to publicly disparage those who are different by reason of belief, birth, or ability, to be anticommunist remains acceptable, indeed even a patriotic duty.

Society's animosity toward the ideology that underpins our identity distinguishes red diaper babies from the children of other outsiders such as Jehovah's Witnesses or Holocaust survivors. Ours is not only a dissident identity but one that challenges a core American value: belief in capitalism as the ideal economic system and the only guarantor of political democracy.

Opposition to the mainstream has its costs. As children most red diaper babies feared ostracism, harassment, losing parents to jail, or worse. Those who reached adolescence during the height of the McCarthy era or who were the same age as the Rosenbergs' sons report some truly terrifying experiences, as do those who participated as children in the labor struggles of the 1920s and 1930s. Many red diaper babies describe having lived double lives, separating their political and public identities. As adults, some continue to perceive life as dangerous. Having been raised as outsiders holding a (potentially) life-threatening secret, some red diaper babies remain perpetual aliens, never allowing themselves to be fully known. Keeping a distance from the broader society may generate ongoing problems around intimacy, trust, and openness.

Countering the reality of being different and not part of the majority are a connection to a worldwide community and a sense of having a role in history. As children, most red diaper babies learned that millions of people around the globe shared our aspirations for socialism, for a more participatory democracy and a more just distribution of societal resources. The triumphs and sacrifices of that extended family became part of our daily lives. Raised with the lore of an international revolutionary culture, we sang the "Internationale" and songs of Loyalist soldiers in the Spanish Civil War, Italian antifascists, and South African freedom fighters with as much fervor as other children sang the latest pop tunes.

Surrounded from birth by left-wing political activism, many of us were raised to believe that we had a critical role to play in the making of history.[15] "As a child I thought it was up to my generation to establish world socialism," recalled Chandler Davis, a red diaper baby and mathematics professor blacklisted during the McCarthy years.[16] As children of scientific socialists, we were taught that human societies could be rationally understood and then radically changed by collective action. Believing that working with others we could affect events of global importance often generated a heady sense of specialness, of personal and group empowerment. (Some recast specialness into superiority, with inevitably negative interpersonal consequences.)

For red diaper girls, the connection to an international communist movement and the ability to "make history" have particular significance. To grow up in a subculture that, at least in theory, validates individuals regardless of gender creates a sense of personal possibility and an ease with authority and decision making that goes far beyond what most young women in this society experience. Many red diaper babies grew up with mothers, aunts, family friends, even grandmothers who served as strong female role models. Perhaps more unusually, some had fathers whose principled behavior in and out of the home qualified them as premature feminists.

Even when we deign to admit that circumstances prevent us from playing a key role in establishing world socialism, the connection between self and history remains visceral, generating, for some, burdensome dilemmas: Are we required to forever confront all manifestations of injustice? Can we be good people if we do not do something to change the world?

Most red diaper babies struggle with the need to adapt the socialist values of childhood to capitalist adult reality, to walk a fine line between individual fulfillment and social responsibility. Getting ahead by placing personal over group needs creates a conflict of, at times, almost unmanageable proportions. Yet some red diaper babies describe childhoods that equipped them to perform well in a capitalist framework. They excelled at aspects of the mainstream game: getting good grades, winning citizenship awards, going on to lucrative careers. Others feel they were not raised with the skills necessary to succeed in the larger society. Many report mixed parental messages: along with "Be a professional" came "Be a professional revolutionary."

The majority of contributors to this anthology are not professional writers. Most have not written previously about their red diaper experiences. Given the opportunity to express themselves on a subject that touches them deeply, these authors have generated profound, often beautifully crafted testimonies. It was difficult for some to come out of the Red closet, believing, as one contributor told us, "that you are violating some important trust not to reveal secrets." For many, going on record as a red diaper baby was a therapeutic experience. For most, writing about their lives in the communist Left was a way to assert—without denying ambivalence or pain and without glossing over failures and flaws—a positive identity and sense of community. All contributors wrote without guarantee of remuneration; if that's not anticapitalist behavior, we don't know what is.

We encourage those who were not ready to go public when we began collecting material to consider doing so now. We hope those who began to re-count their histories for this anthology will continue to document the stories of their lives.

By involving hundreds of red diaper babies in the creation of this book—those who contributed, those who led us to contributors, those who labored long and hard on articles that we were unable to include—we have tried to help the red diaper community name, know, and strengthen itself. In the face of smug de-nials of the relevance of anticapitalist constructions of history, we mean this anthology to affirm the richness of our legacy. In creating a forum for these stories of growing up Red, we honor that inheritance.

Judy Kaplan

Linn Shapiro

Notes

1. Quoted in Saul K. Padover, *Karl Marx: An Intimate Biography* (New York: New American Library, 1978), 295.

2. Ibid., 296.

3. Quoted in Yvonne Kapp, *Eleanor Marx: Family Life (1855–1883)* (New York: International Publishers, 1972), 54.

4. Although statistics on CP membership vary widely, some general trends are evident. By 1929, somewhere between 7,500 and 10,000 people had joined the CP. Ten years later, membership stood at an estimated 75,000 to 80,000. At its height during World War II, the Party estimated its membership to be as high as 100,000. A slow but steady decline in membership began in the mid-1940s, the result of both external repression and internal infighting. In 1955, one year before Khrushchev's denunciation of Stalinism ("'Honest Communists,' Khrushchev declared, 'were slandered, accusations against them were fabricated, and revolutionary legality was gravely undermined'"), the CP reported over 20,000 members. By 1958, that number had dropped to fewer than 5,000 (quotation from Maurice Isserman, *If I Had a Hammer: The Death of the Old Left and the Birth of the New Left* [1987; reprint, Urbana: University of Illinois Press, 1993], 23).

5. For a number of reasons, including its larger size, the CP was able to support a broader range of cultural organizations than other left-wing parties. A former Trotsky-ist, writer Paul Jacobs, recalled: "Despite the sharp political differences that separat-ed us from the Communists, we were culturally dependent upon the Communists and their web of peripheral and supporting organizations, for the American Trotskyist

movement had no folk-singing clubs, no foreign-language associations, no fraternal orders, no hiking clubs, no classes in drama, nor any of the varied other activities which made the 'What's Doing' column in the *Daily Worker* so long every day" (*Is Curly Jewish? A Political Self-Portrait Illuminating Three Turbulent Decades of Social Revolt, 1935–1965* [New York: Atheneum, 1965], 34).

6. Judy Kaplan and Linn Shapiro, eds., *Red Diaper Babies: Children of the Left* (Washington, D.C.: Red Diaper Productions, 1985), 48.

7. Ella Reeve Bloor, *We Are Many: An Autobiography* (New York: International Publishers, 1940), 69.

8. J. Edgar Hoover, *Masters of Deceit: The Story of Communism in America and How to Fight It* (New York: Henry Holt and Co., 1958), 333. This sentiment appears in various formulations throughout *Masters of Deceit*. "The member is regimented from life to death," wrote Hoover (115). "Communists want to control everything," he asserted, "the time your alarm clock goes off in the morning or the amount of cream in your coffee" (8–9). Similar ideas appear in virtually all of his other writing and speeches. In *J. Edgar Hoover on Communism* (New York: Random House, 1958), he described the individual Party member as an "obedient robot" (6) and life in the CP as having "no room for individuality, only conformity" (107).

9. Elizabeth Gurley Flynn, *The Rebel Girl: An Autobiography; My First Life (1906–1926)* (New York: International Publishers, 1955), 59, 60.

10. David Thelen, "Memory and American History," *Journal of American History*, 75 (Mar. 1989), 1129.

11. The phrase "movement culture" is taken from Lawrence Goodwyn, *The Populist Moment: A Short History of the Agrarian Revolt in America)* (New York: Oxford University Press, 1978), 20.

12. Kenneth Keniston, *Young Radicals: Notes on Committed Youth* (New York: Harcourt, Brace & World, 1968), 47.

13. Kathleen Weigand, "Vanguards of Women's Liberation: The Old Left and the Continuity of the Women's Movement in the United States, 1945–1970s" (Ph.D. dissertation, Ohio State University, 1995).

14. Linn Shapiro, "Taking Over the Family Business," in Kaplan and Shapiro, *Red Diaper Babies*, 1.

15. Richard Flacks, *Making History: The Radical Tradition in American Life* (New York: Columbia University Press, 1988).

16. Chandler Davis, "The Purge," *A Century of Mathematics in America* (Providence, R.I.: American Mathematical Society, 1988–89), 413.

1
Family Albums

Photo on preceding page: Communist Party national headquarters, Union Square, New York City, 1930. Courtesy of the Robert F. Wagner Labor Archives, New York University, Charles Rivers Collection. Photograph by Charles Rivers.

Memories from the '20s

Peggy Dennis

Peggy Dennis (1909–93), daughter of Russian Jewish revolutionaries, was born in New York City and raised in Los Angeles's left-wing immigrant community. She joined the Communist Party in 1925 at age sixteen and remained a full-time activist until her resignation from the Party in 1976. Dennis described these experiences in *The Autobiography of an American Communist: A Personal View of a Political Life, 1925–1975* (Lawrence Hill, 1977). Her husband, Eugene Dennis, served as General Secretary of the Party from 1946 to 1959 and then as Chairman until his death in 1961.

Here, Dennis describes the importance of left-wing cultural activities in her childhood and adolescence. A version of this selection appeared in *Cultural Correspondence*, 6, no. 7 (Spring 1978).

Born into a highly insulated counterculture of a large socialist family, my first conscious awareness of the things I believed in came to me through the Yiddish language and literature that dominated my early years in Los Angeles.

First, there was the large glass-doored bookcase filled with the treasured bound volumes of Yiddish poets and writers Mama and Papa loved so passionately. Second, there was the socialist daily newspaper *Forvertz* (*Forward*) and later the communist daily paper *Freiheit* (*Freedom*). Each evening after supper and after a day's work either in the needle trades factory downtown or in the small neighborhood cleaning and pressing shop they operated periodically, Papa read aloud to Mama. First the newspaper was read thoroughly, every word, and then one of the books was taken down from its shelf.

At age four I became a weekly feature at the socialist club meetings of the Jewish emigrés. Hoisted upon a table, I recited one of the Yiddish poems—about a worker who never saw his children because he worked from sunup to sundown, about the horrors of war, about child laborers in factories wanting to see a bird in the sky. To these visionaries who listened with tears in their eyes, the Yiddish was incidental to the socialist content but it was the only form they knew.

At six, my radical education shifted to the English-speaking world when I enrolled in the Socialist Party's weekly Sunday school. My horizons widened as we sang revolutionary songs and played games where familiar "tag" and "tug-of-war" were given "worker versus boss" interpretation. I recall some big program we put on for the adults in which we younger children were tiny flower buds waiting on the vine until the Red Dancer entered, pirouetting around us as a boy with a big sun mask appeared and we tender flowers burst through our cardboard pots to dance toward the sun of tomorrow.

With the organizational consolidation of the split between the Socialist and Communist Parties, at thirteen I joined the Young Pioneers, the children's movement of the Communist Party. For the next three years, dressed in the brilliant red embroidered overblouse of the Russians, I recited frequently at radical gatherings. The selections now were from *The Masses* magazine rather than Papa's Yiddish books. I recall one very long poem about Peg-Leg Johnson, relating his struggles in the mines, the efforts to organize, the loss of his leg, and his cry "A Great Deed Is Needed." I recall, too, reciting with my sobs echoing those of the audience, Ralph Chapman's "Mourn Not the Dead" at the memorial meeting for Lenin in 1924. Interspersed with these dramatic readings, I gave fiery speeches urging organizing the children to carry on the torch of Revolution and Freedom.

At sixteen in 1925 I graduated from the children's movement into the Young Communist League (YCL) and simultaneously into the Communist Party. My main assignment as a young adult was that of being one of five YCL leaders of the children's organizations. Within a year we had some three hundred children in the Los Angeles area, organized according to ages, from seven to fifteen, in groups that met weekly. Songs, games, drama, dance were the sole media through which most of our radical education was transmitted. Devotion to the little *Red Song Book*, which every child owned, preceded by some forty years the fanatic devotion evoked by the little red book of the sayings of Chairman Mao. Those songs and the discussions we stimulated around them expanded the children's horizons as they had mine a few years earlier. The struggles of miners and textile workers, of Wobbly jailbirds in faraway places—all became part of the child's world in L.A.'s Jewish Boyle Heights. The "Internationale," the songs of the Italian, German, Russian movements— these made us part of a worldwide movement and the single barricade of battle. When we rode in open trucks to join the IWW longshore strikers in San Pedro, the port town twenty miles away, our song "Hold the fort, for we are coming, union men be strong" was our armor.

THE YOUNG COMRADE

Vol. I.   OCTOBER, 1924   No. 12

A working class magazine for working class
children

Published monthly by the

Junior Section

Young Workers League

of America.

Max Shachtman, Editor

Send all orders and articles, and remit all
funds to

THE YOUNG COMRADE

1113 W. Washington Blvd.   Chicago, Ill.

Subscription—Fifty cents per year. Single
copies 5 cents. Bundles of five or more, 3
cents per copy.

Entered as second class matter December 12,
1923, at the Post Office at Chicago, Illinois, under the Act of March 3, 1879.

Courtesy of the Tamiment Institute Library, New
York University.

Once a year, to celebrate each anniversary of our growing children's movement, we put on an elaborate event consisting of original song, ballet, drama, and, one year, even original opera—new words set to the known *Red Book*
songs. Every child, regardless of age, was involved in one number or another. I wrote plays and skits; my sister (Mini Carson Boc, who went on to become a fiery strike leader, union organizer, and communist woman activist)
wrote the songs and opera. Everything was quite simple in symbolism but
quite intricate in effort. One of my most dramatic "successes" (later published
in the national *Daily Worker* in story form) was the conflict between a father—
a striking miner—and his son, an eighteen-year-old recruit into the National Guard called out to break the strike. Enter at the last minute the red-bloused
YCL group with their leaflets and their call to "down guns." Lesson, of course:
"Organize the Youth!"

Our adult audience cried and cheered in the right places, and we were all
exhilarated. My sister's operetta carried the story of a child's development
through the various stages and conditions of exploitation and brainwash propaganda—a highly complex production in scenery, ballet, acting, original song,
pathos, and, of course, inevitable victory. Some fifty years later, as I meet
persons not seen for years, I realize that not one of the many hundreds of
children who went through our Young Pioneer movement in the 1920s in
California remained unaffected by that experience.

A California Girlhood

Lillian Carlson

Lillian Carlson was born in Chicago in 1914. Her parents, Harry and Tsivye Dinkin, immigrants from Belarus (White Russia), were active in left-wing Jewish organizations in Chicago, Los Angeles, and Petaluma, California—where they were part of a community of Jewish chicken farmers. Carlson joined the Young Pioneers at age nine, was first arrested—for passing out leaflets—at age fourteen, and became active in the Young Communist League. She joined the Communist Party in the early 1930s and remained a member until 1957. She has lived in Laguna Beach, California, since the early 1970s.

As a young woman, Carlson participated in many of the left-wing struggles of the late 1920s and early 1930s, battles that seem familiar today, over sixty years later: she protested against segregated municipal swimming pools, distributed leaflets protesting U.S. intervention in Nicaragua, helped organize agricultural and garment workers, and planned a statewide children's march against hunger.

When I was nine, in 1923, my family moved from Chicago to Los Angeles. We took the train, and when it stopped in Needles, I got off to stretch and saw my first palm trees. I've loved them ever since.

L.A. was beautiful then, small, clean, with clear skies, trees, flowers, warmth—a wide open space compared to Chicago. We'd run around barefoot all summer. In the fall, I started Sheridan Street School. One day as we walked home, my friend Kate Farber asked, "What paper do your parents read, the *Freiheit* (communist) or *Forwards* (socialist)?" "*Freiheit*," I said. That did it. I was launched into the revolutionary movement. She said there was a children's organization called the Juniors (which later became the Young Pioneers). I joined it and loved it.

From the Pioneers, we "graduated" to the Young Communist League (YCL) and then to the Communist Party. The Party led and controlled both youth organizations.

In the Young Pioneers, we had lots of picnics and we sang songs. The first revolutionary song I ever learned went like this:

We are the builders; we build the future.
The future world is in our hands.
We swing our hammers, we use our weapons
Against the foe in every land.
And we, the workers, who are the builders,
We fight; we do not fear to die.

Another song we sang:

We're Pioneers born,
We're YCL members bred,
And when we die we'll be Party members dead.
So rah, rah for the YCL (or whatever we were rah-rahing
   for at the moment).

We'd wander around the streets barefoot, collect tinfoil from cigarette wrappings, make a big ball, and sell it. The money went to help the starving children of the world—I can't recall which starving children.

Being young revolutionaries, we defied many accepted practices. In an all-Jewish neighborhood, we Pioneers would be the only ones who'd go to school on important Jewish holidays. But we'd stay home on May Day and come back with a note from our parents: "L. Dinkin did not go to school May 1 because it is an international workers' holiday." Many of us refused to salute the flag. We were brave, militant, and committed!

When I was about eleven, my father and a friend, Isaac Epstein, bought a grocery store in Ontario, California, and our two families moved there. I remember orange trees in the backyard and lots of farm animals, cows and chickens. The three Dinkin sisters (Esther was about three and Miriam about seven) decided we couldn't possibly eat those animals, declared ourselves vegetarians, and stuck to it.

My father, Harry, was a communist and couldn't stand the idea of not being a "worker." There were no jobs for him in the area, so he decided to sell the store, where they were making a decent living, and go back to Chicago to become a milkman again. This was in the summer of 1927. The two families and a Jewish poet named Dixel (ten of us altogether) piled into an old Dodge, hooked on a trailer for luggage—in which Dixel and I sat—and started the trek back to Chicago. When we reached the desert we noticed something was wrong. So we dumped the trailer. Dixel, luggage, and I went into the Dodge, and we proceeded on to our destination.

In Chicago, I was very busy in high school and active in the Young Pioneers, took piano lessons, attended Jewish school, menstruated, had boyfriends, went to concerts, and made my first big public speech. I was the Young Pioneer representative at the May Day rally that year at the Ashland Auditorium. When I think about it now, I shudder with fright!

My father had something wrong with his heart; it skipped a beat and he couldn't run up and down stairs, a primary requirement for a milkman in Chicago. So the family went back to L.A. I stayed on with some family friends to finish the school semester and then returned to L.A. alone on the train. I was fourteen.

In L.A. I got super active in the Young Pioneers. We organized a children's demonstration at a park in Los Angeles where Blacks weren't allowed in the swimming pool. There was quite a to-do: media coverage, harassment, the presence of police to scare the children. I remember taking some Black children into the pool with me; we certainly made a "splash."

L.A. was notorious as an "open shop town," which meant no unions were allowed and any attempt at organizing was squelched. There was no law forbidding unions, but workers had to be very secretive and careful when organizing to avoid being harassed, fired, or arrested. The city had a "Red Squad," a group of vicious cops whose only job was to keep track of "Reds," to break up meetings, organize attacks, etc. They monitored the activities of all leftists, young and old; they constantly followed and threatened us. In 1928, for example, the Red Squad beat and teargassed people outside a meeting hall where Communist Party leader William Z. Foster was scheduled to speak.

I was still in high school in the fall of 1928 when U.S. troops invaded Nicaragua. A group of us went to the San Pedro naval base to distribute leaflets to the sailors saying "Hands off Nicaragua." We were arrested for distributing leaflets without a permit. Another gal and I were fourteen and fifteen, so they took us to Juvenile Hall. We were the first Red juvenile arrests in Los Angeles—something to be proud of, I suppose.

We had been trained in how to behave when arrested. A great organization called the International Labor Defense issued brochures stating your rights and how to act if arrested. We knew not to give correct information, not even our names or addresses. We had also read about brave historical figures who had been arrested and went to their deaths singing. We followed instructions, and we sang. The juvenile authorities didn't quite know what to do with us; they'd had no experience with clean-cut kids arrested for giving out leaflets. They went through their usual procedures, asking us pages and pages of questions—about our home lives, allowances—to try to determine what made us delinquent. As instructed, my friend and I didn't give them one correct answer. The next day, we were physically examined to see if we had been "touched," if we'd had sex. They really couldn't figure us out.

The Red Squad knew we were in jail and knew our real names and addresses. My parents were notified that I was in Juvenile, but the Red Squad told my mother, Tsyvia, she couldn't see me because I was very sick and dying. Bastards! My poor mother. Here I was singing, and she was being told I was deathly sick. Only your parents could get you out of Juvenile; eventually between the ILD and others, my parents located me. I had to go through the questioning again and answer properly (the ILD said it was OK), and we got out. The next day in school a kid who had read in the newspaper that some Roosevelt High students had been arrested went on about it to me and others. He didn't make the connection that I had been the one arrested. I was uncomfortable but proud and defiant. Such was my first arrest.

The second arrest occurred because we distributed leaflets urging packing-house workers to organize into a union. Juvenile again. But being veterans, we knew the routine. We were examined physically again and were "clean." I'll never forget being marched through the "unclean" section of Juvenile and all the girls pointing to us and sneering, "They haven't been touched!"

Around this time, the end of 1929, came the Wall Street crash and the beginning of the Great Depression. Our gang of Pioneers were very vocal in school, demanding hot lunches and fighting against the ROTC. In January 1930, I was due to graduate from Roosevelt High. Just before my sixteenth birthday, four of us were called in one by one to the principal, Dr. Elson. We got a verbal shellacking; he told us that we were being denied our diplomas because we were "troublemakers" and "Red menaces" who deserved "to be put up against the wall and shot." He didn't scare me. I had nothing but contempt for him. Although denied diplomas, the four of us thought we'd at least sit in the audience to observe the graduation. When we got to the entrance, the Red Squad was at the door (they knew me well) and wouldn't let us in. So we all went to my house and had a party. The other three subsequently went to another high school for a semester and graduated. They needed to go to college.

For me, having made a commitment to become what we called a "professional revolutionary," and because my family was broke, college was out. I learned to type so I could look for a job, and, boy, did I look, every day for nine months, walking because there was no money for carfare. We tried to organize a couple of places, including the American Can Company and the packing house, were arrested for passing out leaflets and taken again to Juvenile.

At sixteen, as an older Pioneer I was assigned to teach in our Pioneer Training School. I was only one step ahead of my students; to this day I resent some of the kids who asked questions I couldn't answer. I'd use the usual ploys— "What do you think?" "We'll discuss it tomorrow"—and try in the meantime to find an answer.

A basic concept that we had drummed into us was that theory without practice is useless. We decided that our Pioneers needed not only Marxist theory but also some practical experience. By this time, the Depression had set in deeply, and people were being evicted from their homes for nonpayment of rent. Landlords would move the evicted tenants' furniture and belongings out to the street. A movement to stop evictions had begun; people would help put everything back into the house. We heard of an upcoming eviction and took the whole group of Pioneers to put the furniture back. When the cops came and started roughing us up, I got a very small cut on my knee. When they put me in the cop car, I stuck my foot out, gleefully yelling something like "See the police brutality!" Two of us were taken to Juvenile. My sister Miriam recalls that she was also arrested and put in the cop car, but when the cops were busy with something else, I opened the door and told her to run so she wouldn't have to go to Juvenile. I think they kept us there for a week. The Red Squad visited my parents and told them that unless they controlled me, they would put me in reform school until age twenty-one.

I did finally get a job in a huge dress factory with about three hundred workers, about half of whom were Mexican. If you graduated school and were under eighteen, you were allowed to work; otherwise you needed a permit. Officials would come to check the factories to see whether children were being employed. I had graduated but couldn't prove it, and I didn't want them to check with Roosevelt High because I'd be bounced pronto if they found out about my activities. But there was a fine group of lefties in the shop; they would keep an eye out and warn me when officials came, and I'd hide in the toilet.

By this time I was no longer a Pioneer but a "leading" member of the Young Communist League. The left group in the factory where I worked tried to organize a union, the Needle Trades Workers Industrial Union. It was a difficult job, especially in L.A., where every conceivable effort was made to keep unions out. It was also Depression time, and there were thousands ready to take your job if you went out on strike. But we tried, even called a strike, and a small portion of workers went out. As we picketed, the cops would walk behind us and step on our heels. My shoes gave out, so my co-strikers put together two dollars and I got some new shoes, which messed up my feet. Of course, we lost the strike and were all fired, but not too much later the shops were organized. I felt that we had planted a seed.

We continued trying to organize unions in the factories. At regular intervals we'd bring our soapbox to the American Can Company at lunchtime and make speeches. Obviously, no one was going to give us their names while the bosses and stoolies were watching. We got some license numbers and managed to get names and addresses that way. At night we went to their homes to talk to them and get "inside info" about conditions in the plant so that when we put out weekly leaflets or spoke, we had something to say that the workers would respond to. We couldn't organize a union because it's not done from the outside, but I felt vindicated when several years later someone said to me, "I remember you. I was working at American Can when you came around. You *did* have an effect." He was a union organizer for American Can and told me the plant had been organized.

A call went out for a big national demonstration on February 26, 1930, to support the Unemployed Councils' demands for "Work or Wages," unemployment insurance, and an end to evictions. When word came that the date was to change to March 6, we couldn't call off February 26, so we went through with it. The L.A. police were nationally notorious for being the most vicious and bloody! And a bloodbath it was. Thousands turned out, hundreds were beaten, and heads were cracked. Then we tried to prepare for March 6. The night before, everyone was nervous, and little Esther, my baby sister, who was only seven years old, asked my mother, "Why do we have to be communists? Why can't we be socialists?"

Hundreds of thousands packed into downtown L.A. It was arranged that a speaker would get up on one corner and figure on a minute or less to talk before being knocked down, then another speaker would try across the street, and so on. One speaker after another was clubbed down: heads cracked, blood all over, tear gas, horses, arrests. We were dispersed in all directions. Our crowd was chased down 5th Street and constantly assaulted. Miriam, all of eleven and a half years old, saw a friend being beaten, so she picked up something and hit the cop. She was clubbed in return. I got my butt mashed a bit. That was March 6, 1930.

We became expert demonstrators. We always carried wet handkerchiefs for tear gas and a toothbrush and comb in case we were arrested. At one demonstration for the release of Tom Mooney, police used so much tear gas that people in the Biltmore Hotel across the street objected strenuously when it filtered into their rooms.

At this time neither of my parents had jobs. My father looked desperately, mother did housework sometimes, and we got food baskets from the Jewish agency. It was a rough time, but it wasn't grim. Our lives had purpose. We believed deeply in and were committed to what we were doing. We made lasting friends; there was a great camaraderie. And we had fun. We went on hikes and hay rides; we sang a lot; we went to the beach regularly and had full lives.

The Red Squad didn't stop harassing me and my family, so on my eighteenth birthday I left home and hitchhiked to San Francisco. I would be one less mouth to feed, and the Red Squad would get off my parents' backs. I arrived in San Francisco penniless. At first I stayed with a young Finnish woman, her child, and her Italian boyfriend. One of them was working, so I had some food.

We observed May Day with small indoor meetings. I was to cover Petaluma, Chico, Eureka, and a few other little towns as the speaker representing the Party and YCL. Bobby Raport (who was like an adopted son to my mother and was killed in the Spanish Civil War) came with me. Early in the trip, the old jalopy we were using collapsed going up a mountain. The only thing we could do was dump it, so the two of us pushed the damn thing over the side and watched it fall! We hitchhiked the rest of the way and made it to the various meetings.

When I got back to San Francisco, I was appointed Pioneer director, in charge of the organization and children's work. It was the one time in my life I put on weight because I was practically living on potatoes.

During the Depression, the Communist Party organized hunger marches all over the country. We found out that Governor Rolfe would be in his house in San Francisco at Christmastime, so we decided to have a *children's* hunger march. We launched a huge undertaking involving children from all over Northern California—Black, Mexican, Filipino, white—mostly from rural areas. Preparing for it was a monumental task, and I'll never figure out how I had the guts, stamina, or brains to do it. I guess being young, committed, determined, and not realizing the immensity of it helped.

First we had to get into various small communities, seek out sympathetic people, get parents together, and convince them to let their children go. We couldn't take care of the children and their parents, so the children had to go alone. Then we'd talk to the children, arrange transportation to and from San Francisco for them, and arrange adult supervision and care. I remember going to homes where the whole family would sleep late because then they would have to eat only one meal. I felt bad because they would want to feed me. Back in San Francisco, we had to find places for the children to sleep and arrange gathering points for when they drove in. We also had to get food for them—in the depths of the Depression. We did it! This was one of the most satisfactory experiences of my young life. I'm as proud of it as of anything else I've done.

From Red Diapers to Protest Banners

Ruth Hunter

Ruth Hunter was born and raised in Minneapolis, Minnesota. Since 1944 she has lived on the West Coast, where she is active in groups working for social change, for peace, and against nuclear testing. Hunter writes a monthly column for Santa Cruz's women's magazine focusing on local unsung senior heroines. She also publishes reports in local newspapers on her travels to developing countries.

Hunter's memoir provides a glimpse into the life of a politically committed immigrant community. Hunter's anti-religious Marxist father and Sabbath-observing mother found common ground at the Labor Lyceum, a cultural center for Eastern European Jewish Leftists—where the deepest rift was between the followers of Stalin on the left and the socialists on the right.

In our home, growing up as a red diaper daughter meant dancing to two different tunes: Mama's in the daytime, Papa's in the evening.

Papa dominated the household. His Marxist passion, frustrated by his political powerlessness within the capitalist system, found its outlet in rigidly controlling his children. Tightly enforced house rules included selection of the books we read, the clothes we wore, the friends we chose, the essays we wrote. I remember reluctantly changing an idealistic essay praising the North in its war against slavery to Papa's analysis of power and economic control over the South. His lessons, based on Marxist economics, robbed me of the easy textbook answers, shattered myths, overwhelmed me as I grappled with my confusion between history taught in school and his version at home. Coupled with Papa's complete rejection of religious ritual, his daily invasion into our lives created passive and not so passive resentment. During my childhood and early teens, our home was as turbulent as the changing of the guard in the

Soviet Union after Lenin's death, bequeathing me a complex legacy—rebellion against authority, a social conscience, a secular value system.

Mama's tune was quieter but potent, early on sowing seeds of guilt when we defied taboos like the prohibition against writing on Friday night. She lovingly surrounding us with many traditions of our ancient Judaic culture and nurtured our Jewish awareness through games, songs, and food, even though we were denied the richness of Jewish faith, denied participation in religious rituals and prayers, denied observance of Yom Kippur with its traditional singing of *Kol Nidre*, the sacred Hebrew chant, or knowing that Rosh Hashona was ushered in with the blowing of the ram's horn.

Mama recalled her life in the ghetto of Minsk, the burden of working in a crockery store for a pittance as a child of nine to help her widowed mother. She held us spellbound describing her homeward route through a cemetery in a blinding snowstorm and her terrified escape from ghosts that turned out to be drunken soldiers. We never tired of hearing her childhood tales, including the perils of her journey to America at fifteen, fleeing from pogroms terrifying the ghetto. My favorite part was her daring departure, when she was smuggled under a wagonload of hay across the border to safety. Mama's personal memoirs, the Yiddish folklore she read to us (especially the delightful Shalom Aleichem tales of life in the ghetto) and her songs, filled with yearnings for the good life, were an emotional link to our heritage. *Yiddishkeit* began in the cradle as we were lulled to sleep with little Jewish melodies dear to the memory of every first-generation child. Even today, I get a poignant catch in my throat hearing "Unter ahn Yidele's Vigile," a song about a peddler, a small white goat, raisins, and almonds, remembering how many times Mama held me and sang these wonderful words. Mama's tune, interlaced with superstitions, was more than a song of our Jewish culture; it was her atonement for the lack of piety in our home.

I was born in 1916 during an era in which dramatic social change swept the globe. The Soviet Union and I were both red diaper babies. For my immigrant Jewish father the cataclysmic change from Russian czarism to communism was the realization of an idealistic youthful dream. In 1903, Papa, a Torah-trained scholar, fled to the United States, a deserter from the Russian army. I remember vividly a rare time when Papa shared his past, describing his surreptitious introduction in the yeshiva to the literature of radical social change. Under the pretense of studying and praying, he slipped Marxist revolutionary tracts between the pages. I could imagine Papa's excitement reading this contraband material, with Lenin's critique of the existing economic and religious order in Russia providing a vision of social change through revolution.

This vision became part of my father's commitment, his dream of the day workers' pay would be commensurate with production and concern for human needs would have a higher priority than profits. What a contrast with his studies of the ancient Judaic laws in the Torah, which defined morals and ethics through the lens of orthodoxy. And how absolute was his rejection of these teachings when he arrived in the new world. Pleading, crying, and arguments from Mama were useless. There would be no Bar Mitzvah for my brother, no ritual, no prayers. Papa's rigidity, reinforced by commitment to the Marxist theory of class struggle, included his premise that religion made a mockery of social justice. His fierce repudiation of all religious observances in our home created a seesaw, with Mama pulling her weight on one end and Papa on the other. Balanced in between were five kids.

As we grew older, Papa added other limitations in the name of the class struggle. He had rules against makeup, dating, silk stockings, parties, contemptuously labeling them bourgeois luxuries, while the store he owned earned him a living from his haberdashery clientele. For a headstrong teenager these restrictions became catalysts for confrontations as I questioned and resented the basis for my father's rules. Every morning when Papa left for work it felt as if the very walls sighed with relief. Tensions melted away. Mama was easier on us, her permissiveness a joy.

In some ways, we had a Jewish traditional home. On Friday night, the beginning of the Sabbath, we ate the seven-course meal Mama cooked all day, ending with her wonderful strudel. Since Papa forbade Mama the honor of wearing a kerchief, lighting the candles, and blessing the food before we ate, she could only appease her religious conscience by honoring the evening with a white tablecloth. This was part of the ongoing battle between two protagonists: Papa, the Red Doubter, and Mama, the Protector Against Sins. Both were fiercely determined to leave their imprint on our development and as a result often left our young lives in disarray.

Papa mocked his childhood taboo by working on Saturday, but Mama kept the Sabbath undefiled. She did not allow us to sew, work with our hands, or do homework, even though we were forbidden to go to the synagogue. Mama's superstitions pervaded our lives. If we were modeling a dress so she could baste the sleeves or hem, we had to chew bread to prevent the needle from sewing our brains. When Mama returned from a funeral, she went first to an outside faucet to wash her hands before crossing the threshold, scrubbing off the proximity of death to safeguard the hearth. When black-coated religious men with beards and long sideburns knocked at our door haughtily asking for handouts, Mama didn't dare refuse even if she only had a couple of pennies. These chassidic *baucher,* meaning "students of the 'word,'" could put a curse on the house, a house that ostensibly didn't believe in heaven or hell or its wrath. This tension was supreme on the morning of Yom Kippur. Mama would do the traditional fast, giving up her one addiction, the morning cup of coffee. And, only on Yom Kippur, Papa, who disdained cooking, would brew a strong pot, its seductive aroma permeating the house, tempting Mama and making a mockery of the Jewish law so important to her.

One of the burdens I still carry from my red diaper beginnings is the feeling of never quite belonging in my neighborhood or wider community. In our ghettolike Jewish area in north Minneapolis, my father's philosophy excluded us from the culturally rich immigrant activities around the holidays. I remember feeling like a kid wistfully looking into an ice cream parlor and wishing I were inside, wishing I had a new dress like all my schoolmates. We were so few, we children of social idealists, and they were so many. I recall often being uncomfortable, too young to cope with contradictions between home and neighborhood, confused by the mixed signals.

However, on the outskirts of our Jewish neighborhood, we did have a meeting place, the Labor Lyceum. For both parents and children the Labor Lyceum became our home away from home, a center for learning, political education and debate, cultural events, celebrations, and friendships. The Labor Lyceum housed a delicatessen, the branch office of the *Forward* newspaper, meeting rooms (including our *shule* classroom, where we studied Yiddish every day after school), and a large auditorium with a stage.

At the Labor Lyceum, traveling Yiddish theater groups brought melodramas to an audience hungry for plays based on their Russian ghetto culture. And some evenings it seemed as if the adults were just having a good time. I always thought of my parents as ancient and marveled at the way my mother, who probably was in her mid-thirties, danced the *scharele*. She smiled as the women holding arms danced in the round, all seeming young and carefree. Were these women savoring the brief sweet moments when they cast off their defined roles as wives and mothers, twirling to the liberating power of music and dance?

At weekend events in the social hall, I joined the chorus of accented voices lustily belting out the "Internationale," exhorting to revolution the unknown sufferers with "Arise, you prisoners of starvation." Under threats of severe repercussions, we sat through lectures dealing with social issues we couldn't understand. I recall so clearly the volatile speeches and protests reverberating at the travesty of justice in the Sacco and Vanzetti case. Indelibly imprinted in my memory is the outpouring of outrage and solidarity from the members of the Labor Lyceum during the famous trial of the nine Scottsboro Boys. The harmonious sharing of radical issues gradually changed when Stalin supplanted Lenin. Long before discord poisoned the unity in the Labor Lyceum, we children heard about the power struggle in the Soviet Union. My weekend education from ages six through ten was indeed heavy.

The time came when painful schisms shattered longtime friendships in our extended family. I remember criticisms, doubts, and bitter arguments echoing down the corridor of the Labor Lyceum as members questioned whether the Stalin regime was betraying the revolution. In a few short years after Trotsky was ousted by Stalin, the Labor Lyceum was divided into two camps.

Each side carried its own label. I was a child of the Left, of a *linke* father who believed in Stalin, in the Soviet brand of communism as forerunner of global revolution. My best friend was a child of the *Recht*, or the Right. Her parents believed in socialism and change through established institutions. Each side felt betrayed by the other and expressed its anger and passion through shouting matches and acrimonious character attacks. Those on the Right read the *Jewish Daily Forward*; the Left read the *Freiheit*. Both newspapers kept the fracas bitter and volatile. The scars remain. Even today, when my friend and I discuss our memories of the Labor Lyceum, she is bitter when she speaks about my father, reflecting the anger of her father over seventy years ago.

Aunt Bessie was on the wrong side in our family. She was a sweet dumpling of a woman who faced vitriolic political outbursts showered upon her by my father whenever she came to our house. She was a passionate believer in the *rechte* philosophy, although not as bombastic as Papa. Her quiet rebuttals infuriated him. Aunt Bessie was intelligent, a single mother working in a cap factory, and a woman! She had the temerity to challenge his superior masculine intellect, and besides, she was Mother's sister, not his. And yet, when social workers threatened to remove her two young children because she worked long hours, Papa immediately took responsibility for keeping the family together by insisting that her children stay with us during the week. This may have been another control tactic in their ongoing political vendetta.

World War II overshadowed most parochial political contests. Loyal Stalinists scrambled frantically for a logical explanation for the non-aggression pact signed by Germany and the Soviet Union in 1939; in the same year, they struggled to justify the Soviet invasion of Finland. Like those on the Right, I believed that Stalin had betrayed the trust of the internationalists, thus carrying some responsibility for the concentration camps and the evils perpetrated by Hitler on the German socialists and Jews. Somewhere in the '40s, as I reached my mid-twenties, I perceived the reaction of Stalin's followers to be the same as those of Hitler's loyal supporters, in both cases a cult worship of their leaders. This was a painful conclusion for me, as I began to peel off layers of allegiance to my father's passionate devotion to Stalin. And yet it was also liberating as I gradually freed myself from politics' dominance over my life. Liberation meant the freedom to evaluate social issues on their own merits without the trappings surrounding my earlier years. Having questioned some of my father's beliefs, I moved away from extremism in politics. However, I still retained the passion for justice.

During the McCarthy era, disillusioned with both capitalism and communism, I put my energy into my career as an educator, challenging students to think for themselves, to separate emotional rhetoric from real issues, to make connections between global and national decisions and the impact these decisions have on the quality of life.

When I retired, my red diaper past, deeply rooted in my psyche, caught up with me. The basic concepts of justice, compassion, and fairness I had heard so often from impassioned speakers at the Labor Lyceum were still embedded in my social conscience. I moved from the classroom to the political arena and began working with Central American solidarity groups—networking, fund-raising, writing, and speaking.

I have gone through periods of participating in political change, periods of withdrawal and disillusionment, and have been lured back by the compelling social needs in our society. Today, as the pendulum swings to the right, I am challenged by women's issues, homophobia, scapegoatism. I am reminded that the basic issues of the '20s, searching for a healthy quality of life—my father's issues—are the issues of the '90s. The path to social and economic equality takes many turns, carries different labels. Although the goal is elusive, for me and many others the vision lives on.

Daughter and Granddaughter of the Finnish Left

Sirkka Tuomi Holm

Daughter of Finnish immigrants, Sirkka Tuomi Holm grew up in left-wing communities in Minnesota, Massachusetts, Ohio, and Maryland. From early childhood, Holm joined in her parents' political activities, finding herself in situations that demanded physical bravery and difficult ethical choices.

After serving in the Women's Army Corps in World War II, Holm studied at Carnegie Tech and the American Theater Wing on the GI Bill. She lived in Baltimore for many years, working as a secretary and carrying on the family tradition of left-wing activism by participating in the peace and civil liberties movements. She and her husband now live in rural New Hampshire. Holm writes a monthly column for the *Työmies-Eteenpäin* (*Workingman-Forward*), a progressive Finnish-American newspaper, and collects oral histories of radical Finns.

Warren, Ohio, 1931. I was standing with my mother on a picket line of steel-workers and their wives at the Republic Steel Corporation's gates on a warm spring day. The pickets had been holding signs and marching peacefully back and forth trying to dissuade scabs from entering the plant. I heard a yell: "There they come!" All of a sudden a whistle blew. Dozens of cops and company thugs rushed through the barred gates with upraised clubs, yelling and shouting. People began to run. My mother and I stood motionless. It was as if I were watching a faraway movie. I saw a Black striker put his hand on the fender of a car, asking the scabs not to enter the plant. Two white thugs went up to him and beat him on the head again and again and again. To this day I can hear that thumping sound. Blood streamed from the striker's head as he tried to escape his assailants, who were kicking him.

The cops first assaulted the men and then pounced on the women, hitting them with their clubs on the small of the back, aiming for their kidneys. I had never seen a woman beaten before. A big, burly cop ran toward my mother, his hand clenched around a club, arm upraised. He looked like a giant to me. He was red faced and growling, his lips pulled back like a dog. He headed for my mother, and I thought, "He's going to kill her and I've got to stop him." I took a step forward, stood in front of my mother, stretched myself as high as a short ten-year-old could, and glared defiantly at the oncoming cop. My stomach churned. I started shaking all over. My teeth chattered. The cop slowed down, so I stretched upward a little more and jutted my chin out, which was difficult because by now my entire face was trembling. The cop stopped, arm still raised, and we locked eyes. We stared at each other momentarily, and I was surprised to see a look of shame and then one of pity on his face. He lowered his arm, turned away, and started furiously charging at another woman, a friend of my mother's. He didn't hit her but just shoved her. Hand in hand, my mother and I left the steelworkers' picket line; I shook and trembled all the way home.

It wasn't easy being a red diaper daughter.

I was born in Virginia, Minnesota, in 1920, eleven days before the Nineteenth Amendment was ratified, giving women the right to vote. My parents put an announcement in the Finnish-American newspaper, the *Työmies* (*Workingman*) that a daughter was born to the revolutionary forces. Quite a beginning.

I would hardly term myself a revolutionary, but being brought up as a red diaper daughter and granddaughter set me on a lifetime course of political activities.

My father came to the United States from Finland in 1908, and my mother in 1912. They met in Minnesota at a Finnish socialist hall, where they shared the same interests in plays and politics, and married. My maternal grandfather had been one of the ten founders of the first socialist hall in the province of Teuva, Finland. Although he didn't discuss his beliefs with my mother, she listened to his conversations when friends visited and consequently was brought up on socialist theory. After a general strike in 1905 led to universal suffrage, my mother accompanied her father, a sharecropper and carpenter, as he visited every sharecropper in the town to teach them how to mark an "X" in the appropriate box on the ballot for the first general elections. Perhaps that explains in part why my mother became active in the women's suffrage movement in the U.S.

My paternal grandfather was also a socialist. After Finland was granted independence by the Russians, a civil war erupted. In 1918, my grandfather joined the "Red Guards," poor crofters and factory workers inspired by the Russian Revolution to take up arms against the Finnish government, which they felt exploited them. As a young man, my grandfather had been conscripted into the czar's army; having military experience, he became an officer in the Red Guard. When it appeared that the Reds were gaining, the Finnish government imported German mercenaries to help quell the rebellion. After the Reds lost, tens of thousands were put into concentration camps. Some twenty thousand men and women perished, either by summary execution or from disease and starvation. My father came to the U.S. before the onset of the Finnish Civil War. In 1922 he met a man who had been in a cell next to my grandfather and had heard him begging for food from the guards, which they had laughingly refused. My grandfather starved to death in that Finnish concentration camp. I grew up with stories of the horrors committed by the Whites in the Finnish Civil War.

My father worked as an iron ore miner and a timber worker in Minnesota, as a quarry worker in Lanesville, Massachusetts, and as a steelworker in both Warren, Ohio, and Baltimore, Maryland. My mother worked as a domestic. Many Finnish women found employment as domestics, serving as cooks, live-in maids, or laundresses.

I was an only child close to my parents, who constantly explained to me their beliefs in Marxism and their ideals. They worked and fought for a better world, a world in which no one would be hungry and everyone could develop to their maximum and get all the education they needed. My father was especially good at explaining theory, and my mother was the activist. She told me in later years that they almost split up because she was often absent from home attending meetings and demonstrations. She was always out "agitating." I began to see less and less of her, and we weren't as close any more. When I was about eleven years old, my father told my mother that either we survived as a closer family or else he'd take me and leave her. She didn't stop all her activities, but she did cut down considerably. I was happy to see more of her and felt we were again close. However, Mother was wise. Rather than leave me home, she took me with her to meetings, demonstrations, or door-to-door talking to people. I acquired an early education in class consciousness.

Prior to World War I, the large and strong Finnish branch of the U.S. Socialist Party had created dozens of progressive Finnish halls throughout the United States. The Finnish Socialists split in 1920–21 when, inspired by the Russian Revolution, some became more radical. The left-wing Finns formed their own halls; they were called communist halls, but not all members were communists.

My family joined the leftist halls wherever we lived. The hall was a haven and a gathering place for us. There we were safe from the majority of the population that red-baited us, especially the right-wing Finns. The hall served as an extended family; we children addressed all the adult women as *Täti* (Aunt) and the men as *Setä* (Uncle). Plays and operettas were performed; we heard choruses, bands, orchestras, group and individual poetry recitations, and musical soloists, both singers and instrumentalists.

We children were encouraged to give individual performances playing musical instruments or singing. From the time we could walk, we joined the adults in polkas, schottisches, and other folk dances. We were the ones who quickly learned the Charleston and the Black Bottom and encouraged our parents to learn the steps as well.

We even had a Sunday school. It wasn't religious, but it was held on Sunday mornings; we could say that we went to Sunday school and thus were not different from our "American" classmates. We learned to read and write Finnish. We read Finnish literature and were taught simplified Marxism.

We also had athletic activities. Our parents and the elders performed calisthenics, and as we got older, we, too, joined in. We marched into the hall as a pianist played a peppy march (a revolutionary Russian one, of course), then we'd spread out. Our leader would say, "Ready?" and then we'd do our movements. In the summertime, we held outdoor track and field meets attended by hundreds of people.

Usually the children gave a program at the hall on Christmas Eve, and presents and cards were exchanged. One year some of the communists convinced the hall members that Christmas should not be observed—that it was a commercial venture and only made the merchants richer and the people poorer. I was disappointed, but I accepted the decision. We children gave our program, there was the usual dance afterward, and we had soda pop and cake. Nice, but it wasn't like Christmas, with decorations, cards, and gifts; it was just an ordinary festival night.

When we got home I climbed the stairs ahead of my parents to our second-floor apartment and opened the door. My mother put the lights on. There stood a little Christmas tree and beside it a wooden cradle painted blue that my father had made. And in the cradle was a doll! A beautiful doll with eyes that opened and closed, with thick hair, real hair. I was beside myself with joy and actually wondered if there was a Santa Claus, although I had been told years before there was none. In the midst of my ecstasy, my father took me on his knee; my mother sat beside us. They explained that I was not to tell this to anyone, not a soul. They said they would be in trouble if I told anyone, so I promised not to say a word, just to enjoy the presents by myself. Forty years later I told this story for the first time to a group of my childhood friends from Warren, Ohio. Every one of them had a similar experience. They all got Christmas gifts and promised their parents they would never tell anyone about it!

The main thing I recall about my childhood was that there was always a struggle going on. My parents took the time to explain and sometimes involved me directly. For example, I accompanied my mother as she went door-to-door for the International Labor Defense to collect funds for the Scottsboro Boys and for jailed strikers and union organizers. Sometimes my mother and I went out late at night to distribute leaflets. I stood guard on the sidewalk while she ran up to porches to deposit the leaflets. I was scared standing in the dark looking up and down, fearful that someone would walk toward us. At other times I stood guard while my mother mounted a box in the town park near the courthouse. She spoke about workers' rights to earn a decent living. I nervously looked for cops, for they would surely have lugged her off to jail.

When the teachers at school talked about radicals and communists and said they were trying to destroy the country, I wanted to stand up and shout that it was a lie, that we didn't want to destroy anything—we wanted to build a better life. But I kept my mouth shut.

During May Day parades commemorating the eight-hour day, I marched with my fellow members of the Young Pioneers, a communist children's organization. As we marched, I glanced nervously at the onlookers, fearing that I would see a schoolmate who would then tell the teacher that I was in a communist parade. There was no doubt we were different—we were not part of the mainstream—but most of the time I felt secure with "my people."

I shall never forget an incident that took place in grade school. We were in sewing class stitching aprons when the teacher asked, "Is there anyone here who doesn't believe in God?" I was taken aback, but I thought I should tell the truth. After all, I was a good Pioneer and had not been taught to believe in God. I didn't even understand the concept of God. I raised my hand. Silence. The horror on the teacher's face and the faces of my fellow students hit me almost physically. I was despised! My closest friend, with whom I had shared lunch and many giggly moments, walked over to me with a pained expression. She asked, "Don't you really believe in God?" I said, "No." Then I added that I did believe there was a Jesus Christ but he was a real person and a good revolutionary. She pulled away and walked back toward the teacher. They both stared at me with a mixture of anger and tight-lipped disapproval. The girls told the boys about me, and word spread. For the rest of the semester no one talked to me. I was so lonely and couldn't even tell my mother, as close as I was to her. For some reason I felt shame. Or perhaps I was afraid my mother would picket the school and cause a scene. I went to school every day feeling very miserable. At the end of the semester I implored my mother to transfer me to another school, which she did.

Two months into the next semester, our math teacher asked, in the middle of writing a problem on the blackboard, if there was anyone in the class who didn't believe in God. There was another Pioneer in the class, Leo, on whom I had a crush. I thought, I'm not going to raise my hand and have everyone hate me again. But Leo raised his hand high! The teacher turned red and told Leo he'd probably go to hell. I wanted to sink through the floor—I was filled with shame and yet anger that I should have to make no-win decisions.

The next day, we Pioneers had a club meeting in the cellar of a member's house. It was warm, with a big coal furnace in one corner and one electric light bulb overhead. We opened the meeting by singing the "Internationale," and our leader asked, "Pioneers, are you ready?" We shouted in unison, "Always ready!" and raised our clenched fists at right angles to our bodies. Then Leo stood up and pointed at me, saying I was a coward in the face of the enemy. He told about the math class. All eyes were on me. It was the sewing class all over again. The leader asked if I wanted to reply to Leo's charge. I said I raised my hand in class but no one saw it—a lie, of course. I stuck to that story. My mother was told and endured humiliation in front of her fellow communists. She was accused of raising her daughter to be a coward and class enemy. She approached me gently and asked me to tell her the truth—the truth, she said, was all she wanted. I wanted to tell her about everything, but I couldn't. I repeated I had raised my hand but the teacher didn't see it. It took a while for life to return to normalcy.

What did this episode do to me? I vowed that I would never be a coward again and that I would stand up and fight from then on. My test came with the 1931 steelworkers' strike in Warren. When that cop rushed up to my mother and me, I saw my chance. Although I was scared, I thought, now I can make up for not raising my hand in answer to the math teacher's question about God. When I stood between the cop and my mother and the cop left us alone, I felt redeemed.

After the steelworkers' strike failed, all the men were blacklisted. One of the strike organizers was forced to flee for his life because the one-company steel town of Warren instituted a reign of terror and the cops and company thugs beat and arrested union organizers. The organizer's wife couldn't join her husband because she was about to give birth to their first child. When she did, she was "dry" and couldn't feed her infant. No one would sell her milk, so my mother led a delegation of women to city hall demanding that the infant be given milk. We were pushed down the city hall steps by the cops, but it wasn't as bloody a confrontation as some demonstrations. We were unsuccessful, but fortunately a local farmer felt sorry for the woman; he took milk to her in the dead of the night several times a week until she could leave town.

Ohio was a very reactionary state in the thirties, and we were distinctly a minority. There was no tolerance for labor organizers or people who sought civil liberties. At a May Day demonstration in Youngstown, Ohio, a neighboring steel town, Party leaders decided to put the Pioneers first in line in the parade because they thought that cops would not beat up children. The parade formed at a small athletic field: the Pioneers first, then the women, and bringing up the rear, the men. We Pioneers wore our red bandannas. Many of us carried signs saying "Pioneers of the World, Unite!" The adults' signs proclaimed "The Ohio District, Communist Party," "Down with Imperialism," and "Save the Scottsboro Boys." It was a festive occasion. The marchers sang "Hold the Fort," "The Scarlet Banner," and the "Internationale." When we reached the center of Youngstown I suddenly heard a scream; several cops on horseback charged toward us. The horses loomed huge over us, and I saw the cops flailing their clubs at all of us—men, women, and children. They roughly shoved a boy beside me down to the ground and were going to beat him when he agilely rolled from them, got up, and ran. I couldn't move. I looked around for my mother. Her friend, Mary, a Hungarian woman, grabbed me by the hand. She pulled me to the sidewalk, and we ran. I recall that people stood on the sidewalk as if they were watching a show. I wondered how they could just stand there when people were being chased and beaten. We scurried into a linen shop. Mary took off my red bandanna, on which I had painstakingly sewed a hammer and sickle with gold thread, and shoved it into her purse. The sound of people screaming outside was quite loud. There was the stench of tear gas, and we could hear people running. The saleswoman peered suspiciously at us, then a cop entered the shop and stared at us. We looked busily at the handkerchiefs as Mary asked if I liked this one or that one. The saleswoman didn't tell the cop that we were demonstrators. After he left she told us to leave immediately, which we did. The ground was strewn with signs, and I remember seeing horse "biscuits" on the sidewalk. We hurried to the athletic field, where we found my mother and father. I was so glad to see them that when I hugged them I didn't want to let go.

I've devoted my adult life to liberal and progressive causes. I enlisted in the Women's Army Corps during the Second World War and served eight months in the States and eighteen months overseas. I wanted to be part of a force that would destroy Hitler and fascism. I was active in the Progressive Party, protested and organized against the Smith and McCarran Acts, gathered names on petitions opposing the frame-up of the Rosenbergs, and spent many weekends in front of the White House protesting their impending execution.

In 1957, I was hauled before HUAC. It was a spring day when two men knocked at our door in Baltimore. One handed me a subpoena to appear before HUAC in two weeks. I felt as if someone had hit me in the stomach but pulled myself together. Thirty of us were subpoenaed. I took the Fifth Amendment fifteen times, refusing to answer questions about other people.

Before the hearing I bought a new black and white dress and a white hat. I even wore gloves. I could have refused to allow television cameras on me, but I wanted to show the world that I was a concerned human being and not a monster; I thought dressing up and speaking forthrightly in front of the public would make a difference. Regrettably, I was wrong. Afterward, people recognized me on the street and called me "commie" and other names. I became the target of newspaper diatribes that didn't let up for several weeks. I lost a good job as secretary to a steel company vice president, my husband lost his job in a chemical factory, and my sixty-year-old mother lost her job as a cook. No doubt her wealthy employers couldn't stand to have a subversive's mother mix them a batch of waffles with creamed chicken! Two of our front windows were shattered by rocks, and a window in the back was shot at with a BB gun. The neighbors were up in arms about the "subversives" in their midst and passed around a petition telling us to leave the neighborhood, but we never got it. There were many threatening phone calls and other harassments. What really broke my heart was that children I had directed in plays at the Finnish hall were forbidden by their parents to talk to me. It became quite commonplace to see people crossing the street to avoid me.

Many years later, some of the very people who had signed petitions demanding that I leave the neighborhood became good friends and allies in struggles to organize our community. We fought against a hazardous landfill adjacent to a city hospital, a proposed chemical cleanup operation, and the invasion of interstate roads. We also fought successfully for more city services for our working-class part of town.

Growing up as a red diaper daughter was not a grim or joyless experience. Being with others of similar philosophy gave me a sense of security. Belonging to a group gave me strength; I was and still am never alone. My parents taught me about the world, about the class system, and about history. "My people" prepared me for life with the philosophy that there can be no growth without struggle. I shall always be glad that I was born a red diaper daughter and granddaughter!

Passage to Siberia

Doris C. Kaplan

Doris Kaplan, mother of coeditor Judy Kaplan, is a semiretired occupational therapist. She grew up in Brooklyn, New York, and has lived in Philadelphia most of her adult life since moving there to attend professional school. Kaplan is active in the secular Jewish movement and describes herself as still progressive in her approach to politics.

In the late 1920s, Stalin established a "Jewish republic" in southeastern Siberia. Eager to participate in the building of Soviet socialism, left-wing Jews from around the world moved to the Jewish Autonomous Region of Birobidjan. Their experience has not been well documented; Kaplan gives us a unique first-person account from a child's perspective.

In 1931, when I was ten years old, my father came home from work one day with a startling announcement. In a few months we were going to leave our apartment in Flatbush, a Jewish neighborhood of Brooklyn, to go to *Russia*— the socialist homeland. I was excited by the idea but at the same time a little apprehensive. At that age, conformity to a peer group was so important, and I didn't tell any of my friends where we were going because they had such a negative view of communism and the Soviet Union.

My father was a communist and believed that the Soviet Union represented the future for working people. As a socialist, he had been one of the first conscientious objectors in World War I. In order not to "rot in a capitalist jail" (his words), my father changed his identity. He gave up his career as an electrical engineer and became a union electrician active in the IBEW. He took his mother's maiden name as his last name and changed his first name.

We went to the Soviet Union because my father had been asked to accompany the machinery that would be used to construct a small electric power plant in Birobidjan, a territory set aside by the Soviet government to be a homeland for the Jews. The equipment had been purchased by a Jewish organization in New York. We were supposed to stay in Russia for the time it took to complete this project, two years at most.

My mother's family thought my parents were out of their minds to leave a comfortable middle-class existence and relocate to an unknown, primitive, and—worst of all—communist country. But my uncle Abe, my mother's older brother, agreed to keep up my father's life insurance and union dues while we were gone.

The day of our departure finally arrived. Holding my "mama" doll, I boarded what was then the largest passenger steamship vessel in the world, the German ship S.S. *Bremen*. After landing in Germany, we took a boat across the Baltic Sea to Finland. From Finland we went by train to Leningrad. Now! We were here, in this country that I believed was going to make a better life for all people, end war and starvation, and allow everyone to have everything they needed: "To each according to need."

To get to Birobidjan in the far, Far East, we traveled by the Trans-Siberian Railroad. We had many adventures along the way on that unforgettable ten-day trip: for example, when an elderly porter lifted the duffel bag containing my doll to his shoulder, the doll said, "Ma-ma," and the man dropped the bag like a hot potato. Saying "Chort vozmi" ("The devil take it"), he refused to pick it up again.

When we reached Siberia, about five days into the trip, the weather turned cold. Wood, which was available at regularly scheduled stops, had to be collected for the stoves that heated each car. One night the conductor asked me to hold up a lighted kerosene lantern near the door to our section of the train while a group of men, including my father, went for the wood. The lantern was a signal to the engineer that we were not ready to depart. As I stood waiting, holding the lantern, I looked up to see a delegation of husky men in ill-fitting business suits (an official delegation traveling on the train) coming to see who was holding up the train. I was very frightened. They were so big and self-important and official looking; I was afraid they would order the train to leave and my father would be stranded. Fortunately, I was rescued by the timely return of the wood gatherers.

The train carried no food, so we bought things at each station—fat, roasted geese, delicious baked goods, milk, fruit, etc. We had no problems obtaining food, but I did miss cornflakes!

My father kept a diary of the trip, in which this incident is recounted. During the McCarthy period, my mother started to rip up the diary and throw it away, but my father pulled it away from her and saved what he could. It was hidden away along with the communist books and magazines.

When we finally arrived in Birobidjan, we found a hamlet with dirt roads, tents for sleeping, and an outdoor brick oven for cooking. My mother was a nurse, trained in a first-class Brooklyn hospital, and these primitive conditions were not to her liking. My father and I, on the other hand, thought it was great—we felt like frontierspeople—and we took it in stride.

My first Russian words were: "Please give me some eggs." I became the shopper for the family—at my age it was easy for me to learn the language. My parents eventually learned to speak Russian, with heavy accents.

My mother thought she would be working in a clinic and ended up being the only medical person in the village. Because she felt unable to work under these conditions and there was no school for me, within a month and a half she and I moved to the nearby city of Khabarovsk, population 100,000.

My father, who had remained in the village, was having great difficulties. He had come to Birobidjan expecting to assemble a power plant. When we arrived the foundation for the building that was to house the power station had not even been laid. My father was willing to do the necessary construction work, but the person in charge of assigning work in the village, another Jewish communist from Brooklyn, did not consider the power plant a priority. The work force consisted of several hundred emigrés from the U.S., Argentina, France, Germany, and Canada as well as some local residents; sometimes he'd assign one person and sometimes a full crew to work with my father. By the time winter came, very little had been accomplished. The station was left to rust, and my father joined us in Khabarovsk. He got a job in his field, in a factory that produced electric motors. My mother was working as a radio announcer, broadcasting the events of the day in English. She also taught conversational English to adults. The radio station had a wide broadcasting range, and we received postcards from as far away as Australia, which actually wasn't that far from Siberia.

I attended school in Khabarovsk for a year and a half and joined the Young Pioneers. (I still have my membership certificate. I found it to show my daughters when they were studying Russian in high school in the mid-1960s. They were fascinated that their mother had been a member of a communist youth group but didn't think it was a good idea to mention it to their teacher or classmates.) I became fluent in Russian with the help of a gifted teacher, who sensed my dismay and awkwardness at being placed in the first grade. Every day, for one hour after school, she taught me by the "immersion" method. She didn't know any English; she would point to something or demonstrate an activity and name it. Within two months I was in my age-appropriate fifth grade class.

While we were living in Siberia, a reporter from *Good Housekeeping* magazine interviewed my parents. He quoted my mother as saying, "You have to see the new people being born here—the youth that's free for the first time. You have to understand how far they've advanced in order to have young people think of this country as their own, and realize, after hundreds of years of oppression, that they're as good as any one else." Although the author changed their names and professions, and there were many Brooklyn expatriates in Birobidjan, when the article appeared (in February 1933) friends back home were sure that it described my parents. The clincher was his saying that his "keen hostess talked on" and "the rest of us couldn't get in a word."

When my parents decided to return to the U.S., we had to spend two months in Finland waiting for the appropriate papers and permission for my father to enter the U.S. If he could enter the country legally as the spouse of a naturalized citizen, he would no longer have to worry about his undocumented status. The second day we were in Finland, a black car with curtained windows appeared at our *pension* and took my father away. He was gone for about eight hours, during which the Finnish authorities tried to question him about Soviet military and security procedures. We had been afraid that we would never see him again. But they brought him back, apparently convinced he was not a Soviet agent.

We came home on the S.S. *Europa*, the *Bremen*'s sister ship. When we returned to Brooklyn, I found I had lost a year of school. They put me back a year until I proved that I belonged in a higher grade. I never did learn fractions.

For fear of being ostracized, I didn't share my Russian adventure with my classmates. The 1930s were a time in American political life when there was a great deal of anti-Soviet feeling. No one at school knew where I had been, and I refused to speak or acknowledge that I understood Russian until years later.

I lived two lives. In school I tried to be like the other kids; at the same time I was a member of an International Workers Order youth group, where I was accepted and admired for my Russian experience. We met one night a week to discuss politics and went to demonstrations together.

I continued to be quite involved in left-wing politics until the McCarthy era, when people I knew were being harassed and discriminated against. In 1953, the FBI paid me a visit, asking about my activities and affiliations and trying to get me to name others. Since that time, the fear engendered by McCarthyism has limited my level of involvement. I've always participated in some form of political activity—but without the consuming commitment of my late teens and early twenties. During the early 1960s, I belonged to the League of Women Voters and a fair housing group in our community. Today I'm active in a secular Jewish organization that works for social justice.

The duality between progressive political activities and beliefs and the need to "fit in" to the larger society has remained with me throughout my life.

Teachings of Marx for Girls and Boys Infiltrates Alabama

Marge Frantz

Marge Frantz was born in Birmingham, Alabama, in 1922 and lived in the South until 1950, when she moved to California. Since the mid-1970s, Frantz has taught American Studies and Women's Studies at the University of California, Santa Cruz. She has been active in the civil rights, antiwar, women's, and lesbian movements.

Here Frantz describes her father's progression from apolitical scientist to CP leader in the Deep South and her own political evolution. Frantz's father, Joe Gelders, died of a heart attack in 1950 at age fifty-two. Her mother, Esther Zane, whose wit, warmth, and joie de vivre Frantz fondly recalls, died at age ninety-four, after surviving three husbands and a lover.

I hit the jackpot in the parents lottery. My mother was warm, smart, vivacious, a charmer with a sense of humor. She was also a "Southern belle," and as an unregenerate tomboy I didn't properly appreciate her until I was an adult, but I adored my dad as far back as I can remember.

I was his firstborn, and he warmed to parenthood and to me from the start. Endlessly patient, he was full of child-friendly ideas in the John Dewey–progressive education mode prevalent in the 1920s: always explain in elaborate detail whatever you do or demand and expose your child to the widest variety of mind-expanding experiences in a hands-on way. Every time I asked the perennial child's question *"Why, Daddy?"* I got undiluted attention and such full responses I am reported to have once beseeched, "Tell me the short way, Daddy." These were the years before class analysis made the story even longer.

When I was six, he began taking me on hikes every Sunday, rain or shine, in the lovely Alabama woods. One year we studied trees and shrubs; another, flowers or ferns and mosses or mushrooms, complete with books, magnifying glass, field glasses, and projects. And at night there was often star and planet watching. But instruction never stood in the way of sheer enjoyment of hiking and nature.

As a boy he had gone to a camp led by the naturalist and Boy Scout founder Dan Beard. That experience made him an ardent and lifelong conservationist. Actually, everything he did he did ardently.

A physicist teaching at the University of Alabama, my father paid little attention to the political world until the Depression and especially FDR's presidential campaign with conservation as one of his big issues. Dad enlisted me as the "author" of a public letter he largely wrote—I was ten—on the value to future generations of conservation of natural resources. This was my introduction to politics. The story was picked up by the local papers with the headline "A little child shall lead them. Isaiah 5:2."

My dad's enthusiasm for FDR—I remember the excitement of listening with him to the first inaugural address about driving the money changers from the temple—did not last long. When Roosevelt's agricultural policies called for plowing under cotton and destroying pigs to drive up farm prices through scarcity, my father was appalled. With sights of starvation all too evident in Tuscaloosa, the idea of covering pigs with lye and burying them, or dousing oranges with kerosene and dumping them into rivers while hungry children watched, seemed the height of irrationality and made capitalism seem an economic system that was not only unworkable but evil. First and foremost, my father was a rationalist. Like many other intellectuals he decided to investigate socialism and communism.

At the university's library he looked for socialist candidate Norman Thomas's books, but the only book on the alternative-to-capitalism shelf was Stalin's *Leninism*. He took it home, stayed up all night reading, and woke up my mother the next morning with, "Darling, this book has changed my life." And, indeed, it did.

He went to the physics lab, where he was the fair-haired boy, threw the book on the desk of the department head, and said, "Dr. Wooten, this is the best book I've ever read; it's science applied to society." Marxism-Leninism seemed to have all the answers, plus the certainty that history was on its side.

What next? Finding kindred souls in Tuscaloosa was slim pickins. Shortly after, he went to New Orleans for surgery and sent my mother to the public library for all she could find on Marxism, which she then read to him as he recuperated. One day a nurse came in and shut the door. "I've noticed what you're reading, and I think I know someone you'd like to meet." She introduced him to his first live communist, the local Communist Party organizer, who urged him to go to Party headquarters in New York City and look up some people there. He did so at the first opportunity, but the Party functionaries, though friendly, weren't that trusting of, or interested in, a young Alabama intellectual. This was 1934, and proletarians, not college professors, were the ones who would lead the class struggle. However, he was taken to the workers' bookstore to load up on reading matter. On the elevator he overheard a whisper, "Shall we give him Nat Ross's name?" "No, we'll tell Nat to look him up."

He returned with a boxload of books: the eight volumes of Lenin's *Collected Works*, bright red; John Strachey's *Coming Struggle for Power*; lots of pamphlets of Marx and Lenin classics and on topics of the day; and one book especially for me, *Teachings of Marx for Girls and Boys*.

It was a curious book. Its author was William Montgomery Brown, an ex-Episcopal bishop who had been converted to Bolshevism after the Russian Revolution and who had been defrocked after the church held a well-publicized heresy trial. He had published a series of pamphlets with his picture on the cover in full bishop's regalia and titles like *Christianity and Communism*. As a beginning Latin student, I was intrigued with the caption, something on the order of "Bishop William M. Brown, in partibus Bolshevikium et Evangelicum." I don't remember the book's contents, but I recall it more as an atheist tract than as a political argument. But I didn't need to be persuaded by Bishop Brown. Daddy was on the job, and I was his eager acolyte.

He was "working" on me and Mother (my younger sister was only seven) and having much more success with me. I would have followed him anywhere. Mother was another story. She had married this young Jewish fraternity boy from an affluent family with every expectation of continuing her comfortable middle-class life. Now he was talking about going to Russia to be an engineer; the U.S.S.R. was recruiting American engineers to help with the first Five Year Plan. (He had studied chemical engineering at M.I.T. before joining the army in World War I.) That was scary enough, but soon he had decided it was more important to stay in the South and devote himself to the cause of racial justice—far more scary for her. Her family in Montgomery, whose lives revolved around the business community and the Jewish country club, was even more alarmed, as was his. Both families urged her to divorce him, but she was loyal to him, if not his new ideas.

Meanwhile, no local Party person looked him up, so he tried to find the mythical Nat Ross in Birmingham. My dad had grown up there and tried various leads, but the Party was too deeply undercover: no luck. He organized a study group at the university to read Strachey's book, the Marxist text of choice among academics in those days. Many months later, Nat sent someone to check Dad out. Soon our house became the rest and recreation spot for a number of weary young revolutionaries who had come South to change the world, an earlier and smaller version of Mississippi Summer. They mostly worked with the International Labor Defense, a group that organized legal support and public agitation on behalf of political prisoners, which in the South meant, of course, primarily victims of racial injustice.

We had a little house in the woods; Mother was a born hostess and a fabulous cook (as well as an instructor of English literature at the university), and she found the influx of youthful radicals interesting if unsettling. They loved the good food, restful surroundings, and lively discussions. I, now twelve, also loved them, as I was allowed to stay up late and listen to all the talk about their work and "the world situation."

I was learning, but so was Dad. He was horrified to hear firsthand but unreported stories of savage police repression of the union organizing efforts of sharecroppers in the Alabama Black Belt and steelworkers in Birmingham, to hear about the victims of '30s class warfare languishing in southern jails. He developed a plan for establishing a progressive school for the children of political prisoners and began to think about going to New York to try to raise money for it.

Meanwhile, Mother was worrying about the family's economic security. "Darling, you don't understand," Dad would insist. "There's no security under capitalism." But Dad also worried about keeping the family intact; despite the political tensions, he and mother remained very much in love. He proposed moving to New York City for a year to present the communist movement to Mother in a more appealing light by introducing her to colleagues studying literature. The writer and critic Granville Hicks, for example, still a communist in those days, was a big attraction.

The idea was for Dad and me to go for the summer of 1935 and reconnoiter the situation. I was to stay in Westchester County with my father's sister, who was married to a corporation lawyer, and my cousins. When we arrived at their house, my aunt greeted me warmly and said sweetly, "Tomorrow we'll go to New Rochelle and buy you a hat and gloves." That sounded like an ominous summer ahead. When I told Dad I didn't want to stay, he was agreeable. I would go to the city with him.

The cover story in Tuscaloosa was that he would take some physics courses at Columbia, but what he really wanted to do and did do was go to the Party's Workers' School. I was left free to explore the city on my own. What an exciting time! I'll never forget my wanderings on the Lower East Side, beginning on Second Avenue—interesting; then First Avenue—more interesting. By Avenue A, the ghetto really began in earnest and got progressively more fascinating. Totally entranced, I wandered among pushcarts and tenements, a foreign country all the way to the East River. The upper-middle-class

German Jewish communities in the South had not prepared me for this. The colors, the smells, the language, and the whole new world were eye-opening.

At the same time, we were meeting some of the southern communists who had ended up in New York. One of them forthwith recruited me into the Young Communist League. Soon I was selling the *Sunday Worker* on the New York subway. I was a star salesperson because of my thick southern accent. People would buy it just to hear me talk and tear it up in front of me to hear me talk some more. Our plan was to get on the subway at 14th Street, hawk the paper as we walked through the train all the way to 96th, then go downtown on the next train to 14th Street and start over again.

The city was full of enticing meetings and demonstrations. My first demonstration was at a pier to greet a delegation returning from Batista's Cuba; they had gone down to investigate human rights and were refused permission to enter Cuba. Clifford Odets, the leading playwright in 1935, was among the delegation. Here I began to learn movement songs. "Hold the Fort" was the very first. I would become a virtuoso at memorizing all the stanzas of scores of '30s radical songs. I attended meeting after meeting on the issues of the day—the *Daily Worker* had listings of meetings every day—and I listened to all the Party leaders with rapt attention. Birmingham and Tuscaloosa were never like this! What a revelatory summer for a thirteen-year-old. We also went to many Soviet movies and lots of plays; the theater was full of left-wing productions, and tickets for the second balcony were fifty-five cents. Dad also began to meet a wide range of interesting people, and I was welcomed everywhere as "Joe Gelders's daughter." One of his teachers at the Workers' School, who lived on my intriguing Lower East Side, made me part of her childless family, and I began to absorb the culture and politics of the East European Jews and felt truly at home.

Dad lined up a job as executive secretary of the National Committee to Defend Political Prisoners (NCDPP), a group of writers and artists headed by the famous journalist Lincoln Steffens. "Defense" meant organizing delegations, investigations, publicity, and support. The organization had begun with a delegation to Harlan County, Kentucky, where miners' attempts to organize had been met with brutality and violence earlier in the '30s. Dad planned to work in New York for a year and then return to open up a southern office in Birmingham.

The rest of the family arrived and rented a fourth-floor walk-up. My mother, in her usual ability-to-cope style, managed to find a job as a rental agent for a fancy apartment building—no small feat in the jobless year of 1935. That was important because the salary from the "movement" job was uncertain at best. I volunteered in the NCDPP office and learned the office skills that kept

movement organizations alive in those days: mimeographing, all the short-
cuts for folding and stuffing envelopes and sealing and stamping them and
processing bulk mailings.

I entered Washington Irving High School, joined the National Student
League and the Young Communist League (YCL) groups at the school, made
instant friendships, and went to meetings practically every night. That Christmas, the National Student League and the Student League for Industrial
Democracy merged, in new United Front fashion, to form the American Student Union (ASU). Its national office was only a few blocks from our school,
and I volunteered to help its high school director, Celeste Strack. Mostly, I
was given a broom to sweep the office.

But the chapter at Washington Irving was more productive. We participated
in the first national Peace Strike in April, and I made my first soapbox speech,
on the Scottsboro case. We attacked the high school administration for not
allowing us space in the school (I still remember my first leaflet: "An Open
Letter to Mr. Zabriski," the principal). We organized discussion groups and
met with high school organizations from all over New York City to plan campaigns on whatever was grabbing the headlines at the moment. And we developed that kind of close and intense and joyful and soul-satisfying camaraderie that accompanies continuous and committed political activity.

The YCL had a slogan that may sound strange today: "Education and character building in the spirit of socialism." "Character" has become an old-fash-
ioned word, but we took it very seriously. We cared about the quality of human beings in the movement, ourselves, and each other. When we regularly
practiced "criticism and self-criticism," we weren't as interested in how well
you wrote that leaflet or made that speech as we were about what kind of
person you were; were you a credit to the movement? Were you an example
of the socialist men or women we wanted to become? Unselfish, respectful
of others, with the common good paramount. We were accountable to each
other; we tried to make each other better people. To adolescents, especially,
that mattered. And in the South, especially, that mattered. We lived danger-
ously. Our community needed to be very tight, and it was, woven with care
and concern and love.

In September the following year, 1936, Dad went back to Birmingham to
set in motion plans for opening the southern office. Earlier, he had gone South
to organize the first Alabama interracial committee on the Scottsboro case.
Now, he had been there only a few days trying to win the release of a communist organizer who had been jailed for "possession of seditious literature"
when he was kidnapped, driven fifty miles out of town to a deserted spot,

stripped to his shorts, beaten very brutally by four thugs, and told, "If you don't leave town we'll fill you full of lead."

The story hit the headlines in Birmingham and stayed there; many other organizers had been beaten in the labor and racial conflicts of the time, but this was the first time it had happened to a local boy with family connections. The NCDPP generated demands from around the country for the governor to appoint a special investigator, and he complied. A lucky break led to the perpetrators. A stranger saw one of them behaving suspiciously, discarding in an empty lot what turned out to be stuff from Dad's wallet and a baseball bat. His license plate led to a captain and a lieutenant in the National Guard, one of them a member of the local steel company's police force. Not surprisingly, the unfriendly prosecutor presented the case to the grand jury in a prejudicial way guaranteed not to produce an indictment, and the men were never prosecuted. However, the La Follette Committee, a U.S. Senate committee investigating labor violence, held hearings on the case and was able to uncover the direct responsibility of Tennessee Coal, Iron and Railroad Company (TCI), the major power player in Birmingham (and a direct subsidiary of U.S. Steel) for planning the beating. TCI was chastened; the reign of terror against labor organizers ceased.

I was in New York, far from the scene. I remember one of my favorite teachers hugging me the morning after the beating—she had read about it in the *New York Times*—but I remember little else. Clearly, it was too painful for me to deal with then. But five years later, I was reading a novel about labor struggles in Detroit, *The Underground Stream* by Albert Maltz, which tells a graphic story of an organizer's beating, and I suddenly felt what it must have been like for Dad. I sobbed all night.

Late in 1936, the family returned to Birmingham, where I finished high school. It wasn't easy with Dad's name all over the papers, but I had some supportive teachers. It was the same high school he had attended twenty-plus years earlier, and some of his old teachers were still there and offered a helping hand. I managed to organize a peace club, edit the school paper, and recruit one friend to the Party (no YCL in the South), but it was a far cry from New York. A year and a half later I won a scholarship to Radcliffe and left for college, where my ASU activities resumed in earnest.

During the summer after my freshman year, Dad was working on a campaign to challenge a Birmingham ordinance that allowed police to search, seize, and arrest people on unspecified suspicion without a warrant and hold them incommunicado for seventy-two hours. To force a trial on the ordinance's constitutionality, we needed to have some people arrested. Four of us handed out fancy two-color mimeographed leaflets with a drawing of a cop holding a whip and a description of Ordinance 4902. Bull Connor had just been elected public safety commissioner, so I had the honor of my first arrest under his auspices! But at seventeen I was underage and was released without charge. The other three were arrested but soon released to evade a test of the ordinance. However, the publicity generated by the leaflet and the arrests forced the police to stop using the ordinance.

That same year, I organized the Alabama delegation to the American Youth Congress convention at Lake Geneva, Wisconsin: among others the son of a Farmers Union leader, a student from Tuscaloosa, and a young WPA construction worker (who during World War II became an army photographer and took some of the first pictures of Dachau). One night while I was heading back to my tent along the shores of the lake, I heard an unfamiliar voice singing a familiar song, one my mother and father had written about John Catchings, a union leader in Birmingham who had been framed on a dynamiting charge. I couldn't believe my ears; I didn't know that anyone outside of Birmingham had ever heard the song. It's a ballad with lots of verses, and hadn't ended when I got to the tent and joined in. The tall, lanky singer sitting on the floor with his banjo was equally surprised. "How do you know it?" he asked. "My mom and dad wrote it. How do *you* know it?" "I heard it in the Alan Lomax collection in the Library of Congress." I didn't know Dad had recorded it. The balladeer turned out to be Pete Seeger, then unknown; later Pete came south and stayed with us while he collected more songs, and I learned many folk songs from him. Our movement was a singing movement: we didn't listen to others sing; we all sang together. The singing not only lifted our spirits, it empowered us.

When I joined the movement, the so-called Popular Front period was just taking shape, supplanting the more revolutionary rhetoric of earlier years. The change came in response to Hitler's victory in Germany, despite the presence of massive communist and socialist parties there. Catastrophically, they had been fighting with each other instead of concentrating their force against Nazism. Now, in the United States, communists urged socialists and other leftists to join in a "united front against fascism" and in support of the American democratic tradition. Organizing the working class into militant industrial unions, agitating for civil rights, attempting to push FDR and the New Deal in a leftward direction took precedence over talk of smashing the state.

My Dad had stayed in Alabama despite the death threats, despite a fiery cross burned in our front yard, despite shots fired into our living room one night. My mother stuck with him, at first working in his office and then getting a job to support the family. Dad initiated the organization of the

Southern Conference for Human Welfare, the first large interracial organization in the South since Reconstruction, which pulled together southern liberals scattered and isolated in the schools and universities, the New Deal agencies, the labor movement, the farmers' organizations, the media, and so on. Eleanor Roosevelt and Supreme Court Justice Hugo Black were among the fifteen hundred who met in Birmingham in November 1938; sadly, I was away at college and missed the historic gathering. Dad took a full-time job as secretary of the Civil Rights Committee of the conference, working on extending the franchise—through campaigns to abolish the poll tax and to register Blacks and poor whites—in order to undermine the fiercely reactionary southern bloc in Congress, which frustrated New Deal reform. Later, I worked for the conference's youth division, the League of Young Southerners, and collaborated closely with the Southern Negro Youth Congress; still later, I edited the Southern Conference publication, the *Southern Patriot*. These were typical "popular front" organizations.

The Popular Front was the heart and soul of the communist experience for me. I was far less comfortable with the turn ten years later to a "harder" political line. But for a long time, I never thought of leaving the Party; it was my home, my family, my church. I had made a lifetime commitment. After the Khrushchev report in 1956 forced us to examine the crimes of Stalin and socialism—we had never believed the reports of the "capitalist press" on the Soviet Union—some of us thought, wow, now we can make the Party what it ought to be, a genuinely democratic organization. But it was not to be; the hard-liners kept control, and I finally left.

Our worldview was simplistic beyond belief (though no more simplistic than contemporary belief in the "free market"); we blinded ourselves disastrously. The pain of disillusion is profound. But I don't for an instant regret the experience as a whole. I can't imagine another adolescence and young adulthood I would have preferred. All memories are treacherous and made to order, and I have no doubt romanticized my own. But I would not trade the passion for social and racial justice that I inherited from my father for any other way of life. The experience of political community, the power of conviction, and the love that bound us together have sustained me over a long life of radical activism.

An Ordinary Life

Jeff Lawson

Jeff Lawson was born in 1926 to parents who were part of the Twenties generation of artists and writers. By the mid-1930s, his father, the well-known screenwriter John Howard Lawson, had become a prominent Hollywood communist. Subpoenaed by HUAC in 1947, John Howard Lawson—along with other members of the group of writers and directors known as the Hollywood 10—was cited for contempt of Congress, jailed, and blacklisted.

Raised in a world that encompassed Broadway, the film industry, and the American Left, Jeff Lawson learned to value American democracy and to believe in Marxism as the ultimate truth. In this memoir, he explores why those seemingly contradictory concepts did not support him well through the McCarthy years and how, as an adult, he had to "re-create" himself. Lawson is a photographer and writer and is working on a novel.

In the mid-1930s at Christmastime my family and I would visit well-off left-wing friends in their beautiful homes. Their comfortable lifestyles, supported by jobs in the film industry, helped give the sense that they were part of the status quo. Many were Jewish but didn't have strong religious ties. Visiting these radical homes on Christmas Day, I enjoyed the sight of the large Christmas trees with brightly wrapped gifts underneath, the sound of Christmas music, the traditional cups of eggnog sprinkled with nutmeg. Along with all the accoutrements of a merry holiday came the usual serious discussions about politics: what was FDR doing, what about the New Deal, what about the looming shadows of war in Asia and Europe, and what would the Soviet Union do about the likelihood of the capitalist countries ganging up on her?

We usually visited the Lewins in the afternoon on Christmas Day. Albert Lewin was a small man with a sweet manner. I believe he started his career as a schoolteacher, but through some connection with Irving Thalberg, he ended up a very successful and important producer at MGM. Though I am pretty sure he wasn't a communist, he was sympathetic to my father's radical ideas.

Lewin owned a huge modern mansion that had been designed by the son of Frank Lloyd Wright in the early '30s. As a boy I was particularly impressed by the fifteen-foot Christmas tree that sat in front of the huge picture window looking out over the beach and the Pacific Ocean. The setting was luxurious, one suited to a sophisticated wealthy household of the time: deep comfortable couches, displays of expensive glassware, the latest radio and record-playing equipment, fine wines and liquors. What I remember most about it was the comfort, the coziness. It seemed good to be a producer at MGM and partake of this lifestyle. As a child I saw no contradiction between being a capitalist-hating radical and achieving a level of wealth and accomplishment working in the "moom pitcha" business. Why not?

The Christmas celebrations weren't religious. They were social and embodied for these radical offspring of immigrants from Europe the acceptance of American social customs. Though many of my parents' friends hated the idea of capitalism, they did very well under it, and, in spite of their well-intentioned determination to fight the American economic structure, they had a strong desire to accept and associate with American ideals. As descendants of immigrants, the left-wingers I grew up around seemed to try especially hard to fit into the American social scene. We celebrated Easter, Thanksgiving, Christmas, New Year's, the Fourth of July. And, of course, the Hollywood studios that my father and other friends worked for were particularly strong in celebrating, even romanticizing, the American dream.

Though surrounded as a child by Jewish people, I never participated in a celebration of a Jewish holiday in anyone's home. We lived in Greenwich Village when I was in the fourth grade, and the bearded black-robed Orthodox Jews I saw on Bleecker Street as I walked to the Little Red School House seemed strange and forbidding. As I remember, the only time I was aware of Jewish holidays was when Jewish kids at North Hollywood High School in California were absent—often to the tune of sarcastic remarks by the Christian kids, who identified me as Christian, too, and with whom I wanted to be identified because I liked being accepted by the dominant group.

At school, the question of being from a communist family never came up. It was enough that my father was a successful screenwriter and wrote movies in which famous actors like Henry Fonda, Charles Boyer, Humphrey Bogart, and Hedy Lamarr starred. That gave me a certain very limited status, but one that far overshadowed any question that might arise from my father's political views, at least at that time.

I have found that for the most part, middle-of-the-road Americans don't carry strong political grudges. If they like you, they like you, and politics are secondary. I don't remember having a problem in the '30s or early '40s at school because my father was left-wing. In contrast, during the McCarthy period, there were many left or not-so-left people who were either not speaking to or not spoken to because of political conflicts.

★

Even though I was a member of a communist family and was taught all about Marx, Lenin, and Stalin, I was also imbued with American history and culture, and I developed a feel for American life that made me something of a conformist, wanting to accept the status quo. But at that time being a communist was not a total anathema, and there was little contradiction for me in having a Red father, except that he sometimes tried to be more patriotic than the average American.

I evolved a deeply felt and natural sense of patriotism, particularly during the Second World War. My cousin and several friends from high school were killed in the war. The country was so unified behind the war effort that patriotism and even a kind of progressive nationalism seemed natural and normal. Everyone was patriotic, even the Reds. Maybe particularly the Reds.

In the '30s, another kind of patriotism had stirred in the air, somehow endemic to the land and the people. The Works Projects Administration financed projects that explored American urban and rural traditions, values, and history through writing, research, photography, painting, and theater. Photographers like Walker Evans, Ansel Adams, and Edward Weston portrayed the beauty and grandeur of this country and the look of the people.

As a child, I was very interested in photography. By the time I was thirteen, I had my own darkroom, where I processed and enlarged my photos. When I was seventeen, I traveled alone to Carmel and spent a week studying photography with Edward Weston. I tramped with Weston over the gorges, points, hills, and beaches around Point Lobos and learned from him a special appreciation for the American land. That attitude was very much a part of the 1930s.

By a very young age, I already had a particularly strong feel for America's towns, cities, and landscapes. My father worked in Hollywood to make money but often returned to New York to write plays. We traveled the continent dozens of times; a big part of my early childhood was spent hearing the clack of wheels as a crack continental train, the Chief or the Twentieth Century Limited, sped west or east. I experienced a deep romance in train travel; it engendered in me special feelings about the country as I stood for hours on observation platforms seeing plains and mountains, towns and cities flow by. After the mid-'30s we often made the crossing by car, taking a week, stopping for lunch in small-town cafés, and spending the nights in motels in small towns, learning firsthand—even closer than you see by train—the feel of the country's many sections.

Though critical of American society, my father spent much of his time absorbed in American history, reading and writing on the subject. He filled his huge library not just with Marxist tomes but with books about American history. He wrote for the *New Masses* at the same time he wrote for Hollywood.

While my father studied this country's history closely and embraced its ideals, he also viewed the politics of the country negatively, often seeing fascism looming around the next corner. At the same time, he believed that Russia was a paradise and could do no wrong.

He romanticized the Soviet experience and wrote plays and movie scripts in the 1930s and '40s that contained romantic attitudes about love. His line "Take me to the Casbah" from the film *Algiers* became an icon of popular culture. *Blockade*, which he wrote about the Spanish Civil War for producer Walter Wanger and which starred Madeleine Carroll and Henry Fonda, was antifascist and considered radical at the time but also contained an idyllic love story. His patriotic films supportive of the war effort expressed glamorized attitudes toward American ideals, war aims, and the fighting person. *Action in the North Atlantic* showed the heroic work of the Merchant Marine and, uniquely, a union hiring hall, promoting the importance of American workers in winning the war. *Sahara*, directed by Zolton Korda, with Humphrey Bogart, gave a positive, somewhat mythic view of the Allied and American soldier and the values of American life. Rex Ingram, playing a Black soldier from the Sudanese army, was portrayed very sympathetically as a resourceful and appealing man who had only one wife even though religious laws allowed him more.

I think a kind of romanticism was endemic to many '20s writers and certainly to the Hollywood of the '30s and '40s. My father hated the Victorian period and revolted against it. Though on the surface he was somewhat sexually liberated like many '20s writers, I would argue that his love story romanticism was a hangover from Victorian times. I see a connection between the Victorian way of turning a blind eye to sexual reality and my father's way of turning a blind eye to Soviet reality.

I imagine the contradictions in my personality stem as much, or more, from my parents being the children of immigrants as from their being Reds. My mother's parents emigrated from Scotland, lived in Virginia, and then moved to West Texas, settling in Waco. My grandfather was 6'4", so tall, it was said, that he had to have special beds made for him; he evolved from being a tall Scot to being a tall Texan. He died from eating a bad can of peas when my mother was three years old. Though not well off, the family was well accepted in the small community of Waco. Assimilation into the American mainstream was not difficult for a descendant of the Scots. But my mother was very sensitive and had problems accepting the rough-hewn, macho world dominated by Texas males. At about twenty, she went to New York City, attended Columbia University, lived on Patchen Place in Greenwich Village, the home of a number of 1920s writers and intellectuals, and became friends with e e cummings and other artistic members of the "Lost Generation," including my father.

My father's father assimilated against great odds and in the face of prejudice. His goal was to deny his Jewish background and become one with British and American culture. In the 1800s, he traveled throughout the West as an itinerant journalist. Then he went to Mexico City, where he started an English-language newspaper. Being a wily entrepreneur and having an understanding of business, he played the Southern Pacific and Santa Fe railroads against each other to get financing. He was very successful and became wealthy. He moved to Yonkers, New York, and married a woman who was high in society and who had the same desire he did, to shed a Jewish past. Belle Hart was well educated and something of an Anglophile. She named one son Wendell after Oliver Wendell Holmes and my father John Howard after an English lawyer. My grandfather, Simeon Levy, called Pippie, had earlier changed his name to Lawson. He became a Christian Scientist, sent his children to private Christian schools, and rode around in a horse-drawn carriage serviced by footmen. He became the head of the East Coast division of the prestigious British news-gathering service, Reuters. My father often told the story of how his father would make reservations at Catskill resorts using his legal name of Lawson and writing the request on Reuters' stationary. Once the family arrived at the resort, in spite of the coach and footmen and trappings of wealth, they were promptly thrown out because my grandfather looked Jewish and had a thick Yiddish accent.

My father had a typical upper-class education—private schools, good college, and tours of Europe. He had little remembrance of his Jewish background. By the time he reached Hollywood he was already more assimilated than many of his friends. My father was a complex man. I believe his mother's death when he was eleven had a deep effect on him and was part of his anger. But I think what also helped to make him so angry and radical was having a family that tried so hard to gain approval and yet was not totally accepted. He described to me a number of times how at Williams College he had by far the most articles published in the literary magazine and deserved the position of editor but lost it to another student who was not Jewish.

After his wife died, my grandfather never remarried, and my father was raised by nurses and caretakers. He was given an excellent education, but his father didn't spend much time with him. My father was deeply affected by the suicide of his older brother, due in part to my grandfather's insisting that Wendell go into business and give up his aspirations to be a violinist. After that my grandfather could no longer control my father's choice of profession. In 1915, when he was nineteen years old and still at Williams, my father had a play produced on Broadway by George M. Cohan and Sam Harris. Another play, *Processional*, which was first performed in 1924, was experimental and pre-Brechtian in form and showed a Victorian, overbearing, overcontrolling, angry, capitalist father. My earliest memories of my father are somewhat similar to his experience of his father, except mine was not a capitalist but a liberated Twenties radical. I remember an aloof, very, very angry, and driven man who seldom spoke to me, who was not affectionate, and toward whom I felt fascination and awe but also fear. He was not a disciplinarian but was emotionally distant, filled with a frightening ire, and apparently inwardly afraid to be warm and loving to a child. Somehow his angry Victorian controlling father had evolved in him into an angry and driven radical man.

No doubt some of my ambivalence toward my communist upbringing has to do with my early fear and resentment of my father. When I was in my late twenties, he did try to overcome his coldness and self-centeredness and succeeded in some ways; I respect him for that, but it was a little late for me. The communists I grew up with were politically in favor of sharing the wealth, spreading the largess, helping the underdog, the working people, the poor, but in their personal lives were often wrapped up in themselves, self-centered. Though I knew a number of extraordinary human beings, I think my emotional growth was stunted by the narrowness, bigotry, and short-sightedness of many of the people I grew up around. But it went deeper than that: the movement itself, its ideals, ideology, methods, personalities, turned out to be flawed in many ways.

I noticed as a child—and it angered me and was painful at the time—that many left-wingers hero-worshiped my father without the slightest knowledge of what he was really like, of his emotional limitations. Even more, I knew that many of them related to me only in terms of my father. I lived my childhood with people saying, "Jeff, you are so lucky to have such a great man as a father." They were talking, of course, about the father they desired and projected in their own minds. I knew how little these vaunted intellectuals and writers were seeing; it hurt that they didn't see my father or myself as very real. Maybe good old Uncle Joe Stalin was that for them, too, an ideal father. They were captured by grand, great, utopian ideas. They were not bad people. But something was missing from them. Perhaps some were communists and believed so much in saving humanity because it was the only way they could love. Perhaps it was better than nothing, but in my mind not good enough.

In the late '40s and early '50s, most left-wing people I knew were scared. Some went underground or to Europe out of fear of concentration camps. I was harassed by the FBI. Several of my close friends fell apart emotionally. I did, too—but later, in the mid-'50s. We who had grown up in that movement lacked some inner strength. I think it was not just the difficulty of the times but because we had been given rigid and unreal ideals and were taught not to question them. Deep down, they weren't ours. I became disillusioned; I was lost for a long time. I had to try to get rid of the failed dogmatism of the communist movement I had been raised in and slowly, laboriously find other values that made more sense to me.

The blind adulation of a mass murderer that the American communists indulged in was bad enough. But I also question what was in the minds of my father and the other people I grew up with that led them to believe so strongly in such false concepts. What trick of destiny closed their eyes at some important turn in the road? In his eighties, the tragedy of my father's life was that all he had believed in had been turned upside down, not just by the evil Right he had so feared but by professed communists and their heroes. Even though he wouldn't completely admit it, his own ideals had turned against him. What a fate! And what decisions of his own had helped lead there?

My grandfather was an angry capitalist. My father was an angry communist. For a long time I was an angry nonpolitical. But in struggling to deal with the strange contradictions of my childhood and young adulthood, I eventually came to a place within myself where I felt I knew who I was and what I believed without having to rely on the crutches of mechanical ideology, or false gods. I feel a certain contentment with that. No idea is as big as the universe. No one set of ideas ever explains it all. Anyone who thinks otherwise is wrong and, I think, doomed to disillusionment.

The Old Red Granny

Mindy Rinkewich

Born in the Bronx, New York, in 1929, the only child of an immigrant
family, Mindy Rinkewich has been writing Yiddish and English poetry
most of her life. She studied Yiddish at the Jewish schools of the International Workers Order and Slavic studies at Columbia University.
Rinkewich lives in New York City, where she works as a legal interpreter.

Like Pearl Harbor or D-Day for mainstream Americans, the Spanish
Civil War (1936–39) was a world- and life-changing event for U.S. leftists.
Many felt that World War II could have been prevented if fascism had
been stopped in Spain.

This poem first appeared in *Shmate*, 1, no. 2 (June–July 1982).

The old Red Granny lights no Sabbath candles
She has no truck with the Almighty Blessed is He
She hasn't fasted on Yom Kippur since she was fifteen
The old Red Granny turns her hand into a fist and says:
"If they had really stopped them
That time, at Madrid,
Things would be different."

December 1947

Marianne Ware

When Marianne Ware was born in 1936, her father, Max Horwitz, was passing out leaflets for the International Workers Order on a New York City street corner. Her mother, Shirley Zankman, who earned the family's only dependable income, returned to work just a few weeks after giving birth.

In the early 1950s Ware moved with her family to Los Angeles, where she rebelled by negating her left-wing background until Cesar Chavez and the United Farm Workers stirred her to political involvement. Ware has lived in Northern California for almost thirty years. She has an M.F.A. in writing and teaches in the English department at Santa Rosa Junior College.

From earliest childhood, red diaper babies learn that human misery can be permanently eliminated only through radical change in the economic and political structures of society. Yet, for many, this raises a dilemma: what can or should be done about the people who suffer in the painful present while awaiting the socialist future? In this autobiographical short story, Ware explores the collision between a father's rigid political stance and a daughter's attempt to interpret ideology in terms of actual human lives.

That winter, when Barbara was eleven, she and her parents had to vacate a three-room flat on 14th Street in New York City to make space for their landlord's cousin. With the postwar housing shortage still in full swing, all they could find was a one-room furnished "apartment" in a converted hotel on 112th Street.

Each night, a small sofa was let down to make a bed for Barbara, but it stuck out so far that the door to the hall could not open fully and only a foot of space separated the corner of her parents' bed and her own.

Harold usually had late-night meetings at Communist Party headquarters, so Barbara and her mother, May, slept together until his key clicked in the lock and Barbara had to jump up and play musical beds. Often she'd lie awake for nearly an hour after the switch, listening to her father snore and studying patterns on the ceiling made by streetlights seeping in between slats of the Venetian blinds. Sometimes she'd hear her mother thrashing over on her side of the bed and muttering about having to be up at six.

Barbara also had to get up early, so May could make sure she'd brushed her teeth and washed thoroughly in the women's bathroom down the hall. By six-thirty they'd be talking over a breakfast of Wheatena in the community kitchen.

"Here's your lunch: tuna on pumpernickel . . . Stop with that look, Barbara; you need proper nutrition. Promise you'll eat everything?"

"The kids at this school take white bread."

"Leave me alone with that subject. I've got too much on my mind today: the billing and payroll with only four hours' sleep."

After May left to catch the subway, Barbara usually read or did homework at the kitchen table until time to get her coat, gloves, and galoshes from their room. Then, without disturbing Harold, she'd leave for P.S. 96, nearly a mile away.

For the first couple of blocks down Broadway, the cold wind would sear her cheeks and the exposed portions of her legs, but as she came upon store windows with holiday decorations, her physical discomfort faded.

Outside the bakery, Barbara always stopped to drool over a three-humped cake made to look like a snowman. Multicolored jelly bean buttons adorned its belly, and a red icing cap oozed from the top of its head. The eyes were licorice gumdrops, the nostrils two raisins, while the mouth puckered in a cherry sourball grin.

Barbara's next stop came two blocks down at the shoemaker's shop, where the window displayed a group of elves, all dressed in Santa suits, working on an array of tiny footgear. Off to one corner, sleeping children (dolls, really) lay dreaming—Barbara was certain—of a true miracle, new shoes on Christmas morning.

Even the dry cleaners had a holiday display: glittery electric lights on tiny evergreens with a model railroad meandering beneath them. The tracks made loops through the trees and at one curve went round the edge of an oval mirror set down in artificial snow to simulate a lake on which small figures skated.

Jerked back from her fantasies of travel to the land of Hans Brinker, of open spaces and tall, tall trees, Barbara always panicked at that point, realizing she might already be late for school. This gave her an excuse to run the remaining blocks at great speed, with only a glance at the diorama in the butcher's window: the crudely shaped, out-of-proportion cluster of brightly painted animals and humans with that almost sinister-looking infant lying in state before them.

Inside the overheated building, Barbara would try to become as inobtrusive as possible, hugging the wall as she sidled down to her classroom. Once in her seat, she'd slouch and began her usual chantlike internal monologue: Don't let her call on me, not me, not me, not me. Mrs. Gilchrist's favorite expression was "free, white and twenty-one," which made Barbara think of Harold's friend Lester Robinson, whose chocolate skin and beautiful smile had always delighted her.

She'd liked social studies at her other school, where they talked about customs in different countries, but here they'd already spent two weeks just on Russia. An essay on "The Menace of American Communism" was due just after Christmas, and Barbara could not imagine how to write it, especially when she imagined what Harold would say if he ever found out.

At 3 P.M., Barbara always paused in the school yard to breathe deeply and contemplate what she could do with the time of day she had all to herself. May would not be home for hours. There was nothing to stop Barbara from walking slowly past the butcher's shop, nothing to prevent her from moving close to stare at the scene, nothing except the intrusion of her father, his image and his words inside her head. "What rotten baloney! A myth about a damned 'savior' that makes people pawns of this lousy capitalist system. You must see how stupid it is, kid, poor people buying useless gifts with pittance earnings, dreaming about pie in the sky instead of decent wages in their pockets."

The nativity scene always looked to Barbara as if it were a depiction of life on Mars or in Australia, the people's clothing so alien, their faces somber, while the animals seemed about to smile. After a while she'd have to move on, her mind grey fuzz so she wouldn't keep thinking about Harold and because the cold activated a feeling akin to sadness deep within her bones.

When she turned onto the street where they lived, another wave of discomfiture always surged through her body, compelling her to walk past their building, on up to Amsterdam Avenue, where half a block down loomed the Cathedral of St. John the Divine. Like the crèche, it was forbidden to look upon, but she did it anyway, stared at that Gothic structure, mounted its broad steps with her eyes, moved them, curiously, over the high arches, the carved insets, until frigid gusts and the mottling sky sent her racing home.

One afternoon, Barbara came back to find her father stretched across the big bed, reading the *Daily Worker.*

"Make me some coffee," he told her.

"We're out; May said so this morning."

"How do you tell which stuff is ours?"

"Second shelf in the corner closet; bottom rack, left side, in the fridge."

"Well, go fix me something."

"There's only pot cheese, oatmeal, and a can of tuna."

"Damn, why doesn't your mother stock up?"

"There's no room; she buys for supper every night on the way home. If you ate with us more you'd . . ."

"When does she get here?"

"Six o'clock, usually."

Harold returned to his paper while Barbara curled her legs up so she could lie on the unopened sofa.

At 6:30, his snort woke them both. "Where can she be?" he asked petulantly. "I'm starved."

"We could walk down to the grocery," she offered.

"OK, get your stuff on."

The weather had turned particularly nasty. Sleet fell icily against their cheeks, while the wind pummeled their backs. "Where's the grocery?" he asked.

"Five blocks down."

Passing the bakery, she could not resist hinting: "May says after five you can get cheap day-old stuff baked just this morning."

"It's still too expensive. I'm nearly broke, and your mother doesn't get paid 'til Friday."

"Are we going to Philly to see Grandma for Christ——?"

"Not Christmas, dammit!"

They were nearing the butcher's as he spoke, and she, to distract him, pointed at something low to the ground, moving rapidly toward them. "What's that?"

Harold stopped dead and stared. "Christ! Not in this weather," he mumbled under his breath.

"What?"

"That, young lady, is proof of the failure of this rotten culture. Sick people, homeless people, and nobody gives a damn. You'd think it was still the Depression . . ." He began walking again, waving his arms as he talked. As usual, his words made little sense to Barbara, though she soon realized that the moving object was a wheeled cart on which a stub of a man sat, a man with no legs below the knees. He came toward them, moving his torso in a rocking motion, propelling himself with what seemed like arms of extraordinary length. He wore a raggedy pea jacket, hacked off so he could sit without it bunching up on his thighs, which were each wrapped, mummylike, and jutted out in front of him. As he got even closer, Barbara noticed that his fingers, protruding from torn gloves, gripped wooden blocks that clopped on the sidewalk as his arms swung forward to move the cart along.

When he was nearly abreast of them, Barbara could see stains on the white knitted cap he had pulled down to cover his ears and something shiny underneath his nose. Just then, his eyes caught hold of hers. Without thinking, Barbara grabbed her father's hand.

"Whatsa matter, kid?" he asked, veering away to look at something in the gutter.

"I'm just so . . . uh . . . cold. It makes my bones hurt."

"Walk faster; you'll be OK," Harold said, clearing his throat and daubing his nose with a gloved hand.

At the next corner they came to the grocery, and after Barbara helped her father count change from his pocket, they left with a can of chicken noodle soup, Saltines, and some cheap coffee. Halfway home again, Barbara saw that the legless man had stopped in front of the bakery. Now he faced the street, his arm extended, his hand holding what looked like a metal cup.

"Pencils for sale. Buy a pencil, two for a nickel," he called out to them. His breath, like icicles, clung to the air.

"Oh, Harold, please buy some," she said as they paused on the sidewalk.

"Barbara, cut it out!" he whispered. "Sure, it's a pitiful sight, makes your guts ache, but your whining's not gonna help. I don't have any money, and besides, we've got to change the system; charity just keeps the rich rich and the poor miserable."

"But it's cold; right now it's cold. My God, he must be hungry."

"Dammit! don't say 'God'; it shows you think he's real, that all this Christmas crap means something." Harold's eyes gleamed and his voice had turned croaky. Then, abruptly, he began striding away, going so fast she had to run after him.

Almost every store had a few colored lights in the window. They blurred as she passed, even after she'd dried her eyes on the edge of her sleeve. The awful feeling she fought off in the afternoons had taken over her entire body, as if her bones were porous, with the acid of melancholy seeping through them.

Harold rounded their corner without looking back, and Barbara felt his abandonment like a blow to her spine. "What took you so long?" he chided as she stumbled through the elevator doors he held back for her.

May was there, buttoning her coat, as they emerged on the fourth floor. "I was worried sick; why didn't you leave a note?"

"I spent my last cent," Harold complained.

"He still has a nickel and two pennies, May, and this poor, starving man . . ."

"Dammit! She's too sentimental, just like you."

"I didn't expect you for dinner, but I got enough . . . Go rest in the room while I cook," May said.

"Look at her! Look at her face! The kid thinks I'm a monster. The poor bastard got to me, too, but what the hell could I do, take his pitiful pencils for a few lousy cents?"

"I don't understand what you're saying. Just go sit down while I get you something to eat." May gestured toward their door, her other hand patting the sleeve of her husband's topcoat.

"I'm not hungry; stomach's queasy. Look, I've gotta go canvassing tonight. Give me some money for fare. I'll see you both later."

After dinner, Barbara asked May why Harold hardly earned any money even though he talked about the work he had to do all the time. "You don't get paid for making the world a better place," she said.

"But is it ever going to be better? Will people stop being crippled and cold and poor, and when will we have a real apartment again?"

"I don't know, honey. I just don't know."

"Well, you're wrong. He doesn't care about anybody."

"Don't say that, Barbara. He does care; he does. When you were smaller, he got himself thrown in jail for moving a poor Negro family back in their apartment after the landlord put them and their furniture out on the street."

"Well, he doesn't care if I don't have friends 'cause I can't bring them to this horrible place, and he doesn't care about that man on the cart. He wasn't asking for charity. He had those pencils, and he was so cold his bones hurt. I know they did."

"You're too young to understand what your father's trying to do," May insisted. "Tonight, he'll be out in the cold ringing doorbells, trying to convince people to . . ."

"To what? To believe all that Party junk about . . ."

"I won't listen to this," May said sharply.

That next week, when school let out for the holidays, Barbara went for long walks until well after noon, returning only when she was sure Harold had left for the day. She was searching for the man on the cart, though she could not have explained why. Down Broadway to the 80s she walked, then over to Riverside Drive and back up along the Hudson River, turning east at 98th, and finally north toward home. After her long walk, she'd eat some leftovers, collapse on the big bed, and nap awhile before going out again.

It was December 21 when the letter came for Barbara from Harold's mother in Philadelphia. Inside she found three crisp dollar bills and the directive to spend them any way she wanted. At suppertime Barbara told May her plan. "I want to, please? It's my money."

Late that night she heard her parents arguing in whispers. "She wants to buy a few gifts with it. What's the harm?"

"Why not some damned shoes? You're always saying she needs shoes. Christ, I hate this time of year, May. I hate it! So much need out there and all that stupidity and expectation."

"Look, she knows how you feel. She's not asking us to celebrate. Just let her do what she wants, what your mother wants."

"I know the kid thinks I'm heartless, that you're the one who really earns our . . ."

"Shush, she'll hear you. Let her do this one thing and . . ."

"All right! All right! Just leave me out of it. But if she buys me anything, I'll blow my top."

The next day Barbara went to the five and dime and got May a box of stationery and a pin shaped like a starfish. She found some handkerchiefs embroidered with lilies for her grandma and a bottle of "Heaven Scent" perfume for her aunt. Then she chose Captain Marvel comic books for her cousin Bill and Archie and Veronicas for his sister Ann.

After she paid for the gifts, she looked halfheartedly at the men's things but did not make a purchase, leaving the store to wander the streets again. With only two days before they left for their visit with Harold's family, she felt a terrible urgency to search for the crippled man.

It was almost dark when she passed the bakery, and with money still in her pocket she succumbed to its lure, emerging with three eclairs, three brownies, and a loaf of soft white bread.

"You greedy girl," her mother grinned at her. "How much is left?"

"Two quarters. Do you think that's enough to get something for Har——, for him?"

"No! Forget it. You'd only make him mad."

Barbara went out early the next morning just as a light snow was beginning to fall. She intended to go even farther than before, but soon felt weak and chilled, so she turned around and sloshed back home. Harold was still sleeping, and she was about to curl up on her unopened sofa when something prompted her to go to the window, pull the slats apart, and look down at the street. There, rounding the corner onto Amsterdam Avenue, was the man on his cart.

Barbara moved as if in a frenzy, shoving shoeless feet into floppy galoshes, diving into her coat, and lunging for the door. Once on the street, she ran hoodless, gloveless, all unbuttoned, up the sidewalk and around the corner,

Marianne Ware, fourth from the left, at Camp Kinderland, summer 1942. Courtesy of Marianne Ware.

where, with great relief, she spotted him down in front of the cathedral, arm extended, cup in hand.

The coins unstuck themselves like ice cubes from her fingers, clinking as they hit bottom. "Just one," she said. "And keep all the money. We don't need it."

Later that afternoon, as Barbara lay stretched across her parents' bed in a kind of semiwakeful, semisleeping stupor, she imagined Harold in the subway station, saw him reach for his change only to find that long, slim tinfoil package wound round with hair ribbon. Then, in the next instant, she visualized her father inside a train hurtling toward Foley Square as he unwrapped what she'd foisted upon him, to stare, until his eyes began to sting, at that single pencil, the one gift he could not denigrate or deny.

Commiebastid

Albert Vetere Lannon

Albert Vetere Lannon lives in San Francisco, where for many years he was an official with the West Coast International Longshore and Warehouse Union. Lannon is chair of the Laney College Labor Studies Program and performs monologues about snakes and other subjects. He earned his high school diploma at age fifty-one and completed his master's degree in history in 1997, writing a biography of his father as his thesis.

For some red diaper babies, being part of the everyday world of childhood while remaining true to parental values required creative adaptations. Here, Lannon describes his evolution into a tough street kid whose outrageous behavior was often rooted in his own interpretation of left-wing values.

Once again the monsters came at me—Frankenstein, the Mummy, and a malevolent Tin Man. Mom shook me awake, whispering, "They're arresting Dad. Get up. Get dressed." It was June 20, 1951. I was thirteen.

Two giant FBI agents were watching Dad get dressed. No, he couldn't shave. No, he couldn't go to the bathroom alone. They handcuffed him and led him down the stairs from our Manhattan apartment. My sister Karen, who had turned seven the day before, stayed close to Mom, wide-eyed.

Mom got on the phone. Two East 12th Street neighbors, Liz Flynn and Izzy Amter, had also been arrested during the 6 A.M. raids. Mom looked at me with uncommon light in her eyes and said, "Go to school. We'll show them we're not scared." But, oh god, I was scared. I walked the two blocks to Junior High School 60 waiting for someone, some . . . thing to pounce on me. In my homeroom class Ira Slade had a copy of the morning *Daily News*. The huge black headline said seventeen New York Communist leaders had been arrested for "conspiracy to teach and advocate the overthrow of the United States government by force and violence." Ira Slade glanced at me and took the paper to the teacher. He pointed to one of the photographs and whispered, "That's Albert's father!" I wanted to run, to hide, to scream, to be anyplace other than here, now.

In my English class Mrs. Rosenberg—no relation to Ethel and Julius—told the students, "Thank God this is America, not Soviet Russia. People are free to believe what they want here, and if Albert chooses to think like his father that's his business." She stared hatred at me. Later I challenged her definition of the word "hibernation" and I was right—and I would find other ways to strike back.

Freddie Nelson, the toughest kid in school, followed me down the hall chanting, "Commiebastid, commiebastid, commiebastid." I escaped into my gym class. The gym teacher looked around to make sure no one was watching and put her hand on my shoulder. "If I can be of help . . ." Her voice trailed off, and she jerked her hand away as another kid came through the door.

Freddie Nelson found me again later. "Commiebastid, commiebastid, commiebastid." I had to stop at a crowded doorway. Freddie lifted his foot and wiped the sole of his shoe on my dungarees. Something in me went beyond fear and reason, and I wiped my shoe on his neon blue, double white-saddle-stitched pegged pants. He cursed in surprise. I dropped my books and hit him. We scuffled and swung at each other. One of my wild punches connected and bounced his head off the wall and he went down. I was terrified that he would get up and kill me, but I got away.

Running home I saw several cars parked on the block with pairs of giant men in each. I knew they were the FBI. I knew the FBI followed subversive kids. I knew that monsters were everywhere, and that I would have to be on guard for the rest of my life.

Weeks later, when Dad and his comrades were out on bail, released from the West Street jail with strict travel limitations, he and Mom went to the country with Karen, illegally passing through an hour's worth of New Jersey. I stayed behind with my job, soda jerking in the corner candy store. Since I couldn't get working papers until I was fourteen, I was paid less than half the minimum wage.

One night while they were gone I invited two friends to stay overnight. We drank from a bottle of whiskey I found in a kitchen cupboard, and I knew I had found a way to escape my feelings, to run away from my anger.

The anger came from knowing I was afraid, from fear and hatred of a government that could deprive me of my father, the father I desperately craved connection with. I was angry at Dad for being responsible for it all. I wanted and didn't want to be Al Lannon, Junior. But my folks did the best they knew how. They couldn't give me what they had never gotten themselves. We pass on what we know.

★

Mom's parents came from Finland; both were alcoholics. Grandpa Isa was a copper miner and Wobbly who later became a steelworker. He had come to America to escape the Russian czar's conscription. He married Grandma Aiti on a return trip to Finland, this time on the run from a lost strike in Montana. When he returned to Ellis Island with his bride, his name, Bjorklund, was too difficult for the processors, and they renamed him Lund.

My mother, Elvi Lund, was born in Pennsylvania; growing up with alcoholic parents, she became the responsible member of the family at age eleven. She was athletic and found self-esteem through Finnish-American community sports programs. In her scrapbook is a certificate for winning a shot put event sponsored by the Labor Sports Union, a division of the Red Sports International, and a drawing of her made in a Washington, D.C., jail when she was sixteen years old. She took pride in being a "premature antifascist," arrested for protesting the sale of scrap iron to Japan.

When she met and married Dad, at eighteen, her life become subordinate to his and her Finnish support system was replaced by the CP activity dictated by Dad. Mom learned to cook Italian, and I grew up identifying with Dad's side of the family as Italian American, uninterested in my Finn heritage for years to come.

Dad was the oldest boy of eleven living children. His parents came to the United States from Calabria, in the poor southern Italian mountains. Grandpa Luigi was as tough as the land he came from and as hard as the cold walls of the stone house he was raised in, with beatings for those like Dad who dared challenge him. Grandma Caterina was descended from Albanians who had sought refuge from Turkish oppression in the mountains of Calabria some four hundred years before. She was not allowed to speak her first language in Luigi's house.

Dad was raised Catholic and served as an altar boy. He left high school at age fifteen to pick tomatoes and work in a factory. At seventeen he rebelled against his father's tyranny and ran away to sea. He was caught and returned home for being underage, a hero to his siblings. The next time he ran away he decided he had to have a new name to avoid capture, and he found one in a pulp cowboy novel. Anselmo Francesco Vetere became Albert Francis Lannon. And Al Lannon became an alcoholic, a self-described "bum."

Dad bragged in later years how he was known in New Zealand ports as "the wild Yank" and how, after one binge, a doctor told him he would die if he kept on drinking. Released, he promptly got drunk on cheap gin, kicked the doctor's door in, and declared: "You're a fuckin' liar!"

In 1930 his ship went to the Black Sea and spent twenty-three days in Novorossisk, where Dad discovered the promise of socialism. The Soviet workers he met treated him "like a respected person," asking "this dumb sailor" for suggestions on improving the way they worked.

Returning to the United States, Dad stopped drinking and joined the leftist Marine Workers Industrial Union, soon approaching local communists about admission to the Party. The CP put him to work distributing literature. He slept in the union hall and walked miles to the barges at 96th Street, believing his hardships to be a test of his fitness for membership.

The runaway who returned home to organize "Happy Al's" dances at a New Jersey firehouse, the loner trying to impress others with his drunken exploits, the "bum" had found acceptance and self-respect. He was a founding member and strike leader of the National Maritime Union and an organizer hired by John L. Lewis for the Committee for Industrial Organization. After a term at Moscow's Lenin School for world revolutionaries he became a full-time Communist Party functionary.

Dad was a good storyteller, a charming man with intense blue eyes who could sway people with the sheer force of his personality. Sometimes his stories were self-serving and, I realized much later, not borne out by the facts. But I loved his tales of revolutionary heroism: of recruiting seamen to fight with the International Brigades in Spain and the CP reneging on a commitment to let Dad go over as a political commissar; of arming a ship's crew so they could mutiny and return to their newly liberated Eastern European peoples' republic; of carrying court injunctions as picket signs and refusing to a pay a one-cent fine when arrested during a waterfront strike; of throwing a Hearst newspaper courier and his offer of money to turn stool pigeon down a flight of stairs; of being pursued by Murder, Inc.; of pioneering racially mixed union meetings in the South; of dangling a CP emissary out of a window until a directive was rescinded and of a Comintern representative later approving the political correctness, if not the method, of the waterfront comrades.

As I heard the stories I felt that I should have been born earlier so that I too could have fought the fights of the 1930s, when being a Red was acceptable and exciting and communists were on the front lines of a growing world movement against capitalist oppression. It seemed to me to have been a braver and simpler time, when heroes were legion and the masses were on the move toward a glorious socialist tomorrow.

Al Lannon, Junior, age three, on his father's shoulders, accompanied by his mother, at the 1941 May Day parade in New York City. Courtesy of Albert Vetere Lannon.

★

I was born in January 1938, a prewar year of lingering depression in America, but we were never hungry and Mom even had diaper service. Dad left for an organizing trip after taking Mom to the hospital to give birth. Italian family tradition demanded that I be named after my grandfather, but Dad wanted me named after Roy Hudson, his party mentor. In his absence, however, Mom went for the Junior. I never liked that, but it could have been worse: one red diaper baby of my generation was named Mels, an acronym for Marx, Engels, Lenin, and Stalin.

At the beginning of World War II we lived on the Upper West Side of New York, moving to Baltimore in 1943 when the CP transferred Dad; my sister Karen was born there a year later. We moved in with a group from the Italian side of the family in Elizabeth, New Jersey, in 1945 and then to the East Bronx in New York City. After spending a brief time in Biloxi, Mississippi, in 1947, we settled down on East 12th Street on New York's Lower East Side. Moving around as much as we did I never really sank roots. I felt like I was constantly the new kid on the block, the outsider from someplace else. I sought love and attention from my parents to compensate for the isolation, the sense of not belonging anywhere, but they were busy organizing, mobilizing, going to meetings, combating repression.

I soon learned that if I was both outrageous *and* politically correct I could get Mom and Dad's approval. In Baltimore I came home crying one day. I had been pulling my little red wagon around to collect scrap for the war effort and a man had said something bad about the Jews. I wanted the big bolo knife Dad had kept from his seagoing days; I wanted to kill the offender. That won me attention and approval.

During those years there was only one safe haven, the basement kitchen of my cousins' Hungarian grandmother. Fannie Krall baked poppy seed cakes, stocked her icebox with sodas, and welcomed the children with unconditional love. My other lingering memory of Baltimore, however, is of taking one of Dad's mementoes, a Finnish hunting knife, holding it at arm's length, plunging it to my chest, stopping, and wishing I had the courage not to. When Karen was born I realized that Dad did have time for love and affection, just not for me. I became thin to the point of needing medical attention. Later, in Biloxi, Mississippi— where I wasn't allowed to wear a devil mask at Mardi Gras for fear of offending our Bible Belt neighbors—I began overeating compulsively.

Not fitting in was not just about moving and changing schools. I was afraid to let my true self be known. When kids got together and talked about their parents I couldn't very well say, "My father is an organizer for the Communist Party." I learned to lie: Dad was a salesman, on the road a lot. Mom was a secretary. I didn't have to say it was at the Party office. And I was a Lutheran, whatever that was.

At the age of six, just after my sister was born, I began doing loner things that took me to the edge of trouble and beyond: going out on the ice of a forbidden pond and falling in the frigid water, trying to derail trolley cars by putting rocks on the tracks, shaving my eyebrows, demanding attention even if it was all negative.

We moved to East 12th Street in Manhattan when I was ten years old. The neighborhood, just below the screeching Third Avenue El, had a paper factory, a machine shop, a Jewish Home for the Aged (on whose awning crossbar we chinned ourselves), and apartment buildings ranging from once elegant to badly neglected. The candy store on the corner of Second Avenue became my hangout.

We had a large apartment, so Karen and I each had our own rooms. The spare room was rented out, first to Gerhardt and Hilde Eisler, German-born communists who were portrayed in the press as spies and monsters. I remember that Gerhardt often brought home cookies for Karen and me and had a quick smile for us. He disappeared one day, stowing away on a ship to escape prosecution, and Hilde soon followed him to East Germany, leaving most of her considerable wardrobe behind. It was during this time that someone across the street regularly peered into our windows with binoculars. Karen and I were used to the FBI parking on our block and followed instructions never to talk with them.

I began to keep snakes and spiders and other creepy-crawlies as pets. Snake stories continue to be recalled by relatives and my parents' comrades who passed through the house: the corn snake escaping through a front window the morning Dad was arrested; the garter snake who gave birth on the kitchen floor, Mom screaming while she trapped the squirmy newborns under pot covers; the four-foot alligator I was transporting to the Staten Island Zoo that spent the night in our bathtub.

I had a black racer in an aquarium, and I bragged about it to a boy from across the street. Carl Herrmann was five years older than me, smoked a pipe, wore a mustache, *and* had a baby boa constrictor! He became very important to me. Carl opened me up to jazz, Freud and psychology, Civil War history, pork pie hats, and serious herpetology.

Johnny-Boy DeMaria became my best buddy; we nicked ourselves one day on a rooftop to mix our blood and declare ourselves brothers. Carl, Johnny-Boy, and I were a little nature lovers group, sometimes joined by others. Our block had three active reptile collections as well as three arrested Communist leaders. Carl led us on hikes in search of reptiles and adventure; he and I spent a week on a rattlesnake hunt in South Carolina just months before Dad's arrest.

In the woods I felt a sense of communion with something much larger than myself, some sense that there was peace outside of the fear and anger in which I lived. It was not just a kind of spiritual connection that drew me to the outdoors; it was also that I was part of a group and that we could sing and run and climb and swim and laugh and fart and stay up all night and eat pancakes all day if we wanted to. We were free to be the kids we were, and it was the only place for me where that was true. Kids outside of our small group called me "Nature Boy" after Nat King Cole's hit song.

Dad made an effort to share the woods with me once, taking me by train to Pinewald, a jumping-off place for exploring the South Jersey pine barrens, where rumor had it an uncommon hog-nosed snake had been caught by the friend of a friend. Dad had a severe ulcer attack and spent the weekend in our hotel room while I, without the companionship of my fellow nature boys, dawdled around at loose ends. I was contemptuous of Dad's failed effort, but afraid to strike off into the woods on my own.

One day I went to the corner candy store sporting a soft cap, and six older boys, "rocks" wearing black leather motorcycle jackets to proclaim their toughness, took exception to my hat and forced me outside to fight. I ran and they chased me. They pushed me up against a parked car and stood in line, taking turns hitting me. I knew that I could never count on anyone to help me; I was going to have to take care of myself.

Dad's efforts to help me cope with the mean streets were clumsy and strained—streetfighting tips like carrying a beer can opener instead of a switchblade knife because it was effective, nonfatal, and could be thrown away. I would learn to be tough, to build walls around myself and keep others away, but what I really wanted was safety, relief from the fear I carried within me. I read historical novels and science fiction voraciously, escaping into the past and the future. Carl's room was a refuge from the streets and from being part of the hated Red Menace. My folks grew concerned about my spending so much time with Carl and asked me once if there was any "homosexual activity." I wasn't sure what that meant, but immediately hated "queers." Johnny Sepp, a school friend I drank with, joined me in attempting our first mugging before I turned fourteen. We went to Central Park one night and cruised until someone asked us for a light for his cigarette, certain proof of his degeneracy. We hit him with weighted garrison belts, but our victim hollered and fought back, and we ran away. I had lashed out against enemies of my parents. It might be a way to make them love me.

I demanded, and finally got, pegged pants, a chartreuse gaucho shirt, and a red jacket like James Dean wore in *Rebel Without A Cause*. I started smoking, lying to get cigarettes from a store around the corner on my parents' credit. And I continued to drink. Mom and Dad were aware of my drinking but, being preoccupied with the rise of fascism, the trial, and inner-party battles over the decision to send various leaders "underground," chose to ignore it or ascribe it to teenage experimentation

I constantly challenged my parents' authority, as I was beginning to challenge all authority, and found that I could often get away with it if I stuck to the lie. I smoked cigarettes in our bathroom, and instead of flushing the butts down the toilet, I doused them and dropped them down an airshaft. When the first-floor neighbors complained, I simply denied any knowledge of the deeds and pointed to the loudly anticommunist family on the fifth floor.

Mom and Dad found a gun I had borrowed during a dispute with a gang from 21st Street. I passed it off as a blank pistol. Another time I fired a .410 gauge shotgun out of my window. It was during a CP meeting in the living room, and Dad came running back to see what happened. I said it was a firecracker and that I was sorry. Dad's constant anger began turning more and more at me, and at night I sometimes lay awake listening to the murmurs of Mom trying to calm him down, to get him to apologize.

The Communist Party sponsored a youth organization, the Labor Youth League (LYL), where I, as the son of a Smith Act victim, enjoyed some attention and esteem, along with a degree of notoriety for the way I wore my jeans, low-slung and "rocky." For a time I ran with Richie Stein, son of a Smith Act indictee who had gone underground to avoid trial. Richie and Albie were known around the LYL as a team. We affected ultra-hoodlum demeanor and tried to scandalize the young Left, carrying our cigarettes tucked into T-shirt sleeves, acting tough, and trying to get laid. We gave a Johnny Ray album as a birthday present to the daughter of a Party intellectual; she was not thrilled, preferring, perhaps, Shostakovich.

I quit the LYL several times, staking out unpopular positions just as Dad did in the parent organization. I tried to be the most working class, the most militant. Some thought the league needed to broaden itself, while I argued for a return to a Young Communist League. As a more-or-less working-class cadre I was nominated for leadership posts. I attended an evaluation session for several of us nominated for statewide LYL positions, where I was rejected for being a "typical teenager." The main attack came from a Party leader's daughter I had dated once, and I was furious. If trying to get laid disqualified me from leadership in the vanguard of the teenage proletariat, I would leave. Again.

Dad and his comrades were convicted in January 1953 just as I turned fifteen. Sentencing took place on February 3 after the defendants had a chance to say their piece to Judge Edward Dimock. All the speeches had been prepared in advance, coordinated so that they could be published together to point out the fascist nature of the trial to the American people. Words of moral certitude and bravado were rushed into print, with pamphlets issued by the thousands of copies.

On the other side were lurid pulp magazine articles depicting a viciously criminal, Moscow-directed Red Menace. In a *Bluebook* magazine article Dad was portrayed as a gun-carrying Comintern agent who boasted that come the revolution he would "take a machine gun and go down to Foley Square and mow down all the FBI agents." He denied saying that, but he might have.

Not included in the printed texts were Dad's final words to the judge, which began: "When my children cry out in the night for the father that you take away from them . . ." After being sentenced to two years at the federal reformatory at Petersburg, Virginia, Dad left the courtroom tight-jawed and threw his fist into the air in the Red salute. I was thrilled with his defiance, that he cared enough about me and Karen to tell the judge about us.

Dad and his codefendants would remain out on bail for the next two years while the appeals process was exhausted. During that time a bust of Stalin remained in its place of honor on the living room mantle.

During the trial period I hung out in the candy store a lot. One evening, bored, I wrote my first poem, a romantic ode to a girl of my dreams. The store owner's wife read it and asked the question I would get used to hearing from adults, especially teachers: "Did you really write this?"

While my earliest writings glorified the loner image, borrowing from Frankie Laine's "Cry of the Wild Goose," I also began to fancy myself a budding proletarian novelist. Jack London and John Steinbeck and Pietro DiDonato became my literary heroes, and I admired the work of James T. Farrell and John Dos Passos even if they had—as I was told—become "renegades." I began writing short stories, slices of Lower East Side teenage life, and sending them off to magazines. And I began collecting rejection slips.

Mom and Dad encouraged me. Mom showed some of my stories to a Party writer and reported back that my work had been termed "erudite." I didn't know the word and asked her what it meant. She said, "I think it means 'dirty.'"

I was thrilled one day when a rejection slip came back with a handwritten "Sorry" at the bottom. It was a taste of the validation I so eagerly sought. Our neighbor and Dad's codefendant, Elizabeth Gurley Flynn, showed some of my stories to a nephew who edited a semi-sleazy men's magazine, and he wrote that I reminded him "of a young Jack London." It was my best review to date, and I treasured it. He declined, however, to publish any of the stories.

Dad went to prison in January 1955. I was seventeen years old, a month into recovery from mononucleosis, and not drinking by doctor's orders. Since the "second-string" trial in New York, many more communists had been arrested. Ethel and Julius Rosenberg were dead, executed as spies.

Dad spent nearly two years at Petersburg, a minimum security prison. We visited him every other month, sitting on couches under the watchful eyes of armed guards, unable to hug for fear of being accused of trying to pass contraband. It was better than the visits at West Street when Dad was first arrested, where we could only communicate by telephone with a thick sheet of dirty glass between us. Petersburg didn't have high walls, but the cyclone fences and barbed wire and lookout towers made it fearsome enough.

Dad told us that prison life was OK. He was well fed, was learning the painting trade, had found a few Marxist books in the library, and was able to preach the class struggle to fellow inmates, southern bootleggers and minor felons. He accepted prison, I think, because it was the physical manifestation of his life's work. Whatever doubts he might have had as Party policy tried to keep up with the twists and turns of Soviet policy, and he admitted to none that I ever knew of, were laid to rest. He and his Party were real threats to the system; theirs was a real movement whose repression showed that their challenge was taken seriously.

★

While Mom worked with the Families of the Smith Act Victims committee raising funds for appeals and publicity and living expenses, I was attending high school less and less, spending more time on the street, sitting up late on the stoops smoking cigarettes (and ignoring Mom's admonitions not to smoke). I broke up with my first real girlfriend, an Irish cop's daughter, scared because I had let her get behind the walls I had built to protect and hide myself. I continued to drift in and out of the Labor Youth League, once having a meeting in my room on 12th Street while Johnny-Boy watched television in the living room, waiting for me to go prowling in Greenwich Village with him, looking for girls or trouble.

With Dad in prison and me acting out it wasn't any surprise that Stuyvesant High School wasn't going to let me graduate in June 1955. I had taken the entrance examination for academic Stuyvesant mostly because my junior high school teachers didn't think I could pass it. Once there, it was simply another place to not fit in, to rebel against. I had failed twelve courses, chemistry five times, and was officially logged as being absent or late some 20 percent of the time. My transcript states: "Very disorderly and impudent—reprimanded most of the term for his very poor conduct and absenteeism." Well, what the hell, they were a bunch of fascist bastards anyway, and so what if I didn't graduate? Dad never finished high school, and I shared his contempt for education.

In September I went to the first day of classes, obtained a subway pass that allowed me to ride free, and quit school. I was seventeen and a half years old and had a job cleaning rat cages in the research section of a medical center. Not exactly "basic industry," but it paid for booze and cigarettes. Like Dad, still in prison, I was finally a man.

Proletaria and Me:
A Memoir in Progress

Dorothy M. Zellner

Raised in New York City, Dorothy M. Zellner has been an activist since adolescence. She went south in 1961 and spent the next ten years as a civil rights worker with the Student Nonviolent Coordinating Committee (SNCC) and the Southern Conference Educational Fund (SCEF). Back north since 1983, she works as the director of publications at the Center for Constitutional Rights. Zellner's historical article "Red Roadshow: Eastland in New Orleans, 1954" (*Louisiana History*, Winter 1992) won her a New York Foundation for the Arts Fellowship in 1990.

Zellner is writing a memoir, on which "Proletaria and Me" is based. Here, Zellner captures the texture of daily life as experienced by many red diaper babies growing up at the height of the Cold War.

Until I was a teenager, our family lived in a red brick five-story tenement on Second Avenue between 18th and 19th streets in Manhattan. The neighborhood, a mixture of storefronts, tenements, and run-down brownstones, had no name and was rather shabby and gray, unlike the more interesting districts of the Lower East Side and Gramercy Park, each a few blocks away in opposite directions.

My parents, both immigrants, ran a Mom-and-Pop operation—a dentist's office—in our apartment, a dark six-room railroad flat several feet below street level. The office, which faced the street, occupied three rooms, and the five of us—my parents, sister, brother, and I—lived in the three back rooms.

My father did not enjoy being a dentist. He had wanted to be a teacher, but in Canada of the 1920s—where his family had migrated from England, coming before that from Russia—Jews were not hired as teachers. He did enjoy having an audience, though, being more than a bit of a showman, and he often told jokes or gave long political monologues—in the English accent he had carefully preserved—to some poor patient trapped in the dental chair, while one of us children played on the floor nearby, occasionally with that squiggly and uncatchable substance, mercury. True to his eccentric personality and leftist political views, he was completely uninterested in money or professional status and saw himself as a neighborhood tradesman who provided a service, just like the shoemaker two doors down.

The war was a central focus of my early childhood. In the morning, in the evening, and between patients, my father raced to the back of the apartment to listen to the war news. He alternately cheered or cursed at the radio, waving his arms or banging his fist on the table, depending on whether the Red Army was advancing or retreating. When the news reported a particularly horrible atrocity by the Germans, my father would bellow, "Nazi swine!"

I was seven years old the summer of 1945 when a new family moved into the apartment on the fourth floor of our building. Alice, the mother, smiled a lot and had very blue eyes. Freddy, then six, was dark haired with a dimpled smile. Carlie, a brown-haired four-year-old, lisped in an amusing way. The father, V. J. Jerome, was a high-ranking official of the Communist Party of the U.S., what the press termed its "cultural commissar," meaning that he had responsibility for all the Party's intellectual and cultural work.

The stereotype of an intellectual, Jerry was short, plump, had thick glasses, smoked a pipe, and taught Freddy how to play chess instead of baseball. He used very long words. My father, delighted to learn that Jerry had spent part of his childhood in London after migrating to England from Poland, immediately struck up a friendship. Soon he and Jerry sang English vaudeville songs together, energetically and off-key.

The Jeromes became very important to our lives. Alice, a nursery school teacher, was quite modern in her child-rearing techniques, unlike my mother. Alice used words like "sibling rivalry," a concept, like other dynamics of childhood, that my mother never quite grasped. We soon began to run up the four very steep flights of stairs to the Jeromes' house to play.

Neither Alice nor Jerry cared anything for possessions. Their apartment was dowdy and completely devoid of style. Oblivious to fashion, Alice wore crumpled clothes, too long or too short. She cropped her hair straight across below her ears and held the front back by a bobby pin or a barrette. She never wore any makeup. Jerry wore plaid shirts under the suspenders holding up his pants. Alice could not cook at all. From the beginning we children understood that whatever food we ate at the Jeromes' would be undercooked or burned, or sometimes both at the same time.

What Alice and Jerry had, however, was more fascinating than any material object: they knew things. They knew a lot more than my parents, even my father, whose politics were more emotional than analytical. The Jeromes loved to explain, explain, explain, about why some people were rich and other people were poor, why it was terrible that Black people were discriminated against, why the Soviet Union was such a wonderful place, why such glorious events as the Warsaw Uprising had happened, why the Depression was so bad. I loved Freddy from the start. A mischievous and imaginative little boy, he was the most interesting person I had ever met. He was the one who thought up the games we played; he was the one who said the most interesting things. "Lenin was a great man," he announced to me one day, at age seven. "Who is Lenin?" I said. A year younger than I, he was my teacher.

One Saturday morning early in June 1951 my mother and I took the Third Avenue bus to go to 34th Street to shop for clothes. As we held on to the steel handgrips and swayed back and forth, my eyes fell on a headline in a tabloid newspaper, which I could see over the shoulder of a man sitting near me: second-string Commies arrested. There was Jerry's name! I waved frantically to my mother, pointing at the newspaper. She looked terrified; without saying anything, we leaped off the bus at the next stop. My mother hailed a cab, a sure sign of imminent disaster, and we returned home, breathless.

My mother finally reached Alice on the telephone. The FBI had come to get Jerry at 7 A.M. As in the movies, the family was awakened by persistent ringing of their doorbell, followed by very loud hammering on the door. Freddy and Carlie watched as Alice opened the door to several FBI agents, who barked, "V. J. Jerome is under arrest." Jerry got dressed and went away with them. Freddy would not tell me how Jerry said good-bye, and he resolutely did not cry.

For the next ten days, Alice raised money for Jerry's bail. Most of the donors refused to sign checks because they were afraid of the FBI, so Alice collected cash in her purse, a mashed-up brown bag with a handle, which she carried everywhere until she had the requisite $10,000.

Soon Jerry got out of the West Street jail on bail. But we knew that no matter what kind of defense would be made at his trial, he was going to be found guilty and would have to go away to prison. The worry on my parents' faces turned into rank fear.

About a week after Jerry was released from jail, my father, age fifty-two, had a massive heart attack. The only thing that saved his life was his close proximity to Beth Israel Hospital, where he arrived only moments after experiencing severe crushing chest pain. When he came home he could not or would not work for three months and lay, inert and wan, on the couch, not even picking up the *Daily Worker* to read.

During his convalescence, my sister, brother, and I were sitting on the stoop of our new house around the corner when a man unfamiliar to me but looking remarkably like Alfred Hitchcock walked by. He asked, "How is your father?" Naturally taking him to be an FBI agent who would enact yet another June catastrophe, I assumed my older sister pose and shepherded my brother and sister inside, saying loudly, as I had been taught, "We don't have to talk to you!" This man, a doctor whose office was down the street, never talked to anyone in our family again.

After the three months were up, my father evidently decided he was fated to live. He quit smoking, quit eating butter, began working again, began playing bridge, began reading the newspapers, began shouting about the McCarthyite beasts, began to play "Oh, Them Golden Slippers" on the harmonica, began to be my father again.

He and Jerry resumed singing their English music hall songs, and our family went to rallies and meetings to defend the "Smith Act victims," a group that surely now included us even though we had not been personally charged with violating the Smith Act.

By 1953, when I was fifteen and in my second year of high school, Ethel and Julius Rosenberg had been on Death Row in Sing Sing for two years. I lived and breathed their case. I wrote letters, signed clemency petitions, went to rallies, and stood on street corners winter and summer with the Rosenberg committee giving out leaflets and asking for signatures from passersby. I knew as much about the Rosenbergs—people I had never seen—as I did about my own relatives and certainly cared more for them than for some of the people in my life.

My political friends shared this passionate involvement: even as young teenagers we were able to cite all the arguments—legal, moral, and political—supporting the Rosenbergs' innocence, and we understood all the legal maneuvers and the appeals. Hour after hour we read the letters the Rosenbergs wrote to each other and studied the photos that appeared in the newspapers and the Rosenberg committee literature. In a sense, the Rosenbergs were our movie stars and we their teenage fans. But it was more than that: in the extreme anticommunist hysteria of the '50s, the Rosenbergs represented the possibility that we could actually be charged with something fantastic that we never did and "fry in the electric chair," as the New York dailies so delicately put it. Simultaneously we also became Michael and Robby, children whose parents could be taken away forever.

The date for the Rosenbergs' electrocution was set for June 18, 1953. As a last desperate effort, the leaders of the Rosenberg defense committee organized demonstrations throughout the country to pressure congressional representatives and President Eisenhower for clemency. Alice, my mother, Freddy, and I joined a special train of thousands of people in Penn Station that morning, hoping that an eleventh-hour miracle might occur. After arriving in Washington, we spent a few futile hours pursuing hostile congressmen up and down the halls of the House Office Building and then joined a picket line at the Treasury Building of several thousand people marching ten or fifteen abreast, carrying signs urging presidential clemency. In the afternoon, the picket captains passed the word that Supreme Court Justice Douglas had granted a one-day stay of execution. Alice and my mother had to get back to New York, but Alice told Freddy that he could stay if he wanted to. I begged my mother to be allowed to stay. Somehow or other, Alice convinced her: "Sara, it's so important!"

Freddy and I volunteered for the 2 to 4 A.M. shift in front of the White House, where about a hundred hardy souls walked around and around close to the black iron White House fence. The area was dark, silent, and almost completely deserted of pedestrians or automobiles, except for the occasional car that cruised by, plastered with signs suggesting that the Rosenbergs burn in hell.

After sleeping a few hours on the floor in a youth hostel, chosen because it was one of the few interracial places to stay overnight in Washington in 1953, we went back to the White House. By day there were several hundred people picketing, and we marched up and down, holding our signs up, waiting for some word about whether the full Supreme Court had continued Justice Douglas's stay of execution. Finally, the word came. Our picket captain, a plump woman in her forties, stood inside the line and said over and over tearfully, "The Supreme Court has not upheld the stay. The vote was six to three. The execution is scheduled for eight o'clock tonight." Disconsolately we tramped back and forth, back and forth for the next two hours.

Across Pennsylvania Avenue, in Lafayette Park, a tremendous crowd gathered, smelling blood. They booed and screamed at us. At the precise moment of eight o'clock we picketers turned, put our picket signs down, and silently faced the White House. The crowd across the street shrieked with joy.

Numb, we were escorted by police to our waiting chartered bus and arrived back at home about 3 A.M. The next day the New York papers dwelt lovingly on every detail of the executions, including the fact that wisps of smoke came out of Ethel's head after the switch was pulled. I broke down and sobbed for hours, kneeling on the floor with my head on my bed. My mother, alarmed at my grief, refused to let me go to the Rosenbergs' funeral. Some days later, I bought myself a bracelet of silver links in honor of Julius and Ethel and swore the adolescent promise that I would wear it "always."

I did—for a few weeks.

When school started in the fall, I wrote a paper for my English class about the trip to Washington to save the Rosenbergs. Normally I was somewhat cautious when it came to revealing my full political views, even in a school as liberal as the High School of Music and Art, but the experience overcame my reticence. When the teacher, a nervous, rabbit-faced person, returned everyone's work, he cleared his throat and announced that contrary to his usual procedure, he wanted one of us to read the assignment aloud to the class. Much to my surprise, he meant me, and I went up to the front of the room and read the whole article. When I finished, the other students were utterly silent, but after class a few of them came up to me and asked me sympathetic questions.

Only much later did I realize that my teacher's request revealed more about him than I could appreciate at the time.

My particular peer group of red diaper babies, born in the late '30s or very early '40s, were mainly first-generation American children of European immigrants, though our group sometimes included a child or two of Black leftists or even the occasional WASP. Our timing was unlucky: we were too young to enjoy the few years of wartime respectability bestowed upon our parents by the short-lived U.S.-Soviet alliance against Hitler, and by the time we started ed school, the Cold War had started, too.

As a quasi-Bohemian I was indistinguishable from any other art student at my high school: I wore paint-spattered jeans and sneakers instead of cashmere sweaters over blouses with Peter Pan collars and sneered at such bourgeois affectations as going to proms and being "pinned" by boyfriends (the pin always attached at the left breast near the stiletto point of the '50s bra).

But I was careful not to reveal my other life, my life in the Left, which contained a completely different set of people and activities. As a member of the Labor Youth League, I did things that the typical high school student did not do: I went to "meetings," I attended "study groups" and "lectures" about the "principal questions of the day," and I went to "rallies" about the Rosenbergs or banning the H-bomb or against the House Un-American Activities Committee. This required some juggling: I couldn't actually say to my high school friends that I was going to a meeting—what fifteen-year-old goes to meetings? I tried to deflect inquiries from friends about where I was going; if they really pressed me, I invented boring and inconvenient family functions where my presence was mandatory.

Our language became specialized. At home we said "Smith Act *victims*," but in my civics class at school I was careful to say "Smith Act *defendants*" if the subject came up. A slip of the tongue could give you away to some alert fascist-type teacher, who could torment you in class, flunk you, or report you to the principal as having "subversive" ideas. But this very same slip could also identify you to a fellow red diaper baby who, like you, was in disguise, pretending to be like everyone else.

Some words we used deliberately out of a sense of political pride. I made sure to say "Negro" instead of "colored" and "Soviet Union" instead of "Russia." I tried to avoid saying "Red China," which was repeated so often it virtually became one word, but rather "China." I substituted "Eastern Europe" for the term "Iron Curtain," but I'm not sure I said the risky phrase "Socialist bloc."

In school I watched with fear and satisfaction if a braver red diaper classmate challenged authority. One day, my high school history teacher, a stiff young man with heavy horn-rimmed glasses, remarked that slavery was not all bad: in fact, owners had given slaves food, shelter, and medical care. Emily, a red diaper friend who was the daughter of a prominent leftist, waved her hand frantically to be recognized and when called on, burst out, "How dare you say anything good about slavery!" The young teacher literally backed into the blackboard, stammering a defense that he was being "objective," but he never reported her.

I was incapable of shouting at a teacher, so I used other methods. If I was having trouble holding up my end in class, Sol, my father's best friend, would look for clippings from the *New York Times* or some other irrefutable source that I could use to bolster my position.

Fortunately for me, my first name called up nothing more than an association with Toto or the Cowardly Lion. Not so other red diaper babies whom I heard about. Their parents had given them exotic Red names in the more militant '30s: a set of twins in California who bore the first names Marx and Engels; a boy named Lesta (for Lenin and Stalin), later adjusted to Lester; a girl named Commilda—"C-o-m-m" for the Communist Party, combined with "i-l-d" for the International Labor Defense; Bira (for Birobidjian); Stalina, who became Nina; Ninel (Lenin spelled backwards); and finally, the ultimate, Proletaria.

While the parents of some of my red diaper baby friends urged their children to carry the Red banner heroically forward into the future, as immigrants many of them also wanted their children to be "popular" and "successful." These confusing signals were difficult to follow. Though frightened by the McCarthy hysteria, and especially by Jerry's arrest, my mother and father did not, like some other leftist parents, restrict my political activities. My father in particular was rather proud of them. But socially, my dilemmas were endless. How was I to succeed in typical American tasks (be popular, get married, get a good job) and still remain what I was and what my parents had taught me to be—an outcast in American society?

I could remain more safely within the confines of the red diaper group, but it was so small that the prospect of securing boyfriends was dim. Besides, politically we didn't want to become inbred, even though it was a lot more comfortable. So we sometimes went beyond the group; in our political vocabulary, this was called being "broad," as in the "broad" masses.

I was briefly and madly in love with a "regular" boy with an extremely short crewcut whose hair stood up in soft black spikes that I loved to touch. One night while he was waiting for me before going out to the movies—the fashion of the times requiring that the girl be almost but not quite ready when the boy appeared—he idly riffled through some newspapers that were stacked on a table near the front door. Someone, probably my mother, had carefully put a *Daily Worker* into the center of the pile to hide it from view. As I came to meet him I saw him pull it out and begin reading it, his eyebrows climbing higher and higher. I almost fainted with horror. Since there was nothing I could say to explain the presence of a communist newspaper, I tried to pretend it hadn't happened. He was kind enough not to say anything either, but I knew that he would never think of me in quite the same way again.

When my social life was in the doldrums, which was often, I occasionally turned my politics to my own benefit: I became quite adept at provoking a needless political argument midway through a dull date so that I could avoid the customary fumbling kiss goodnight. I would say something like, "I can't understand how people could possibly believe in God," knowing perfectly well that the discussion was bound to escalate from there. When we got to my door, the boring date would invariably stomp disgustedly off into the night, leaving me contentedly kissless.

With a few slipups here and there, I thought I was pretty successful in passing as a fairly normal American teenager. Many years later, however, a few of my "regular" high school friends told me, laughing, that they knew all the time I was up to something unusual, though they didn't know exactly what.

Southern Discomfort

Maxine DeFelice

Maxine DeFelice was born in 1938 in New York City but returned immediately with her mother to St. Louis, where both parents, Clara Wernick
Fiering and Henry Fiering, were union organizers for the CIO. The family moved frequently; her parents said, "Wherever the union needs us, we
will go." A political activist most of her adult life, DeFelice lives in Marin
County, California, where she works as a psychotherapist.

From 1946 to 1953, the CIO waged Operation Dixie, an organizing
campaign in which left-wing unions such as the United Electrical, Radio
and Machine Workers of America took the lead. Although ultimately unsuccessful as an attempt to organize unions, Operation Dixie was successful in challenging racism in southern workplaces and communities. DeFelice's childhood memories remind us that parents who are engaged in an
exhilarating frontline battle for social change can be insensitive to the
needs of their own children.

Bleak is my image of our year and a half in Winston-Salem, North Carolina.
My family moved there near the end of 1946 when I was eight and a half years
old. My parents had been assigned by the United Electrical, Radio and Machine Workers of America to take a leading role in the CIO-Dixie campaign
to integrate southern union locals and try to equalize working conditions for
Black workers.

The neighborhood we moved into, on the edge of the poor white section of
this industrial city, had nothing of appeal to me. I recall wide, flat blocks with
dusty vacant lots stretching endlessly. Our family of five shared a large house
with another organizer, his wife, and two children. My favorite space in the
house was an area on the floor about two feet wide between my bed and the
wall. I could hide there for hours with my books transporting me to other worlds.

Every evening and on the weekends our house was filled with people. It was truly a momentous time. R. J. Reynolds was on strike, and the FTA—the Food, Tobacco, Agricultural, and Allied Workers Union—was working to ensure that the picket lines would be integrated. Our house was stoned several times because of the mixed meetings of Blacks and whites. I can remember rocks crashing through the windows, flying pieces of glass, and trembling with fear for hours afterwards. Pete Seeger, Woody Guthrie, and Paul Robeson came to sing at the rallies, and they also participated in a meeting at our home. Sylvia Thompson, an old friend of my parents, recently told me, "There was always a place at the table for anyone showing up at dinnertime. Your mother welcomed anyone, anytime." I hung out on the fringes, an observer.

Even though I excelled scholastically, I hated school. Maybe because it was my fourth school in three years, maybe because everyone else had a different way of speaking and my accent stood out. Maybe because I was the only Jew and isolated because everyone knew my family's politics. During my first week there, each day I stole a dollar from my mother's purse (a lot of money in 1946) and bought a large bag of candies. I came onto the schoolyard, calling out, "Does anyone want some candy?" Schoolmates gathered around me; my hopes grew. They grabbed the candy to the last piece and ran off. I stood alone with the empty bag. After several more tries I gave up on the candy.

Due to numerous articles in the local newspapers, one with a picture of my father with arrows pointing to each corner and the caption "This Man is a Communist!" no one in the neighborhood talked to us. They called us "the nigger lovers" or "dirty commie Jews."

Not long after we moved to Winston-Salem, as I left for school one morning, with no warning, stones were thrown at me. Running to crouch behind a car, I heard a loud adult's voice yelling, "Nigger lover." After a quiet moment I stood up to continue on my way. "Ping, ping," stones were flying toward me again. I ran crouching from car to car as the voice yelling "Nigger lover" followed me throwing stones. Finally, when I was off the block, the stones stopped. I ran as fast as I could the two miles to school. I don't remember much of those days except the fear that gripped me every time I left for school. The stoning happened more than once, but exactly how long it went on I can't recall. I knew we were part of an important struggle. I knew I couldn't complain to anyone, and I knew I had to run fast.

One afternoon, I was walking home from school on a deserted street, humming, scuffing my shoes, looking for gum wrappers on the ground. In the postwar years foil was being reclaimed, and you could get money for a large ball of rolled up foil. It was a muggy day; the air was still. A group of eight boys about fourteen or fifteen years old appeared suddenly, surrounding me, shouting, "We're going to vuck you!" I never knew if I was singled out or if I was chosen randomly. Looking back, I know I had learned resignation at an early age, and it wasn't in my nature at that point to fight back, even if I could have.

They pushed me against a large tree. It had a wide trunk and thick bark and full leafy branches overhead. Pinning my arms back, pulling my dress up, and underwear down, they came at me one at a time. I can clearly see today their bug-eyed, leering grins; their taunts, laughter and jeers floated through my senses. The rest is a blur. I imagine that they raped me, though I don't really know. I became numb. I went into a trance. When they finally let me go it was nearing dusk. My dress was torn and dirty. I cried as I pulled on my underpants and tried to smooth my dress. My braids were loosened, and strands of dirty wet hair hung in my face. I felt filthy all over, and I was.

They ran off, and I made my way home. When I got there, two hours later than I should have, there was a meeting going on about the next day's strike action. The living room was so full that many people were sitting on the floor. I walked over to my mother, she looked at me, but I guess she didn't really see me or the shape I was in. I leaned over and whispered in her ear, "What does 'vuck' mean?" She looked at me angrily and said, "Don't you ever say the F-word again! We're having a meeting, can't you see? You know better than to interrupt a meeting. Go to your bedroom!" At that, she turned back to the room full of people.

Withdrawn, resigned, and sad I went to my room, changed my clothes, sat down on my spot on the floor, and proceeded to read. Sometime later I crawled under my bed, where I spent the night. No one knew, no one noticed. Important things were happening.

When I think of the things that kept me sane, I think first of my baby sister, Bobbi, and brother, Freddy, both of whom I loved to pieces and who gave me back the pure love and joy only children can give. I think of my 1920s bicycle with 32-inch wheels that I bought for five dollars. The seat was so high that I had to climb on a wall in order to get onto it. I could only stop by jumping off and letting the bike fall, but oh, how I loved riding.

There was our friend Sylvia Thompson, who was in her early twenties and had come to live with our family for the summer to learn about organizing from my parents. She saw my loneliness and took me on an outing once in a while. She gave me my first book of folk songs, *Lift Every Voice and Sing*, which I still have. I remember sitting and listening to her playing guitar and singing. She opened me up to what became a lifesaver and a passion throughout my life: folk music, guitar playing, and singing.

There was Moranda Smith, an FTA leader and one of several Black women with whom my mother worked closely. She came to our house when I fell out of a second-story window and tried to locate my mother after the ambulance took me to the hospital alone. Once she took me shopping downtown. We sat in the rear of the bus. The bus was filled, and a burly white man came up and shouted, "Let a human being have that seat." I started crying, but Moranda remained calm. "Shush, honey, don't pay him any mind; we're getting off," she said.

There was my world of books and learning. As painful and lonely and scary as the weeks were, I had my weekends organized. Saturday mornings I rode a bus to the library and took out the maximum ten books allowed. I started with the *A*s and worked my way through the alphabet. I had a contest with myself to read ten books a week. Most weeks I did. I read everything written by Willa Cather, and I loved *The Secret Garden* and *Caddie Woodlawn*, which I read over and over.

Sundays would be church. One day at school I had overheard some girls talking about a church. It sounded interesting, so I found out where it was and decided to go. This was the beginning of a long search for some spiritual or community connection. Every Sunday I woke up early, got dressed in my favorite plaid dress and polished my brown oxfords, tiptoed out the door at 7:00 A.M., and walked the few miles to the church. It was a small Baptist Revivalist Church. (I had never been in a church or any religious place before. I had learned and could recite the story of evolution by the age of three and knew we were atheists, which meant we didn't believe in God, we believed in Science.) I remember the first time I walked in. Families filled plain wooden benches. I sat in the back. Instantly I liked the calm, warm, friendly, family feeling. The choir, people of all ages, paraded in wearing long periwinkle blue robes with broad white collars. As soon as the singing began I was completely absorbed by the sounds of the gospel music. I knew immediately that I wanted to be part of it. The whole place seemed filled with a kind of joy I had never witnessed.

I returned every Sunday and soon became a member of the choir. Wearing my own robe and belting out "We are climbing Jacob's ladder" and "Rock-a my soul in the bosom of Abraham" nourished my being in some way that overshadowed the bleakness, the incredible aching loneliness and estrangement that pervaded the rest of my life. I won a bible for best attendance, which I still have.

When the preacher came to our house one Sunday after church to ask my parents' permission to baptize me, they said I couldn't go anymore. They explained to him our Jewish background and reminded me why we were atheists. I knew all of that. To me it wasn't about God or evolution. Nor did it involve my parents. I had found the church myself and managed to get myself there and home. I craved belonging somewhere. I had that in church. Every time I went to church people seemed happy to see me. They knew my name and smiled warmly at me. My heart opened for those brief moments when I was singing. I always walked home as slowly as possible, not wanting the feeling of belonging to end. I don't remember anyone at home ever asking me anything about church. No one even knew how much I liked the singing.

Red Sisters of the Bourgeoisie

Rosalyn Fraad Baxandall and Harriet Fraad

Rosalyn Baxandall is a professor of American Studies at the State University of New York at Old Westbury. She is the author of *Words on Fire: The Life and Writing of Elizabeth Gurley Flynn* (Rutgers University Press), coeditor of *America's Working Women: An Anthology of Women's Work, 1620–1970* (W. W. Norton and Co.), coauthor of *The Rise and Fall of the Suburban Dream 1945–2000* (Basic Books, forthcoming), and coeditor of *The Encyclopedia of the Women's Liberation Movement, 1964–1976* (Carlson Publishing Co., forthcoming). A feminist activist, Baxandall was one of the foremothers of the women's liberation movement of the late 1960s.

Harriet Fraad is a practicing psychotherapist whose published work centers around the intersection of class analysis and intimate life. She is coauthor of *Bringing It All Back Home: Class, Gender, and Power in Modern Households* (Pluto Press). An activist for over thirty years, Fraad helped organize the Hill Parents Association, a civil rights group; AIM, a socialist organization; the New Haven Green Party; Save Our Schools; Citizens Concerned about Childbirth; and New Haven Women's Liberation. She is the president of the Association of Economic and Social Analysis and a founder of its journal, *Rethinking Marxism*.

Fraad and Baxandall grew up in a Left family that was atypical in its affluence and in the fact that both parents and three of four grandparents were U.S.-born. The authors describe the contradictions and tensions created by their parents' diverging views of women's roles and of the place of politics in everyday life.

It's hard to separate the influences of the Communist Party from our parents' particular quirks and the environment in which we grew up. On the surface our family of three girls—Rosalyn, born in 1939, Harriet, born in 1941, and Julie, born in 1947—a doctor father, and a housewife mother seemed as ordinary as the family of Dick, Jane, and Sally in the primary school reader. But things were seldom what they seemed in our family.

During our adolescence in the 1950s no one mentioned the word "communism." We didn't realize until the 1960s that our dad had been in the CP. Our mother still denies knowing that her husband was a Red. We're not sure about her, although she worked for many CP fronts, like Russian war relief and the Angelo Herndon and Scottsboro Boys campaigns. It wasn't until our dad was vulnerable and near death in 1990 that we actually dared to ask him direct questions, like when he joined the CP (1919) and when he left (1957). Generally we were discouraged from asking direct questions. Our family was ruled by the Fifth Amendment.

Most of our socialist upbringing was caught rather than formally taught. But we had moments of explicit, inspiring, political indoctrination, usually spurred on by alcohol. Dad could be quite didactic and indignant about the "bourgeois crap" that we received in school or from the media. We had far less media input than we wanted. We didn't own a TV for many years, and comics were forbidden and censured in the Soviet style. (*Little LuLu* escaped the "Red List" because it was rumored to have been written by a fellow traveler.) When our grandmother died in the late 1950s we inherited her TV, which was placed in the basement, where our father was spared its presence.

Our upbringing was far from mainstream. No junk food, soda, potato chips, or nickel candies were permitted. For such special events as the first day of school we were forced into matching knitted dresses made by our grandmother, worn with sturdy oxfords. When wearing chartreuse and fuchsia was the "in thing" to do, we wore burgundy and olive green. Our parents "redlined" American popular culture, which they held in contempt. They identified with the European elite, preferring classical music, "high" art, and theater. Neither parent listened to the radio. When we reached high school and they actually purchased a phonograph, pre-Beethoven classics and Left performers like Pete Seeger and Paul Robeson were the only kinds of recordings they sanctioned. Like other families that adored the masses, we lived with our contradictions. When we pointed them out, Dad said, "Nothing's too good for the working class, even if they have false consciousness!"

Three of our grandparents were born in America, not typical of most Party members. Only our mother's father was born in Russia. Our father, one of six brothers, was the only leftist in his extended family. One of his brothers was denied promotion to three-star general because our dad was a Red. Two others followed their dad's example and went into business. Unlike our father, they became proud millionaires.

Dad worked for the Comintern in Vienna from 1932 to 1936. We never knew exactly what he did or how he landed the job. Maybe it was because he spoke German like a native and looked Aryan. We gather from his stories that he had a printing press in his apartment and printed leaflets for the Comintern. He also carried packages, money, and letters across the Austrian border. Mother joined him in Vienna, where, although unmarried, they lived together. These were the glory days of our father's life. He referred to them wistfully on those rare occasions when, oiled by goodly amounts of liquor, he spoke about his past. He regaled us with stories of workers risking their lives during the failed 1934 communist uprising to save books from burning buildings. Dad's recounting of this period left us with a sense that even when struggles were not successful, Party life was filled with adventure and camaraderie.

In contrast to our father, our mother was a pedigreed leftist. Her father, Horace London, a socialist and a lawyer, managed his brother Meyer London's political campaigns. As a lawyer to many wealthy cotton merchants, Horace earned the money that helped to support his brother's family and his work. Uncle Meyer was a famous social democrat and among the first socialists elected to the U.S. Congress. Although he faithfully served his constituents from the Lower East Side, he was evicted from Congress for voting against World War I. Legend has it that Meyer was run over by a cab driver while crossing the street deep in thought about a call to once again run for political office. His parting words defended the working class: "It was my fault. Don't blame the cabby."

Our maternal grandmother was a multitalented, beautiful woman with powerful ambitions. When she graduated from secretarial school at fifteen years old, she applied for the most prestigious possible job, lying about her age and qualifications. Overwhelmed by her beauty and spunk, our grandfather, fifteen years her senior, hired her. He was impressed that she stayed late at night studying his law books, which she did to conceal the fact that she had no training as a legal secretary. After mastering the secretarial aspect of her job, Grandma earned her high school equivalency at night. When her three children were old enough for junior high school, she earned her law degree at Fordham University (at that time one could go directly from high school to law school). Like many Left men of his era, our maternal grandfather wanted his family life and wife kept separate from his career. Although Grandma joined the law firm briefly, Grandfather preferred that she stay home. When he died, Grandma took over the law practice.

Grandma joined the CP after her husband's death in the early 1930s. As a youth she had marched in suffrage parades. As a widow she lived in an apartment hotel to avoid domestic labor. She didn't remarry until she retired at age seventy.

In spite of Grandma's feminist leanings, the earth revolved around her only son. Her ambitions for her daughters expressed her contradictions; she wanted them to be useful citizens and also the ladies of leisure that she had never been. Our mother, Irma London, was a dutiful daughter. In 1922 she entered the family law firm even though she detested the practice of law. She had been a modern dancer and loved writing clever lyrics, dancing, singing, and theater. Throughout our lives she wrote and sang sparklingly creative songs for occasional PTA productions. Although energetic, highly articulate, and bright, she never developed an independent life, her own friends, or a lasting career. After the Second World War, mother found herself trapped at home. Too guilty to continue a career that took her away from serving Dad and managing an elegant home, she was also too angry to enjoy her children. When we were growing up, Mom was a frustrated housewife who didn't admit that she was miserable. She had to beatify our father in order to justify her life. She transformed his character defects into charming eccentricities, attributing his emotional neglect of his family to the pure dedication of the doctor, scholar, and man of principle.

In spite of her Left credentials, Mother was the liberal to our Dad's radical. She discouraged our father's political engagement with us, telling him to stop feeding us communist propaganda. Dad's personal attention was a rare commodity for which competition was fierce. Mom was uncomfortable with both Dad's politics and his occasional attention to us.

When we were toddlers, Dad enlisted in the U.S. army, where he served formally as a doctor and informally as a Party recruiter. Without consulting Mother, Dad volunteered to combat fascism overseas in spite of the fact that Mother was pregnant, had two toddlers under three years old, and opposed his leaving. He, like many communists of this era, held to principles of collective decision making as long as they were applied outside of his household. When Dad volunteered for overseas duty, Mother contracted tuberculosis. When he was about to be transferred overseas, Mother miscarried, collapsed, and was sent to a sanitarium for a recovery that lasted three years, until Dad returned.

With our father away and our mother hospitalized, this was a period of upheaval. We lived with a series of conservative, religious, anti-intellectual relatives. We held on to part of our father by adhering to a childhood version of his values: self-sacrifice, hard work, and antifascism. Stoically, we did not complain about loneliness. Marginalized in a series of families none of whom wanted the care of two young children, we intensified our identification as outsiders. We cultivated a kind of fierce independence as well as interdependence that came from being unable to depend on anyone but each other.

Although we adopted our dad's politics and values, we were in our own way deeply aware and deeply angry that these values did not apply to us. Dad loved humanity and put others first—unless they were members of his immediate family. In our own inchoate childish ways we picked up on this contradiction. We wondered why we were not worthy of his love or the special attention of the relatives with whom we lived.

When the war ended our father continued his education on the GI bill. A two-year residency in pediatrics meant another two years in which he lived at New York Hospital away from us. When Dad finished his residency, our family was finally united after almost five years. He returned to live with us, in a fashion; he developed a private pediatric practice that kept him away late into the night.

We experienced the nurturing CP community during our earliest years before we had any idea that this surrogate family network was labeled "communist." We didn't know then that we were the Red menace we heard about at school. However, we knew that we were different. The day that the Rosenbergs were executed we were the only ones at Public School 81 who grieved.

In the mid-'50s, we spent three summers on Shelter Island in a colony of bungalows rented by communist families, where topics of discussion among the adults included politics in general, McCarthy in particular, and who was sleeping with whom. McCarthy was so often the center of discussion that we thought he was president of the United States. Adults took us crabbing, swimming, boating, and had good political as well as personal talks with us, giving us a sweet taste of social mothering. Mother never took part in these activities. She stayed home with the housekeeper and our little sister.

In this communist community in which many of the wives had careers, the traditional division of labor prevailed. Women maintained homes and children; men, including our father, visited on weekends. It was Dad who taught us to swim and took us skinny dipping in the moonlight.

Communist values were our social and cultural identity, as religious identification, ethnicity, and nationality were for other kids. The children's books our father gave us introduced us to poverty and oppression in the midst of North American prosperity and denial of such realities. We read biographies of Haym Solomon, George Washington Carver, Marie Curie, Isadora Duncan, and

Helen Keller. We were alone among our classmates in the knowledge that many of these famous people were socialists.

Even in the 1950s, the age of U.S. dominance and insulation, we learned a version of internationalism. A Yugoslav who had been a Loyalist general in the Spanish Civil War stayed at our house and taught us radical Spanish songs. French friends taught us words, games, and chants in their language. We celebrated the birthdays of the Russian and French Revolutions. With our Dad and other Left parents and children we sang at "hootenannies," where Pete Seeger, Tony Kraber, and other blacklisted folk artists taught us international songs. We celebrated a friend's birthday at Café Society, the first racially integrated night club in New York City, owned by Barney Josephson, a communist. We learned multiculturalism and racial integration long before they became liberal icons of political correctness.

The McCarthy period was difficult politically as well as personally. Our communist community was shattered. Some of our parents' friends went to jail. Some were deported. Others informed or, as we heard it, became "rat finks" and "stool pigeons." Our father, in one of his few serious conferences with us, explained in no uncertain terms that going to jail did not have to mean that you were bad. His friends, he said, went to jail because they were courageous and would not betray the things they believed in. "We should be proud of them. They are our red badge of courage."

During McCarthyism, the worst crime in our family was being an informer. Rosalyn reported to a neighbor that Harriet had destroyed the neighbor's vegetable garden. Both parents lost control, screaming at Ros that she was a stool pigeon.

As red diaper kids we reacted to the McCarthy period with bravado. Maybe because we weren't afraid of our parents disappearing. They already had disappeared. We threw Tampax at the FBI agents who parked outside of our home for two days after my father refused to speak with them. We giggled dirty words into the phone when told that it was tapped.

Although generally a liberal, mother was radical when it came to local school politics. She was one of a handful of parents who openly opposed corporal punishment, air raid drills, teachers' loyalty oaths, and patriotic assemblies that featured songs from every branch of the armed forces. Mother not only protested but became a leader, the president of the PTA.

When Mrs. Devereaux smashed Harriet's head against the blackboard for the insolent suggestion that the tradition of burning the Yule Log was to toast Santa Claus, Mother protested. Henceforth Mrs. Devereaux had to say, "May I touch you?" every time she shoved Harriet or anyone else. Rosalyn got into trouble for using such obscenities as "oh God" and "damn it" and bringing a sex education book to class. Our CP influence permitted us to do the impermissible: ask questions, laugh at contradictions, and admit sexual curiosity.

Even though we rebelled against conformity, we also strove to become popular and blend in. We acted up in the anti-authoritarian ways our friends supported and were accepted in the popular crowd under false pretenses. No one knew that our family questioned God, country, and sexual Puritanism. Although we didn't know to keep sexual curiosity hidden, we knew to keep our parents' politics secret. Popularity proved a Pyrrhic victory. We were counterfeits in the currency of '50s popularity.

Dad broke with the CP in 1957 when the Party no longer fit his ideal of serving the masses. His departure was not dramatic. He maintained his class-conscious, humanitarian values and never denounced the organization.

Medicine replaced the Party as his primary service to people. He was an exceptional doctor and dearly beloved. The children of economically hard hit, blacklisted families he treated free of charge, quietly leaving money behind him after house calls. His former medical students tell of his wry, practical teachings and his skepticism about drugs and so-called "advanced" technology. He helped organize one of the first unions of interns and residents and the Manhattan Hospital Insurance Plan (HIP), an early inexpensive group practice, raised funds for medical supplies for Cuba, and edited the *Medical Letter*, a journal evaluating medications on the basis of research independent of drug company financing.

Values and politics were among the few meaningful things that our father allowed us to share with him. We were taught distrust of established authority, the media, and the official U.S. line even when it was correct, as in the Stalin trials. When we saw or read murder mysteries, Dad theorized that the priest or the capitalist was the culprit. From him we learned to eschew the liberalism of charity politics; he advocated joining with others to free ourselves. His exciting and ennobling legacies included hard work and the importance of serving others and your community, of being what Dad called "solid citizens" and "Stakhanovites." We also learned a set of values that in retrospect is redolent of Christianity—dividing the public and the private, the mind from the body. Things personal, emotional, relating to the body and home were degraded, not worth discussing. Labor and politics were the arenas where men, and exceptional women, made worthwhile contributions. Personal need equaled weakness and could only interfere with progressive politics. Although Mother may have disagreed with Dad's evaluation of the personal, which was her sphere of life, she did not contradict him. She heartily endorsed his view that personal neediness is anathema.

Throughout our lives we held on to the political solidarity that our father taught us. In high school when there was little Left activity, we worked for the Committee for Nonviolent Action—picketing nuclear submarines in New London, Connecticut—and with the American Friends Service Committee in the ghettos of Philadelphia, painting houses, cleaning up streets, supporting rent strikes, and accompanying accused tenants to night court. In and after college we participated in local Civil Rights Movement activities and committees to end the war in Vietnam. We were among the early members of the abortion rights movement. In 1968, we were founding sisters of the newly formed radical Women's Liberation Movement in New York City and New Haven, Connecticut.

We have gone through life together even though we have lived in different cities throughout our adult years. We have tried to overcome the division between the personal and the political that our parents' generation rigidly upheld. Our own children, although raised outside of the Communist Party, are third-generation red diaper babies.

What Did I Know
and When Did I Know It?

Sonia Jaffe Robbins

Sonia Jaffe Robbins was born in Newport News, Virginia, and grew up in Maryland, Washington, D.C., New York City, Connecticut, and Pennsylvania. A long-time feminist, Robbins helped found the Network of East-West Women, which links women activists from Central and Eastern Europe and the former Soviet Union with feminists from North America and Western Europe. A writer and editor, Robbins teaches journalism at New York University.

Unlike most authors in this anthology, Robbins grew up in suburban and semirural communities. She sensed that her family's values differed from those of the people around her, but it was not until adulthood that Robbins asked her parents if they had been members of the CP. Here she recounts the process of uncovering a hidden past, the answers she received, and her reaction to learning of her heritage.

I didn't even know I was a red diaper baby until 1963, when I was twenty-one. A politically active housemate, raised a Southern Baptist, explained the term to me. I wasn't, in fact, very sophisticated about any sort of politics. This is what I did know.

In the late 1940s, my parents, my younger brother and sister, my mother's parents, and I lived in Brooklyn, in "Bensonhoist." ("Benson-*hurst*" my mother said carefully, when I used the local pronunciation.) Our apartment topped a dusty-windowed storefront on 20th Avenue, which had become a warehouse for old refrigerators. The other storefronts on the block had no apartments above them, and their tar-paper roofs beckoned to us to run and play. We climbed out the windows to clamber over the walls separating each roof until our mother or Granny called to us to come back in. Behind the storefront lived a family whose teenaged daughter, Rhoda, was our baby-sitter. Behind their apartment was a garage. We lived "toppa Rhoda, toppa garage."

Our apartment ran the length of the building; the front was ours, the back my grandparents'. In the living room my father set up a dark wood cabinet almost as big as I was, with two doors that opened in the center. On the right, a tiny gray screen showed programs in the evening and a test pattern in the afternoon. On the left was a record player that slid out. When I was six or seven, I listened over and over to the two-record set of *Ballad for Americans* sung by Paul Robeson. When Robeson's deep voice sang, "In '76 the sky was red, thunder rumbling overhead; Old King George couldn't sleep in his bed, and on that stormy morn, old Uncle Sam was born," I imagined the red sky, the black thunder, and an old man with wrinkled face and nightcap tossing and turning. My favorite part was near the end. When a bossy woman's voice asked, "Are you an American?" Robeson replied, with a chuckle, "Am I an American?" and rattled off all the kinds of American he was, ending with "check and double-check American." I didn't know that Robeson was saying, "Czech and double-check American," but I loved the sound of the words. It was my first American history lesson.

When the grown-ups didn't want us to know what they were talking about, they spoke Yiddish. These mysterious conversations remained hidden to me. I was a good girl, and if they were going to speak in code, I wasn't going to try to unlock the code. Even when they spoke in English, I sometimes didn't ask for explanations.

I remember my parents and grandparents sitting around the kitchen table talking heatedly about "Affa David." Who is Affa David? I wondered, and why is everyone talking about him so much? No one told me, and I never asked. Years later, the pieces slipped into place. I knew my grandfather had been an officer in the Fur and Leather Workers Union in the 1940s. (A leather-bound copy of the history of the union written by Philip Foner sat on my grandparents' bookshelf. As a child I had marveled that a real book had a picture of my grandfather.) In a college history class, I learned that the Taft-Hartley Act required union officers to sign a non-communist *affidavit*.

My childhood world consisted of family, school, friends, neighborhood. In 1950 we moved to West Haven, Connecticut. On a country road, amid open fields surrounded by post-and-rail fences, my father built a small red-brick house on an acre of land. Dark-red tea roses and raspberry bushes bordered the gravel driveway. The backyard sloped down from a concrete patio to a vegetable garden where I spent loathsome hours picking rocks out of the dirt and pulling weeds. Beyond the garden my father eventually built a small wooden barn and chicken-wire fence to hold the goat my mother milked.

Although I didn't know I was a red diaper baby, I was beginning to notice that our lives were not quite like our friends'. They had their own toys, for example. We had to share our toys with each other. "There's no such thing as 'mine,'" my mother reproved me when I objected to my brother playing with the Lincoln Logs that had been given to me. "The toys belong to all of you."

At dinnertime we ate in front of the television set in the living room. John Cameron Swayze reported the world news from 6 to 6:15. Solemnly he intoned a report on Red China or Red Russia, and dark spread across the map on the screen. I asked my mother a question; I don't remember what. She replied, "Just because you see something on television doesn't mean it's true." My nine-year-old mind processed this into an axiom: The opposite of what you see on television is true. When John Cameron Swayze reported the evil deeds of the commies and the purity of Americans, I now knew that meant the commies were good and the Americans were bad. It wasn't so hard to flip-flop the categories. When we watched Howdy-Doody, we rooted for Mr Bluster and against the goody-goody Howdy-Doody.

One day I saw my beloved sixth grade teacher's car parked among the cinders in the parking lot behind the school with a "God Bless Joe McCarthy" bumper sticker. I was stunned. At home I had learned that teachers are to be respected and listened to, but I had also learned that Senator Joseph McCarthy was a bad person. This was an incomprehensible contradiction. When I went home to ask my mother about it, she told me we had different beliefs from other people but we had as much right to our beliefs as they did.

In 1956 we moved to Levittown, Pennsylvania, offspring of the original Levittown on Long Island. This was the real suburbs, with spacious, three-bedroom houses, lots of lawn and saplings. In high school I devoured Ayn Rand's novels. My father was horrified. "She's a fascist," he said. But the message in favor of selfishness and against socialism gave legitimacy to some of my feelings. My parents' insistence that my brother, sister, and I share all of our toys had not instilled a sense of community in me; it simply made me vow that when I grew up I would possess my own things. When my parents told me that no one was better than anyone else, I had felt embarrassed by my intellectual abilities. Ayn Rand's novels said it was good to own things, it was good to be smart (even for a girl!), and it was wrong to make people feel bad for having things and being smarter than others.

Political activities didn't exist in my school, and I probably wouldn't have been interested if they had. I didn't know if any of my classmates had family beliefs like mine; we simply never talked about it. My feelings of rebelliousness focused on cultural issues: when two boys were sent home from school for growing mustaches, I thought the school authorities were silly. A young English teacher organized an after-school discussion group, where we read *Catcher in the Rye*, but while everyone else enthused over this book "speaking to our generation," I felt alienated from Holden Caulfield's self-conscious cynicism.

When the first Black family moved into Levittown, a cross was burned on their lawn. My mother was acquainted with them and wanted to show a welcoming presence. I asked to accompany her when she visited, but both my parents said no, it was too dangerous.

The summer I was fifteen I joined a world affairs group organized by the American Friends Service Committee. The group was gathering people to participate in the Philadelphia portion of a march from New York to Washington commemorating Hiroshima Day, and I thought it would be a worthwhile thing for me to do. Of course, I had to ask my parents. To my surprise, my mother said no. My father had a new job, she explained, and it might be dangerous. If anything happened to me, if my name were in the newspaper, my father might lose his job. Why might he lose his job? I asked in amazement. Didn't I have a right to my opinion? Only recently did I learn that the FBI had visited my father soon after he'd started this new job, asking for information about some people he had known fifteen years before. This heightened his sense that the FBI was still watching and that we should all be careful.

This was the beginning of my realization that our being "different" was more complicated than I originally thought. I knew my parents were Democrats; in rural Connecticut and suburban Philadelphia, being a Democrat was difference enough. In 1952 we didn't like Ike when everyone else did. In 1956 I was the only one in my class to vote for Adlai Stevenson in our mock election. My grandmother talked about "progressive people." I knew it was bad to call communists "commies." I knew that "Negroes" were just like "you and me." I knew that Alger Hiss and the Rosenbergs were innocent. But none of this added up to a coherent way of thinking about politics. I never heard of dialectics until I was in college. While we might occasionally discuss current events at the dinner table, we didn't argue politics. Political opinions were important, but how they were arrived at was vague to me. Disagreement could be dangerous, whether it was my parents' disagreement with mainstream politics or, possibly, my disagreement with my parents' ideas. My parents' hypocrisies seemed clearer. When my mother, standing in the fancy kitchen of our big new house on Philadelphia's Main Line in 1959, said, "Comes the revolution," I could only think, "Comes the revolution, you won't get to keep this house." I was too much a "good girl" to say that, however.

I don't remember when I learned that my grandfather was a communist, possibly because that fact was so at odds with the picture of "communists" laid out by popular culture and education. Grandpa was no doctrinaire zombie. He was a sweet and loving and playful man who talked to children as if we were on the same level. My grandmother was political only because her husband was. I remember her telling me, "The *Guardian* [a left-wing paper] is a beacon of light," but I don't remember her ever talking about politics.

My father was close-mouthed about lots of things. When I learned, in college, about the four-way presidential election of 1948—within my lifetime!—I asked my parents who they'd voted for. My mother said she'd voted for Henry Wallace, and she hinted that she and my father had disagreed. But when I asked my father, he replied, "The ballot is secret." I'd already learned that he wouldn't tell us anything he didn't want known by anyone outside the family. When we'd asked him how much money he made—so we could compare figures with our classmates, a common topic of conversation—he'd said, "It's nobody else's business."

"We won't tell anyone," I'd said, disingenuously.

"If somebody asks you, I don't want you to have to lie," he'd replied.

So I had to screw up my courage in the late 1960s to ask the Question.

"Dad, did you belong to the Communist Party?"

"Yes, but a long time ago and not for very long," he replied, after a hesitation. He'd been part of a group in Washington during the war ("A cell?" I asked excitedly. "If you want to call it that," he shrugged) until they learned that a woman in the group was talking to the government about them. He quit so he wouldn't lose his job.

I leaned back, satisfied for the moment. No matter that the story had holes in it; I'd asked the question, and I'd gotten a definitive response.

Recently, I asked the question again. This time my father said he'd never been a member of the Party but had been in the Young Communist League. He repeated the story about the woman who had talked to the government. He said she had caused him to be blacklisted from a job at Johns Hopkins after the war because of his political background—this was news to me. I asked him who the woman was, and he said, "I don't remember her name."

"How could you not remember her name?" I said. I would never forget the name of someone I thought had betrayed me.

"I made myself forget a lot of things," he said. "There were names of people I didn't want to come out at the wrong time, so I just made myself forget."

When I first learned about red diaper babies, I tiptoed around the identity. I wanted to embrace it, but I thought I would be doing so under false pretenses. My parents weren't active Party members, and I was in my twenties when I learned they were both red diaper babies themselves. I hadn't gone to socialist summer camps or grown up in a community of other leftists. We didn't have to fend off the FBI, though we kept them off the TV: we never watched "I Led Three Lives." I didn't think of myself as a socialist, though I did consider myself a leftist of some sort. When my housemates in 1964 called our apartment "the 19th Street Soviet," I cringed. I never read anything about the Russian Revolution until after I saw the movie *Reds* in 1981. When I learned about anarchism in college, I embraced that more readily than I did socialism. Self-government seemed much more dependable, if much more work, than either soviets or markets.

On the other hand, being a red diaper baby seemed to give me a certain cachet with my friends. Some people I met even seemed to envy my growing up "inside" what they had only come to as adults.

The fall of communist governments throughout Eastern Europe made me think about my relationship to this identity more clearly than I ever had before. Talking on the phone to my father the week after the failed coup in Moscow in August 1991 (he saw the hand of the CIA at work), I felt liberated, as though an anchor I hadn't even known existed, an anchor as ephemeral as a soap bubble, disappeared with a ping. I began working with feminists in the "post-communist region" and found a curious mirror-image in the backgrounds of red diaper babies in the United States and the children of dissidents in Eastern Europe: the feeling of difference from mainstream culture, the fear of expressing family opinions in public, the need to hide who one was. I also heard firsthand about living under "really existing socialism," and the stories made my parents' beliefs seem illusory.

Writing this memoir has made it possible for me to talk to my parents about this aspect of their lives and mine as I had never before felt free to do. Each story I've remembered has led to phone calls to verify a fact or ask for their version of events. My father still worries about red-baiting and witch-hunts. There is a hesitancy in his voice when he answers some of my questions; he's cautious about people's names. I learned that my mother didn't think of herself as political at all because she thought being political meant leafleting on the street and mastering dialectics; she preferred curling up with a good book. She remembers her father talking to her, as a child, about the class struggle and workers and capitalists. She remembers that his explanations seemed clear and sensible and that she felt no desire to argue with him. Even in her fifties she refused to read Solzhenitsyn's books because she didn't want to learn bad things about the Soviet Union.

What I knew and when I knew it has become less important than the satisfaction of opening up a conversation with my parents about our lives. My father is uncomfortable with introspection, and my mother is firmly planted in the current moment, yet I'm glad that they have both responded encouragingly. In return, I judge them not as harshly as I once did, when I knew less about who they were.

Black and Red All Over

MaryLouise Patterson

MaryLouise Patterson was born in Chicago and grew up, from the age of six, in New York City. Patterson received her undergraduate degree and trained as a physician in the former U.S.S.R. After living for twenty years in California, she has returned to New York City, where she works as a pediatrician. Daughter of well-known and widely respected left-wing activists— her father a CP leader and her mother an important political and cultural figure—Patterson describes growing up within the Party's upper echelons.

One night, in bed, surfing the TV offerings, I chanced on a PBS program showing Alexander Solzhenitsyn on his first return to his ex-homeland, looking like a modernized version of an eighteenth-century Russian monk. He was enjoying a train tour of Russia with the traditional bread and salt reception at every stop. From the train steps he'd rail against the former rulers: the vicious demons who, calling themselves communists, ran the show for seventy-plus years, oppressing the people, creating a new privileged elite and a monstrous bureaucratic state, throttling "free" thought and expression for the sake of the "party line" and the "ideological war."

The demons he denounced were the very people I grew up hearing about with reverence. They were struggling against tremendous odds to create a new man, woman, society. The name Stalin meant the defeat of fascism, the electrification of the U.S.S.R., the personification of a world free of racism, gender and national chauvinism, class exploitation, and human degradation.

I grew up living two parallel lives. On Monday through Friday, I went to school, socialized with my friends, and never let on that I was the offspring of the "enemy within." Weekends were spent with my parents and the families of their many political comrades. During the witch-hunts of the 1950s, I dreaded being "found out" by my school and neighborhood friends; there-fore, I was never completely comfortable with them. I kept a certain safe dis-tance and grew up with a fear of discovery, public denunciation, and rejec-tion. At the same time, I was proud of my parents. I believed in what they did yet was often reluctant to bring friends home because my dad might "let the cat out of the bag." My dad knew of my fears and respected my dilemma, but he never missed an opportunity to engage, then politically enlighten, some young Black man or woman.

My father was William Lorenzo Patterson, a lawyer and a member of the leadership of the U.S. Communist Party. He was widely known outside the Party because of his involvement in mass protest and the Civil Rights Move-ment. Perhaps because of this broad base he wasn't as viciously or publicly hounded during the '50s as so many others were—although he survived an attempted deportation effort and served time in prison for contempt of Con-gress and later for contempt of court.

My mother, Louise Thompson Patterson, had been involved in the Har-lem Renaissance and Black cultural and civic life in New York City and Chi-cago; she was introduced to the Left in that milieu. She then organized work-ers for the International Workers Order (IWO). After she and my dad married, she worked in Black community organizations until I was born in 1943. When I was six, we moved from Chicago to New York City, where my mother worked, among other places, for a U.N. housing organization and for Local 1199, the hospital workers union. She was always the main breadwin-ner in the family; the Party had little money for its full-time functionaries.

My mother toured the country with Paul Robeson during the worst of the McCarthy times and organized a national group of Black women, the Sojourn-ers for Truth and Justice, a formation in part inspired by Ida B. Wells and Mary Church Terrell, which sought to advance the cause of Negro liberation and opposed state-sanctioned or mob lynchings of Black men.

I acquired my political consciousness, my political identity, and my dreams by direct observation, participation, and osmosis. With fierce devotion, my parents lived their beliefs, shared them with me, and included me in many of their political activities.

I grew up going to meetings and demonstrations, learning how to make stencils, running mimeograph machines, collating, stapling, stuffing and seal-ing envelopes. What I liked best—but never learned completely—was the switchboard. Most of the time I enjoyed participating, feeling a part of some great invincible yet clandestine force.

I had many hours of fun at Party headquarters, an old mansion affection-ately called "Twenty-Sixth Street." It was a solid and impressive red brick townhouse; I found out much later that the building had originally belonged to a rich family and was bequeathed to the Party by one of the family's way-ward descendants. There was a rickety old self-service elevator, big enough for two, with a folding wrought-iron gate. The winding marble stairway had a highly polished dark wooden banister that beckoned me to slide down—when no adult was watching, of course.

Children were tolerated at Party headquarters, but the atmosphere was heavy and serious. Many a Saturday with me in tow my mother and father would go to Twenty-Sixth Street to do Party work. My mother always did clerical tasks while my dad disappeared behind a heavy wooden door. On rare occasions, I'd catch wedged glimpses of the men in their meetings when the door would unexpectedly open while I was playing in the hallway. I was too young to think about, much less question, the division of labor. It seemed to me that my mother's work was very important (and it was), and I enjoyed doing it with her.

Other times I would be taken to the "Jeff School" (the Jefferson School) for recreational classes. It was a wonderful place where children and adults from the Left and the labor movement studied everything from art and dance to political science and labor issues. The Jeff School had a bookstore where you could browse forever—and I did as often as I could.

My parents always had people visiting the house, people staying or living with us. For the most part they were my parents' political allies and comrades, and I grew up with a natural sense of family connection to all of them, Black and white.

My dad's family was god-fearing, respectable, and middle-income, many with government jobs. For the most part, they had excommunicated him, and my mom barely knew most of her family because she had not grown up among them. When my mother was four years old, she and her mother moved to the West Coast from Chicago following her father, but the marriage soon dis-solved, leaving my grandmother, who had no marketable skills, to fend for the two of them. My mother grew up all over Oregon, Washington, Idaho, and finally California.

Our political comrades were Black or white, which never seemed to mat-ter, although race was always discussed in our house. My dad was a "race man" as well as a communist; he defended everyone's rights but placed special em-phasis on the fight for the rights of his own people. I grew up hearing the stories of many courageous and honest white people who devoted their lives to the full inclusion and participation of Black folks in society: from aboli-tionist John Brown to South African freedom fighters Ruth First and Joe Slovo to many lesser known others from all over the world.

We always marched in May Day and Labor Day parades. I'd avoid looking at the faces of angry bystanders for compassion or reason while trying to dodge the rotten eggs and tomatoes and epithets. My parents must have inspired in me a certain confidence with their own courageous posture as their hands tightly gripped mine; I always wanted to carry the banners or placards and always shouted the slogans. Perhaps I was seduced by the sense of danger and by their bravery.

Both parents, but especially my father, were acutely aware of the need to talk with me to actively counter the daily barrage of anticommunist propaganda in the media. I was about eight or nine the first time my father was jailed. From prison he wrote me long, wonderful letters, urging me to believe in "a world without hungry children" where "strawberries and cream for breakfast for everyone" was possible. I believed that the men who ran our country, allowing lynching, segregation, hunger, joblessness, ghettos, and hopelessness alongside an idle rich class, should and could be overthrown.

Our closest family friends were other Black communists and their families. My best friends were their children. Many of us lived near each other in Brooklyn. For several summers I was sent to a Left children's camp called Higley Hill, a truly magical place in the woods of western Vermont. For the children of persecuted leftists, it was a breath of fresh air, a place where we could be ourselves and express our real beliefs unencumbered, where we reinforced those beliefs and that identity by trying to briefly live a happy communal lifestyle. Years later we learned that the cook was an FBI informant.

What exciting times as I was emerging out of childhood: the 1956 bus boycott, the 1959–60 lunch counter sit-ins. During my high school years I helped organize a chapter of the National Council of Christians and Jews, organized three busloads from my high school to a march on Washington, joined the Labor Youth League (which replaced the Young Communist League) and then the Du Bois Club (considered a CP front by the federal government).

In high school my homeroom teacher, who was also my social studies teacher, called me "Little Stalin" and another classmate "Little Lenin." Perhaps I hid the Party connection, but not the politics: I always challenged the teachers' and textbooks' anticommunism and distortion of American history, especially the part about slavery.

During those years I irregularly attended a large Black Baptist church (because "the guys" were there playing basketball), was a cheerleader for the high school basketball team, and had two boyfriends. One knew my "true" identity and introduced me to poetry, jazz, Greenwich Village, and a wonderful, inexpensive, tiny, left-owned Chinese restaurant in Chinatown that we haunted. He was my true soul mate. We could talk forever about politics, poetry, music, life, and our futures. The other was the star basketball player, the most handsome guy on campus (even the white girls were crazy over him), with whom I was for a time totally infatuated (the day he joined the army I dressed in black, and I then wore black for an entire week). We talked about his other girlfriends, current R&B singers and hits, our daily lives. We danced a lot. He introduced me to Bed-Sty (Bedford-Stuyvesant), the Black community of Brooklyn, where he lived.

I graduated from high school in 1960. Several months before my graduation, my dad left for a long trip to Europe. The State Department had just restored passports and the right to travel to my father and many others, including Paul Robeson and W. E. B. Du Bois. My dad had two daughters who were born in Leningrad during the 1930s from a marriage that terminated abruptly because of Stalin's banning of foreigners (at least that's my understanding of what happened). After the three-year siege of Leningrad during World War II, he'd tried to discover their fate and was told that they probably hadn't survived the siege (plausible, since two million hadn't). When he finally got to Leningrad in the summer of 1960, he serendipitously found them, alive and well.

Meanwhile, my mom and I prepared to make the trip to join him. When we got to Moscow, we learned that he was in China, so off we went. I wasn't to return home to live for eight years. Initially, I was going to study in Beijing, but this plan proved too "complicated" for my father—due to the impending Sino-Soviet split, of which my mother and I knew nothing—and for my mother, since maintaining regular contact with me would have been extremely difficult. So, after a wonderful two-month stay, we left China for the U.S.S.R. I had wanted to stay, as I found China fascinating.

My dad had worked out an agreement for a new university in Moscow, People's Friendship University, to take five African American young people; we met the admission criteria because we represented a neocolonized people. I was the only one of the five who went. For some reason, the U.S. Communist Party never carried out the plan. Had it done so, my boyfriend would have gone as well.

I entered People's Friendship University in September 1960. I officially studied medicine. Unofficially, I learned politics, life, and love. I met and married a Cuban student. I participated in political activities, had my first child, and traveled through parts of Europe and the U.S.S.R., to North Africa and Cuba.

In the U.S.S.R. I saw bureaucracy (which I learned was largely a vestige of czarist times), sloppiness, inefficiency, drunkenness, waste, and abuse of privilege and position. Those with authority, power, and prestige in the U.S.S.R.

lived much better than the general population. But I saw no unemployment, no hungry children's hollowed eyes, no open prostitution, a highly educated populace, and wonderful culture available to and enjoyed by all. I also saw promise for a more equitable distribution of wealth. I saw real assistance to national liberation struggles; free excellent education for all; free adequate health care for all; real protection of children, the elderly, and the disabled.

I left the U.S.S.R., a doctor, in 1968 (after time out for another child and a year in Cuba) and returned to the United States determined to dedicate my life to making a difference in the lives of those who are oppressed, dehumanized, discarded, undesired, and feared.

I work as a general pediatrician and participate in community activities, lecturing to schoolchildren, working with African American teenage girls, speaking at rallies and demonstrations, participating in efforts in solidarity with Cuba. I could probably be more involved, but perhaps my edge has been dulled by the saccharin sweetness of petit bourgeois life.

When Life Was a Party

Stephanie Allan

Stephanie Allan was born in 1943 in Detroit, where she grew up and graduated from high school. After holding a variety of jobs, she settled into a career as business agent for a blue-collar union. She lives in Berkeley, California.

Allan was raised in postwar working-class urban America. She describes a happy childhood and warm family life, interrupted when her father, a leader of the Michigan CP, was jailed under the Smith Act.

An association between food and good times—at home, in the neighborhood, and at political events—is woven through this memoir.

My father, William "Billy" Allan, was born in Glasgow, Scotland, in 1907. His mother died when he was six months old from drinking unpasteurized milk. His father was a house painter, a socialist, and a drunk. To the extent anyone raised Billy, it was his grandmother. She had been a weaver of Paisley shawls, and her fingers were in a permanent claw from years of mill work and arthritis. At age five, my father went to work in a stable, caring for Clydesdale horses so huge he barely came up to their knees.

When Billy was six or seven, his father took him down to the Glasgow docks, where the senior Allan made speeches against the war in Europe (World War I) and in support of Irish revolutionaries. A conscientious objector to the war on political grounds, my grandfather didn't think workers should fight for imperial England. He served at least a year in prison for refusing to enlist, to the disgrace, apparently, of the family. After his father's speeches, Billy would take his cap off and pass it around for donations for the Irish to buy guns to fight the British.

My father's schooling ended when he was twelve, as tuition was required to go further. He left school with a love of reading, his escape from a miserable home life. He was apprenticed as a baker, which became his trade and later his hobby. At about age fifteen, to escape the increasingly violent alcoholic binges of his father, Billy shipped out in the merchant marine. Although the hours were long, usually twelve or more a day, he had the peace of his bunk in which to read. He also met sailors who introduced him to new ideas, including political economics. Billy took part in the 1926 general strike in Britain and, like thousands of other activists, found himself unable to work when the strike was broken. He headed for the United States, where he landed in the spring of 1929. He rode the rails and eventually ended up in Detroit, where there was a large Scottish community and the hope of jobs in the auto plants.

Billy found work as a baker and quickly joined the fledgling Bakery & Confectionary Workers Union Local 32. It was dominated by German socialists and communists who had fled the collapse of the Weimar Republic and the rise of National Socialism. They made Billy secretary of the local because he could read and write English. They also continued his political education and were instrumental in his decision to become a communist.

A mixture of radicals, socialists, anarchists, communists, populists, and trade union militants, many of whom had fled the collapse of democracies in Europe, shaped the political climate in Detroit. The battles to organize unions and to fight the ravages of the Depression were physical, immediate, dangerous, and, I believe, exhilarating. Billy plunged into them with complete dedication and total involvement, taking part in virtually every major labor struggle in Detroit. A skinny little guy with glasses known for his sharp tongue, fearlessness, and commitment, he became an unpaid organizer for both the Communist Party and the CIO. He had to raise his "salary" through contributions and sales of the CP newspaper and often bunked with friends when the contributions didn't pay the rent for what he called a "flophouse room."

My parents met through the Communist Party and were married in 1938. My mother, Stephanie, supported Billy throughout his life, both as a partner and as the primary breadwinner while he worked for the Communist Party newspaper.

In 1953 the Rosenbergs were executed, and my father was arrested under the Smith Act for "conspiring to overthrow the U.S. government by force and violence." I was ten years old.

The Rosenbergs had two sons, the same ages as myself and my sister Martha. I knew my parents had worked hard to save the Rosenbergs and shared their ideas. I was terrified by the executions and frantic that my parents would be killed. I never spoke to my parents about this, and I don't think it ever occurred to them that it was something a kid would even think about. I knew I was expected to be mature and help them, so talking about such a fear was not something I thought I should do. But I can remember crying myself to sleep night after night, praying to Mother Nature, hoping that no police officers would take my parents away to jail and put them in the electric chair.

My father was arrested standing at a bus stop, going to work. The FBI drove up with several carloads of agents, who jumped out and handcuffed him. He spent some months in Jackson State Prison while bail was raised. I remember it being a long drive to go see him. My mother, my sisters—Martha, who was about five, and Jeanne, who was just two and still in diapers—and I would make the trip to visit him.

Prison guards would search all of us, even looking in Jeanne's diaper. We used to giggle and joke, hoping Jeanne would properly reward them. It seemed to take forever for them to clear us, and we'd be jumping up and down, frantic to see Daddy. We missed him terribly.

Finally they'd let us into a big room with chairs and tables, where he'd be waiting. We were only allowed to kiss and hug him when we arrived and when we left. The rest of the time we had to sit apart from him, not touching him. There were always guards standing and watching, listening to everything we said. The only point of interest in that dreary room was a machine that dispensed soft drinks. My mother would let us get one while we were there, a rare treat.

Both my parents were firmly convinced that this effort to silence my dad and the political movement they belonged to would be defeated. "The workers will defend us," my dad said. I became proud of him rather than scared he wouldn't come home. How my mother hid her fear, worry, and exhaustion during that time, I'll never know, but I'm grateful to her because it meant that we as kids focused on the effort to free Billy and fight the injustice of the Smith Act rather than on our loss.

Ultimately, the $10,000 bail, an astronomical sum in those days, was raised, and Billy came home. He and my mother plunged into the work to prepare for the upcoming trials, the fund-raising, political organizing, and defense of their beloved Communist Party against government attacks.

While our parents were totally immersed in the political defense movement, we had birthday parties, went to concerts and picnics, and had friends over to camp out in our front yard. We lived in a housing project in Detroit called Herman Gardens. My mother would hang a blanket over a clothesline and make a tent for us and the neighborhood kids. She made Kool-Aid, and my father produced quantities of cookies, pies, and cakes, which were enormously popular with all our friends. Sometimes my mother would take an old diaper pail and use it as a frying pot, making plate after plate of french fries, which were a special treat. Kids used to love to come over because my parents welcomed them all and allowed us to play in and around the house with few restrictions. I never knew we were poor. I thought we were about the luckiest people I knew. We had a lot of friends, and we always seemed to be doing something or going somewhere interesting. There was a lot of talk in the house, books, toys (thanks to two bachelor uncles who filled in a lot of the financial cracks), a television, music, and my parents, who always had answers when we had questions.

When Billy went on trial, along with five other people, the pictures and addresses of the "Michigan Six" were splashed across the front pages of the local newspapers. Suddenly, life changed for us. Some people wouldn't let their kids come over anymore. Rocks were thrown through our windows, and obscene, threatening phone calls began to make us afraid to pick up the phone. I walked about a mile to Herman Elementary School, and men began to follow me in a car. Gangs of kids would also follow me, yelling insults and threatening to run us out of the projects.

The worst insult they could think of was that people like my father didn't believe in God. I was a militant little atheist and argued with them. How could they be so sure there was a God, I asked. Had they ever seen him? I believed in Mother Nature, I said, and they could see proof of her everywhere. In adulthood, I developed an appreciation of a more spiritual view of the world, especially after working with the Quakers in the anti–Vietnam War movement. But at age ten, I had a certainty about the world that enabled me to slug it out verbally with my tormenters. I was absolutely sure that my dad was right, and I would defend him and our family without hesitation.

Billy was convicted under the Smith Act. When the Supreme Court overturned his conviction, the government tried to revoke his citizenship. I was convinced I was going to have to grow up in Scotland. The government alleged that Billy had lied on his citizenship application by not admitting he was a member of the Communist Party. His attorney, George Crockett, who later became a judge and then a member of Congress, proved that Billy had never been asked about his political affiliations.

That was the end of the official political persecution, but the hard years of the '50s took their toll on my parents. The organization they'd devoted themselves to was first splintered and then destroyed. The attack on the labor movement and the destruction of the Left in the unions was, I think, even more painful for Billy. Despite his lifetime commitment to the Communist Party, he was essentially a union activist with a Marxist viewpoint. He had two articles of faith that he attempted to instill in his daughters. One was that workers were good and bosses weren't; the other was that the Soviet Union was a force for peace in the world.

During those years, though, we continued as a family to march in nuclear disarmament demonstrations, support picket lines, and take part in political events. We also had a warm, loving family life. My mother had a rule: four nights a week for meetings, but Friday and Saturday nights and Sundays for the family. We ate dinner together almost every night; only something extraordinary interfered. After dinner, one or the other of my parents had a meeting to go to, and we had homework. I remember being startled to find out that other kids' parents didn't go to out to meetings every night. What do they do, I wondered. It was clear to me and my sisters that we were expected to do something about the world we lived in, and it never occurred to us that others didn't share that perspective.

Both my parents worked half days on Saturdays; in the early afternoons, we'd all go to Eastern Market in Detroit, a great open air farmers' market where you could buy every kind of produce, meat, live animals, and wonderful treats like maple sugar candy. Then we'd go get fresh bagels, still warm and soft, from a local Jewish bakery. Saturday nights there were fresh fruit and bagels with cream cheese. After dinner, we'd watch the Lawrence Welk show, roll back the carpet, and dance.

Shortly after my dad went on trial, we had to move out of the projects. The official reason was that my mother had gotten a $5 raise and we no longer qualified, as our income was too high. I later learned that we were forced to leave because the FBI pressured the housing authority. They also visited the doctors for whom she worked in an effort to get her fired.

Eventually we moved to a big, old, two-story dwelling with a full basement and a wonderful hidden entrance through a closet to an attic crawlspace. My sisters and I pretended that if Joe McCarthy ever came to arrest us, we could hide up there and he'd never know where we were.

I got a strong sense from my parents and their friends of a multiracial, multiethnic community. My mother would identify people by their country of origin: he's a Bulgarian or she's a Serbo-Croatian. We would go to Hamtramack to buy smoked sausages and look at the signs in the stores, which were in Polish. We went to Greektown to buy bread. Very little, though, was ever said about Scotland. My mother said that when my dad came to this country, he decided to become an American. He worked hard to lose his accent and never talked about his native country.

Some of my best memories are of baking with my father. He always baked in huge quantities as though he was feeding the Russian army, as my mother would remark. It was a weekend ritual, and we loved to help him, kneading the dough or licking pans. Billy also baked for all the political events we took part in, bazaars, picnics, banquets. He could always be found in the kitchen, baking or cooking, then would take off his apron and make the collection speech. We girls used to help by taking the baskets around while Billy made the pitch. My mother, who was a bookkeeper, took care of the money at such events. It was a family affair.

My mom and dad were loving parents who didn't put the movement ahead of their family but rather joined their family and politics to the benefit of both. But Billy was a complicated, difficult man. A prickly, somewhat egocentric person, he had a terrible temper and would spank us if he lost it. My mother intervened constantly; gradually, but not completely, she put a stop to the physical punishment. There were a lot of loud, yelling arguments, especially since we felt perfectly free to dispute, disagree, and challenge our parents. But I also remember many long conversations with my father about things that were bothering me or questions about what was happening to us and our friends during the '50s. When I became an adult, he valued my opinion and sought it out.

Fifteen-year-old Stephanie Allan demonstrates for "security through disarmament," 1958. Courtesy of Stephanie Allan.

In the seventh grade, I wrote a report for my social studies teacher about banning the atomic bomb. He gave me an "A" and congratulated me on my inquiring mind. Both my parents were enormously proud of that paper and grade. Until I entered high school and ran into the brick wall of peer pressure, I freely and openly expressed my usually different views and didn't seem to suffer much social ostracism. I was opposed to saying the Pledge of Allegiance with the words "under God" (and remain so to this day) and thought that Flag Day celebrations were anti-peace. I never felt that I couldn't or shouldn't speak out about these ideas, which were, to say the least, a minority view in the 1950s. However, I was coming into conflict with my parents on certain issues, starting with music. I loved Elvis Presley, and they thought rock and roll was an abomination.

In high school, my rebellion took the form of resisting my parents' politics. I was militantly apolitical, the quintessential conformist. My parents suffered through this period without criticizing or pressuring me. Eventually, through the Quakers, I became politically active in the anti–Vietnam war movement. I felt some urgency about this because the Cuban missile crisis had left me with the fear that if something wasn't done about the madness of nuclear war, I'd never live to see thirty. My parents took justifiable pride in my activities, especially my dad, who'd quietly despaired of me through my teen years.

While my dad was the dominant political force in our house, I realized in later years that my mother had given me a great deal as well. She had been raised in a family of Ukrainian immigrants and was the first one in the family to graduate from high school. My grandfather then tried to sell her off to an older man in exchange for a chicken farm. An older sister intervened, and my mother remained at home, working full-time as well as cooking and cleaning for her father and two brothers. They expected her to get their permission to go out with friends and certainly not to go anywhere with a man alone.

My mother's rebellion against her home life had a lot to do with the kind of family my sisters and I grew up in. She was determined we'd have a family in which things were shared, where the women didn't sit in the kitchen after dinner while the men sat in the living room drinking, smoking, and talking. She was determined that her daughters would be independent and self-confident. She wanted a family that did things together and where there was love, not servitude. My father, who was raised on the streets and never had a family life, recognized her strength in this and to his credit became a full partner with her in it. I don't think this was a Marxist approach or a result of their involvement in the Communist Party, although the kind of communism my parents practiced was certainly in harmony with an egalitarian, humanist view of the family.

My parents drilled into us that we could always rely on our family and should take care of each other. They expanded that idea to society as a whole, but the foundation was our family. I am grateful to them for giving me that solid ground to stand on. It has sustained me through the most difficult periods of my life and helped me to develop my own politics and ethics. Even though I can look back and see the shortcomings in my parents that I try to make up for with my own son, I can also see their love, their commitment, and their unwavering belief in me and my sisters and the possibility of a better world for us to grow up in. I was lucky to be a red diaper baby.

A Memoir

Rachel Fast Ben-Avi

Rachel Fast Ben-Avi, born in New York City in 1944, grew up there and in Teaneck, New Jersey. She studied at Wellesley College, the Neighborhood Playhouse, and the Herbert Berghof Studio, worked as an actor and model, and taught high school English before becoming a clinical psychologist and psychoanalyst. Ben-Avi was on staff at the Institute for Rehabilitation Medicine of New York Medical Center and had a private therapy practice until 1990, when she and her husband, also a psychoanalyst, retired. Ben-Avi now works as a writer. Here she describes the complexities of a childhood lived among the Red and famous.

Daddy was a saintly heroic figure, Mommy his apostle. Daddy was a sinner, a wicked commie, Mommy his dupe.

Daddy was not only a famous writer but also a great patriot, revered around the world for both his moving stories and his utopian idealism. Daddy turned his back on democracy, conspired with Americans who were bent on overthrowing the government of the United States. He was the loyal devoted ally of our arch enemy.

The communists were good people, our closest friends. The communists were evil.

Anticommunist hysteria was rampant, everywhere in the media. The vast majority of Americans hated and distrusted us.

It was not romantic, the actual daily life. It was not thrilling and did not imbue me with a glorious sense of transcendent purpose. Much of my childhood, in fact, was grim and confusing; the political atmosphere that colored it, unnerving, intimidating. Tranquility and the assumption of safety would have made for a less troubled upbringing, but while I suffered the emotional dis-comfort and insecurity that would seem a necessary concomitant of the rad-ical life, I was privileged to grow up in the company of the men and women in the communist movement. Though they may be faulted for naïveté, for denial, they were special—smart and principled, courageous, analytical and thoughtful, fair-minded. They had humanitarian values for which they were willing to and did sacrifice much. And I hold dear the admiration I felt as a child and still feel as an adult for my father's courage (and my mother's too—though less enthusiastic, she stood by him and the Party loyally) during one of the most terrible times in our country's history.

1950. I was six. My father had been found guilty of contempt, sentenced, and was about to serve three months in prison. My parents, after consultation with a psychiatrist, agreed to conceal the particulars of this upcoming event from me. It was the opinion of the psychiatrist that my knowing my father was in prison "might create trauma." My father told me the truth when I was some years older.

I laughed aloud when I read "might create trauma" in Father's book *Being Red*, a memoir about his involvement from 1944 to 1956 in the Communist Party. A series of traumas tarnished my childhood—no absolute disaster like the one that befell the Meeropol boys, but disruptive incidents that did punc-tuate our day-to-day lives, did take their toll.

I assume many of my red diaper "brothers" and "sisters" emerged from their McCarthy-era childhoods politically astute and involved, bold, strong. The events of the time, terrible enough intrinsically but exaggerated by my father's fiery rhetoric, his aggressive suffering and theatrical outbursts, frightened me into silent, sometimes sycophantic submission and a stance for peace-and-harmony-at-any-price in almost any threatening situation. By the time I was six or seven I was clinically depressed. There are photographs of me that were taken then. In them I look sad, beaten, angry.

I became politically stupid (that stupidity has persisted, despite efforts to overcome it, into my middle age), deaf to political news on the radio or tele-vision, blind to the news in print. Though I marched for civil rights in the Sixties and against the Vietnam War, it is only in recent years that I have be-come outspoken (to call myself an activist would be to exaggerate grossly) on issues that touch my heart—AIDS and gay rights, the right of women to choose, peace.

I would give much now for total recall. Or so says my conscious mind. When I was old enough to experience the anxiety and anger floating around our house like a miasma that, though invisible, compromises respiration, my unconscious determined I needed an escape hatch: the less I remembered the better. I imagine I sensed the omnipresent fear before I had language.

I was born in May of 1944. *Citizen Tom Paine* had already been published. Father had finished *Freedom Road* that April. People at the Office of War Information, where he worked, drew him and my mother into the Cultural Section of the Communist Party. My parents would devote themselves to the Party for the next twelve years. The troubles and miseries of the world became my father's personal woes, the Party his raison d'être. He writes, "Active involvement in the Communist Party commanded the whole life process. One ate it and slept it." So did one's children. Because of his assumption of the world's burdens, his obvious goodness, and because he was my father, I made excuses for him, whatever the accusation leveled by whoever the accuser.

The Roosevelts invited my mother and father to a luncheon at the White House on January 19, 1945. The framed invitation still hangs in my parents' house. It was a heady time for them. Father was famous, admired; Eleanor Roosevelt loved his books. The McCarthy era, the blacklist (which would affect us from 1949 to 1956), the witch-hunt of the future, these were unimaginable.

My childhood was spackled with excitement, lit by special experiences other children who were not red diaper babies could not, would not ever know, the comrades and camaraderie, the parties, the singing, the sense of belonging to an almost holy inner circle that was part of a great and noble good, a movement that would do away with inequality of every sort, usher in a true "brotherhood of men." We would abolish all manner of prejudice and bigotry. We would love and respect each other. Everyone would have enough of everything necessary for the good life. There would be no more hunger, poverty, war.

Father was omniscient. Or at any rate, he seemed certain he was, or that is the way I remember his being and apparently needed him to be, so we made an unspoken pact. I was, he told me, to think, to accept nothing without question, yes, even to question him. It delighted him when I did. He would laugh, applaud my "brilliance." When we argued, though, his was the last word. I do not know if other Communist Party members were as fanatically certain they had a corner on the absolute and pure truth or whether that conviction was peculiar to my father. He has always been the proud possessor of certitude, always insisted my mother, brother, and I (everyone, come to think of it) believe him, whatever the subject, however obviously he bent truth to suit himself, however glaring any evidence to the contrary presented by whoever the authority.

I am lying on my parents' large bed on one of those white bedspreads covered with little round knobs of cotton. I am two? three? four? The *New York Times* is spread out before Father and me. It is our daily morning guest masquerading as a neutral informant, in fact a con artist likely at any moment to mislead, we know. Father attacks the paper, combs it for untruths. He reads to me, explains the events of the day, points out distortions, anticommunist propaganda, outright lies. I try my best to understand. Sometimes I challenge him. "You're not listening, Rachel," he reprimands. "You must listen," he pleads.

There are pictures of me, taken throughout the years of my childhood, concentrating with every brain cell I can mobilize, eyebrows knit, forehead creased. I look pitiful in them, I think now, trying so hard to be a little intellectual, to listen well enough to understand, well enough to please him.

My mother watches from a distance, hovers somewhere in the background, her arms around her body; she holds herself tight. She is tense, sometimes frightened, often disapproving, angry.

I always felt she hated Father's politicizing me so young, his demanding I respond as if I were forty when I was only four.

★

As soon as I could, I asked, "How do you know you're right—communism is good, capitalism evil—and everyone else in America is wrong? How do you know? Convince me." I needed Father to be right so that he, so that we would not be despised, ridiculed, haunted. I wanted, I said, a wand that could change things, wished to be able to effect the great social change instantaneously, *presto*, to end the omnipresent conflict, tumult, and scary high-drama of our lives, FBI banging on the door in the middle of the night, whispers of comrades arrested, beaten.

Father's desperate desire for a more compassionate and evenhanded society, his faith that change was possible, inspired me. As an adult I earned a Ph.D. in clinical psychology and a certificate in psychoanalysis, practiced for fifteen years in hospitals and privately. I don't doubt that Father's passionate conviction that he could change the world contributed to my notion that I could and ought to help people change themselves, a more modest, less public, and certainly less risky endeavor.

Hiroshima and Nagasaki had been bombed by the time I was a year old. The fear of nuclear annihilation was a constant topic of conversation in our house. I suspect the horrific but unlikely possibilities were transmogrified into imminent probability by Father's descriptive gifts, his tendency to histrionics, hyperbole. I had repetitive nightmares, from which I awoke in terror, of bombs dropping all around me, enormous silent bouncing black spheres each of which threatened to kill with its next strike. The Communist Party would save us from the madness of the capitalists in power.

On April 4, 1946, my mother's twenty-ninth birthday, my father testified before the House Committee on Un-American Activities. He was a member of the executive board of the Joint Anti-Fascist Refugee Committee, which had been raising money for a hospital in Toulouse that cared for Spanish antifascists and their families. My parents took me with them to Washington; I was not yet two and have no conscious memory of this experience. Father refused to hand over to HUAC a list of contributors to the hospital and was cited for contempt. A second subpoena delivered a summons for him to appear in Washington in October 1946. In March 1947, the House indicted the entire board of the Joint Anti-Fascist Refugee Committee not only for contempt, punishable by as much as a year in prison, but also for conspiracy, punishable by up to five years. A trial was set for June 11, 1947, a little after my third birthday.

Father went alone to Washington, D.C., for sentencing. According to his memory, I watched bewildered, frightened, while he and Mother parted, weeping. He was sentenced to three months in prison, to commence in the spring of 1950.

The FBI hounded us. Federal agents followed my parents. I was aware of the constant surveillance, enough the eavesdropper to hear conversation about it. From 1945 on, our telephones were tapped. One night when my parents returned home from an evening out, Father, sensing something was amiss, stepped onto the coffee table in the living room, reached over his head, searched inside the top of the chandelier. He stepped down, a "bug" in hand. The baby-sitter had been an FBI informant. I can see now the look of astonishment, disbelief on his face, despite his having suspected the bug would be there, despite his having been right. I remember the three of us staring at each other in mute horror.

During these years my parents drank too much, fought a good deal.

While this harassment was going on, we were surrounded at home by people whom I remember with fondness and admiration. Our brownstone on the West Side of Manhattan was constantly filled with people, many of whom I was told were important, famous. I enjoyed the excitement of company, dinners, cocktail parties, even meetings. We dressed up often. I was allowed to pass hors d'oeuvres. Mother, always chic, circulated about the living room, wearing black velvet, smoking, drinking martinis.

In 1948, Alger Hiss was indicted for perjury. I had repeated nightmares in which a fox and a wolf cooked me in a large iron cauldron.

Paul Robeson was a frequent guest. When he visited, he held me in his lap, sang to me. "Ma Curly-Headed Babby" to this day makes me cry. I have, I imagine, idealized memories of Paul. He was perfect, a great gorgeous man with a deep voice, a gentle manner, prodigious intelligence and courage.

In the spring of 1949, a third subpoena was served at midnight one night. I was five, my brother Jonathan, one. Violent pounding on the front door tore through the quiet. Our upstairs was suddenly crazily ablaze with lights. Shaken awake by the noise, the glare, and my parents' activity, I threw myself from bed to run to them. Father flew down the stairs. Mother stood rigid at the head of the staircase; I huddled against her. There was shouting back and forth through the closed front door. Father was raging and yelled obscenities at the process server. The police came. I was terrified. I remained at the top of the stairs clinging to my mother's knees, trembling, crying. Eventually the process server left, to return in the daylight.

My parents' marriage was in tumult. I have no doubt that the terrors of the time contributed to their troubles, exacerbated tension, anger, resentments already present.

In 1949, Mother and Father hired a housekeeper named Juliette, also a communist. She was a big Black woman, warm, protective, dignified, and tough. She cooked, cleaned, took care of us. Mother trusted her and at the end of the summer left to go abroad for a month. Juliette, Father, my brother, and I spent that month in Croton, New York.

Pete Seeger called Father one day. There was to be a concert in Peekskill, New York. He would sing with the Weavers; Paul Robeson would sing, too. Pete asked Father to come to speak at the concert. Father said he would and he would bring me and Jonathan. I was joyous, as always ecstatic at any opportunity to see Paul.

Juliette heard there would be trouble and was determined to prevent Father from taking us. She barred the door, her body plastered against it like a massive human portcullis. There was a mêlée at Peekskill that day. Anti-leftists wielded bats and threw stones. People were hurt. Juliette had promised Mother to look after us and had. I never forgave her. She vanished one day to return to her home in the South to see to a sick relative. Or that is what I was told. We never heard from her again. Except for the Peekskill incident, I do not remember that summer at all.

Now and then gifts arrived from the various embassies of communist countries, large cartons containing bottles of vodka, jars or tins of Beluga caviar, strange wines.

My parents dressed me up, took me to embassy parties with them. There were almost never any other children at these affairs, and I suspect it was fairly inappropriate that I was there, but I loved those parties, primarily because of the food. And because I felt special there, being the only child.

On a Wednesday in the beginning of June, in 1950, Father went to Washington, D.C., to serve his sentence. Mother and Father told me that he had been summoned to Paris for three months. He wrote postcards to me from prison, sent them to a friend in France, and the friend sent them on to me so that they would have French stamps and postmarks. Years later, when Mother and Father told me the truth, I was enraged. They had betrayed me. Why couldn't they have trusted me to have the maturity (at six!), the strength to know the truth and to cope with it? I could have helped, somehow. I was sure of it.

Mother took Jonathan (only two at the time) and me to the New Jersey shore, where we spent the summer of my father's incarceration with my grandparents. Jon asked compulsively, "Where's Daddy?" Daddy was in Paris. I wonder, did I sense the lies? Mother's anxiety? How did they keep me from seeing the newspapers? From overhearing gossip, conversations?

According to my mother's memory, only one friend called her—and only once—during the three months we were there and Father was in prison. I asked her recently why she thought that was. She said, "They didn't give a shit." Minutes later she said, "They were afraid. Everyone was afraid. Paul and Peggy Stuart walked right by us in Sardi's one day, pretended not to see us. You remember how dear he was, how affectionate? They were afraid. There were agents watching, everywhere, noting who knew whom, who talked to whom. We understood it. You can't imagine how it was. It was a terrible time. Terrible."

In the early '50s, I watched Father, on our first television set, ridicule, sneer at, shame Joseph McCarthy before his Senate subcommittee. Father's eloquence, his nerve awed me.

In 1952, while Julius and Ethel Rosenberg were in jail awaiting execution, someone, I don't remember who, took me to a Christmas party given for their two sons, children just about my age. The party was in the basement of someone's house. I don't remember whose. The room was dark, the mood somber despite a lighted tree and gifts. There was much whispering. I remember huddling in a corner somewhere as far from the Rosenberg boys as I could get, afraid even to look at them. I cried through the party. To process this experience without extrapolation was impossible—that is to say, there was no reason to believe that what was happening to their parents could not happen to mine.

Six months after the Rosenbergs were executed, Father was awarded the Stalin Peace Prize. Paul Robeson had received it the preceding year. I sat on a platform with my father and mother, Paul and his wife Eslanda Cardozo Robeson, W. E. B. Du Bois and his wife Shirley Graham. I was nine. I was puffed up with pride.

Having the notion he might be able to effect some sort of real and immediate change if he held public office, Father ran for Congress in 1952 but lost. Despite my mother's objections, he took my brother and me on the sound truck with him occasionally. Campaigning was exciting for us, but I was always frightened. I was always worried someone would attack him, the Communist candidate, the Red.

The government would not give us passports; we could not go to Europe, so we spent the summer of 1954 in Mexico. The purported purpose of our sojourn was to remove Father from the United States so that he could not be sent to prison a second time. One needed only be found guilty of contempt to be sentenced, and one could be found guilty for simply refusing to answer a question. Although Congress had passed the Communist Control Act, which made membership in the Communist Party punishable by twenty years in prison, we returned to the United States in the fall. I cannot imagine why. Was Father convinced he would not go to prison again? If so, why had we gone to Mexico in the first place?

At my parents' request, issued from our retreat in Mexico, my maternal grandparents found us a house across the street from them in Teaneck, New Jersey. If Father went to prison again, Mother would have her parents and her sister and brother-in-law there; we, our grandparents and an aunt and uncle down the block. Father did not go to prison again, but we spent the next six years in Teaneck, the first two while he was still in the Party, the last four after he had left. He hated the suburbs, was deeply depressed during these years.

I had a framed picture—a gift to my father from the Russian Consulate—of Stalin standing in Red Square, holding pink-cheeked children in his arms, surrounded by thousands of smiling admirers, flowers everywhere. He appeared the soul of kindness, benevolence. He was God. Goodness incarnate. I desperately wanted to hang the picture on the wall of my bedroom, in suburban New Jersey. Mother objected strenuously. Father objected to her objections. There was heated debate and, in Mother's face and voice, an edge of panic. The picture remained on a shelf in my closet.

Life in suburbia was pleasant for me. No one seemed to have heard of us. The only incident I recall was seeing "Go back to Russia" scribbled next to my name on the posted honor roll list. It made me laugh. How naïve these children were! None of us had ever been in Russia.

One evening, Paul Robeson drove out from the city to have dinner with us. He pulled up across the street from the house, a police car behind him. I had been watching for him at the living room window, yelled when he arrived that the police were outside with him. After a few seconds of mayhem in the house, Father ran out. He returned with Paul, both of them chuckling. The officer had given Paul a ticket for driving with a broken muffler. The policeman had no idea who Paul was, no idea who Father was either. We were delighted, jubilant. So fearful were we, a ticket for a broken muffler was cause for celebration.

After Father and Mother left the Communist Party, we never saw Paul again. The politics that had earlier bound us later separated us.

In 1956, Khrushchev made his speech revealing, detailing Stalin's atrocities. Father was shattered. He resigned from the Communist Party immediately, loudly, publicly.

Friends of ours, Russian Jews, had years earlier disappeared into the Soviet Union, never to be heard from again. How could my father have not known about the many crimes of the regime: purges, imprisonments, repression of civil liberties, and the like? How could it possibly be that none of our comrades knew?

Believing that people who remained loyal to the Soviet Union would shun us, my parents withdrew not only from those people but also, inexplicably, from all the comrades, supposedly close friends, who left the Party when they did. We never again saw most of them.

In 1957, Joseph McCarthy died. His is the only death I ever remember celebrating.

When it finally dissolved, it was almost impossible for me to believe that there was no more Soviet Union. I watched, on television, scene after scene of Russians trying to learn how to manage in their new system, and I had the powerful, albeit irrational, conviction that the change was not only temporary but also, as improvement, suspect. I knew, of course, "normal" had been dreadful but hoped senselessly that life there would be "normal" again soon.

My irrational visceral reaction reminds me of my senseless sentiments and unconscionable impulses, both of which persisted years after Khrushchev forced us to confront the truth about our idealized, in fact, altogether imaginary Stalin. I continued to have gooey feelings about Stalin similar to those a four-year-old holds for Santa Claus, despite what I knew was true; I continued to have a pressing impulse to defend him against any pejorative despite constant reminders to myself that he was not the man we had so wanted him to be. Now, in the sixth decade of my life, the sentiments, the impulses have thankfully, finally, truly changed.

But I believe still—and am glad I do—that the ideal of an integrated community, of common aims, shared wealth, of a socialist society continues to be valid. Had I, by magic, the option to relive my life in a family of which the government of those days would have approved, I would refuse it. The gifts I received from both my talented, principled, passionate parents and from their exceptional circle of friends compensated for the Sturm und Drang of the life we lived; I would not trade the childhood I was forced, by circumstance, to navigate—although I might wish to have navigated it, from time to time, with more dignity—for one the world would consider "normal."

From *Pledge of Allegiance*

Mark Lapin

Mark Lapin describes his family as having radical politics and fragile psyches and his childhood as having been spent "trying to reconcile Marxism at home with McCarthyism at large and confusion within." Lapin reports that he "dropped out of several fine universities, smoked away years in the Haight Ashbury, drifted for more than a decade as an expatriate in Europe and Japan, and learned to eke out a tenuous living as a hack writer."

Lapin's novel *Pledge of Allegiance* (Dutton, 1991), from which this selection is excerpted, is the story of a young boy growing up in New York City in the mid-1950s. The protagonist, Josh, is the younger child of a Party leader who has gone "underground" to avoid persecution under the Smith Act. In this depiction of Josh's interactions with adults and other children during a fund-raising party, Lapin captures a child's perspective on the nuances of Party terminology.

We were getting ready for a Party party at our house. That's what I called it when everyone who came belonged to the Party. We used to have them all the time at our apartment in San Francisco, but this was the first one my mother had given since we moved to New York. . . .

I liked meeting people at the door. They all knew me and said something friendly about how fast I was growing or how much like my father I looked, and almost everyone brought something to eat on a big plate or in a paper sack or wrapped up in tinfoil. By the time I finished doorman duty, our kitchen table was covered with salads and sliced meats and platters of light and dark rye bread and bowls of rice and stuffing and potatoes and gravy. The desserts were on the counter by the sink. . . .

The bar was in my mother's room by the window. Fat Peggy Mendolsohn was bartender. She stood behind a card table covered with bottles and bowls of ice cubes and stacks of paper cups and a white coffee can for people to put their donations in. The coffee can had a label around it that said SMITH ACT DEFENSE FUND.

Before I reached the table, Joe Lester put his hand on my arm. He was the tallest man there. He bumped his head going through doors and kept his shoulders slouched over like he was trying to bring his face down to the level of other people's. He had a hook nose and a vein that stood out on his forehead when he got excited. The vein was pulsing now. He was arguing with a dozen people who stood in a circle around him.

"Let's ask this young man," he said, drawing me into the circle. "Now what do *you* think, young Josh?" He pointed a long finger at my face and looked at me seriously. "Is it really five minutes to midnight?"

I couldn't see why they needed to ask me the time when they all had watches and I didn't. But Joe Lester was always asking tricky questions like that.

"It's nowhere near midnight," I told him.

"How do you know?" he asked.

"Because the party just started," I said. "And by midnight it'll be all over."

"Out of the mouths of babes," said Joe in a loud satisfied voice, turning back to the group and pointing a finger at Leo. "Out of the mouths of babes. It's nowhere near midnight and the party's just started. I tell you, we have to . . ."

They started arguing again. My mother's room was hot and smokey, and I didn't feel like talking to grown-ups anymore. I put my platter down on top of the bookcase and squeezed through the crowd to Vera's room.

Her door was closed, so I knocked.

The door opened a crack and Simone's head peeked out. Simone was . . . Vera's best friend. She was sleeping over tonight. She wore glasses and braces like my sister, but instead of reading all the time like Vera did, she carried a white slide rule everywhere she went.

"It's your brother," Simone said to Vera.

"You can't come in," Vera called, "unless you want to play Party Meetings."

"Groan," I said. But I went in anyway. I knew all about Party Meetings because the only time Vera and Simone let me play with them was when they needed somebody else for the game. Vera was crazy about meetings. We weren't supposed to listen when my mother had one at our house, but Vera would crouch on the kitchen floor with her ear pressed against one of the painted-over panels on the door to my mother's room and listen for hours without getting bored.

She was sitting on her piano bench with her legs crossed and a notebook on her knees when I came into her room. She had on red knee socks and a plaid skirt. They were all set up for the meeting with Monopoly money to pay dues and coffee cups from Vera's dollhouse and even ashtrays from the kitchen with rolled-up pieces of paper for cigarettes.

"I'm Org. Sec.," Vera told me. That meant Organization Secretary.

"And I'm Sec. Org.," said Simone. Sec. Org. meant Section Organizer. It was like chairman, so Simone sat at Vera's desk by the window with her slide rule in her hand to call the meeting to order.

"You're the rank and file," Vera said to me. "You sit with them." I sat down on the gray rug between the desk and the piano bench with four or five of Vera's dolls. They were the rank and file until I came along.

Vera started the meeting by taking roll and collecting dues. I had to pay for myself and all the dolls. Then Vera sold literature because she was Lit. Org., too. The literature was lined up on Vera's orange bedspread. There were green-and-white pamphlets called *Monthly Review* and heavy sets of books with leather covers and gold print from our bookcase. Vera made me buy the thickest book of all.

"I'm sure you'll find it enlightening," she told me. "It'll correct your left deviationist tendencies," she added. "If anything can."

When Simone took over, she made us report on our activities. We had to tell about our work with Mass Orgs. and how many leaflets we passed out and how many "subs" we sold that month. The last time we played I said I sold a thousand "subs" to the navy, but they expelled me for that because "subs" weren't submarines like I thought. They were subscriptions to the Party newspaper and Vera said I ought to know about the paper because my own father edited it.

When you got expelled, first they brought you up on charges before the review committee. And if you couldn't explain what you did, they took a vote and threw you out. Then you had to leave the room and no one would talk to you and you couldn't go to meetings or Party parties anymore. Usually they found some way to expel me before the meeting was over, but I didn't mind because, after using Monopoly money to pay dues and buy books, all they did was talk.

They talked about Problems and Questions. There were lots of Questions. Like the Negro Question and the Woman Question and the Peace Question.

"Tonight," said Simone, "we will hear a report on the Negro Question from our junior member, who"—she scowled at me—"needs considerable education on the subject." She tapped her slide rule on Vera's desk and nodded at me to begin.

"The Negro Question's getting a lot better," I said. "Because before they wouldn't even let Jackie Robinson play in the majors. But now we've got five Negroes just on the Dodgers alone." I counted them off on my fingers.

"There's Jackie, and Campanella behind the plate, and Newcombe and Black on the mound, and this season Junior Gilliam at second base. And he might even win Rookie of the Year."

Vera and Simone looked at each other, shaking their heads and making *tsk tsk* sounds through their closed lips.

"I think we have to bring him up on charges," Vera said.

"White Chauvinism if I ever heard it," nodded Simone.

"Don't you know that even if they let Negroes play a stupid game and get traded for money like slaves, they're still lynching them in the south?" Vera asked me. "Haven't you read your own father's articles on the Emmett Till case?"

"And what about Male Chauvinism?" said Simone, waving her ruler at me. "Did you ever stop to think that all your precious ballplayers are men? What about the plight of the colored woman?"

"He's left deviationist and right opportunist both at the same time," said Vera.

"Clear cause for expulsion," said Simone.

"Out," shouted Vera, pointing to the door. "Most definitely and incontrovertibly and irrevocably out!"

What's Red Hot
and What's Not: Circa 1950s

Norma Allen

Norma Allen describes herself as part of the mandarin class of Washington, D.C. The '50s were her formative years. Here, she boldly captures
the essence of that decade, contrasting the icons of New York City–area
communists with those of their neighbors.

P.C.	Non-P.C.
Progressive	Liberal
Moiseyev Dance Ensemble	New York City Ballet
Paul Robeson	Paul Anka
Hollywood 10	10 North Frederick
Salt of the Earth	*Gone with the Wind*
Edith Segal	Sylvia Plath
Silver Jewelry	Gold jewelry
Negro	Colored
Howard Fast	Ayn Rand
The Kremlin	The Alamo
Saturday afternoons at Washington Square	Saturday afternoons at Bloomingdale's
Daily Worker	*Daily News*
Julius Rosenberg	Orange Julius
UE	IUE
Dodgers	Yankees
Jackie Robinson	Roger Maris
YCL	YMCA
CIO	CIA
Union hall	Church hall
North Korea	South Korea
Peace	War

American Heritage

Nina Olff

Nina Olff is a poet, artist, educator, and researcher living in Cambridge, Massachusetts. Her poetry has been published in *Women's Review of Books* and *City River of Voices* and will appear in the film *Whistling Women Is Up to No Good.* She is writing a screenplay in which one of the main characters is a red diaper baby, son of an Abraham Lincoln Brigade veteran.

Born in 1955, Olff grew up in the Brownsville section of Brooklyn. This poem is an exploration of her multiracial and left-wing ancestries.

I am alive,
born
from a Black
Man

whose tribe
conquered
northern
Brooklyn

and
settled
in southern
Manhattan.

My uncle went back
to the spear,
injected rhythm
into his vein;

he heard the voices
of Africans and Mohawks,
the Surinamese
and the Dutch,

the holler and the
"Tacki-tacki,"
Sra-nan-tango
in his feet.

His march on Washington
was a ritual dance—
every month
he had the dream.

He made sense
when he was stomping
raising hell
when he was jumping.

I am alive
born
from a White
Woman

whose father
cursed
in
Yiddish;

every
corner
was
a podium,

with his Russian-Polish
fist,
he created
a crowd.

His white brow
and steel blue eye
went blind
in the face of madness;

you could see rage and blood;
the bombs in Spain
were leaving him
with ghosts.

He made sense
when he was yelling
raising hell
when he was vocal.

My mother and father
raised a ruckus when they bore me,
they ditched back the dirt
that covers my ancestors' graves.

On my birth certificate
were the faces
of women
from the last century;

their names
came pressed together
like seeds
buried under stones,

a swarm of eyes
from Dresden and Hiroshima,
fireflies carrying
old spirits.

In their faces
I saw their dances,
and the songs
of their children,

dragonflies
and caterpillars,
tucked away
in petals

like the silence of sleep
broken
only by the nightmare
or the scream that wakes the dreamer.

A tongue
is a vow
against
silence,

voices cry out
from graveyards in Guernica, while
a multitude of bees
gather nectar.

Each ascendant
hears the vow
to march against death,
to raise hell.

The Little Red Superego

Gilda Zwerman

Gilda Zwerman is an associate professor of sociology at the State University of New York at Old Westbury. She has written extensively about the lives of radical women imprisoned for their participation in political violence. Her articles have appeared in publications such as the *Feminist Review* and *Social Justice*, and she is also the author of *Martina Navratilova* (Chelsea House, 1995). In 1993, Zwerman received the prestigious SUNY Chancellor's Award for Excellence in Teaching. She serves on the board of the Rosenberg Fund for Children.

With wry humor, Zwerman recounts her life in an atypical left-wing household. While the parents of many red diaper babies combined radical politics with social conformity, Zwerman's upbringing was marked by an absence of restraints. Her parents' approach to child rearing was as casual as their explanations of their political beliefs, and for Zwerman, those beliefs were often expressed through actions that made her uncomfortable.

Unlike the family albums of most red diaper babies, filled with pictures of outings at Camp Kinderland, picnics with extended political kinship networks, and memorable cultural events, my album is empty. My parents didn't own a camera. They didn't send me to camp. They didn't have a network of left-wing friends. I was, in every sense, an only child.

My daily existence—in an urban ghetto in the Brownsville section of Brooklyn—was freewheeling and unstructured. I spent almost all my waking hours in the streets, and when it was warm enough, I slept on the fire escape. Beyond compulsory schooling, I was given no extracurricular activities, no "lessons," no afterschool programs. I was not encouraged to study. Indeed, conditions at home were hardly conducive to concentrating on anything. There was no desk in the apartment, not many books, and no encyclopedia.

Summers were spent playing in empty lots and running through water sprinklers in the school yard. As I got older, I graduated to sitting in front of a gushing fire hydrant. Eventually I was allowed to go to the Betsy Head Park, where I was usually the only white kid in the pool. I became a very fast swimmer.

My exposure to culture outside Brownsville was limited. When the school term ended, I would be taken to the Abraham & Strauss department store in downtown Brooklyn and given money to buy one recording of a popular Broadway show of my choosing. (I never saw the show, of course.) I would play the record over and over, memorize the lyrics, and act out all the parts (as I imagined them) in front of a wall mirror. In that way, I toured parts of the Midwest and made repeated trips to Siam.

For one week at the end of the summer, we packed up pots, pans, and bed sheets and headed for a dilapidated bungalow colony in the Catskills, where the kids ran around, the adults sat around, and everyone told dirty jokes. Every Sunday night during the rest of the year, we drove to La Polina's restaurant on Avenue P in Bensonhurst and ate ravioli with some of the families from the bungalow colony. All the dirty jokes were retold as reminiscence.

My father went from job to job, as he was unskilled, uneducated, and un-ambitious. At night he played pinochle in a dark storefront filled with cigar smoke. On the weekend he woke up at noon and in the afternoon polished the car and took me "for a ride." We would arrive at Aqueduct race track in time for the daily double and return home by 4:30 to watch the replay on television. At the time, I did not understand that my college tuition was gal-loping around that track.

My mother rarely changed out of her housedress or left the kitchen. When she did, it was to rummage through secondhand "junk" stores and fill her drawers and closets with things she, or others she knew, might wear "some-day." Nothing was ever discarded, and eventually we moved to a larger apart-ment because she needed a separate room for her junk. The room was referred to as her "office."

Yet, beneath this lowbrow lifestyle, beneath the cigar smoke, the dirty jokes, and all the junk, there was another dimension to family life: my parents were radicals. My father had been a member of the Young Communist League during the 1930s and early 1940s and then became an organizer for the Amer-ican Labor Party after the war. He served as a security marshal for both or-ganizations and has a six-inch knife scar across his cheek to prove it.

My mother never joined anything, on principle. She watched Garbo mov-ies, read the *Village Voice*, and listened to WBAI on the radio, all in the kitchen. As the Civil Rights Movement emerged in the early 1960s, she became fascinated with the persona of Malcolm X. I knew this because she put a picture of him on the refrigerator door next to the one of Garbo. She said that they made a sexy couple and that we'd all be better off if they ran the country.

In 1964, she finally left the kitchen in order to terrorize the white, lower-middle-class neighborhood adjacent to Brownsville, advocating "forced" integration and community control of schools by Black parents. I suspect that part of her motivation for supporting Black nationalism was that she would never be asked to join.

In my family, no political idea was ever labeled or formally discussed. I never heard any references to socialism or communism or any social movement. I was never told what to think and only rarely told what to do. I remained within the small, circumscribed, world of the street and the school yard. And even when given the opportunity to do something different—go to a museum or a concert—I generally declined. I did ask and was taken to see *Some Like It Hot* seven times, where I learned "nobody's perfect." Yet, by the time I was a young adult and ventured into the world outside Brownsville, my view of the government, of the Vietnam War, of racism and inequality, and my sense of obligation to construct a life in which personal need and material comfort are subordinated to the imperative of social change were as radical, as internalized, and as articulate as those of any alumna of Camp Kinderland. How did this happen without the aid of left-wing books, camps, friendship networks, organization, or any ideological indoctrination?

My childhood, which appears so unbridled it borders on neglect, was, in fact, incredibly harnessed. Not by coercion, or rules, or didactic beliefs, or by an identification with a cohesive political community, but far more powerfully, through the nuances of family interaction, kinesthetic experience, and my parents' eccentric, but principled and consistent, responses to their immediate environment. It was the pentimento of Greta Garbo, Aqueduct race track, and Betsy Head Park pool that formed the indelible layers of my "little Red superego."

It was the summer of 1957, and I was four years old. I was sitting on the curb digging up dirt in a crack of the sidewalk with a stick. My friend Juanita had said that the devil lived under the ground and that if you dug deep enough you could touch the tip of his horns. Behind me, I heard a window opening and a screen lifted. My mother stuck her head out and asked if I wanted to go "swimming" in the sprinklers at the school yard.

By then, I already knew the hitch to such an offer.

"Will there be any junk stores?" I inquired.

"Yes, one, on the way back," she answered.

My mother always kept her word, and if she didn't, if there was some change, an unexpected grand opening of a dirty, rancid, storefront filled with cartons of secondhand rags that she couldn't resist, a new deal would be negotiated: it usually involved either chocolate or salami, my two favorite foods.

We walked through the streets, my mother wheeling a baby carriage and me next to her, taking hold of the handle when we crossed the street. The carriage had been mine, but now she used it to cart her junk. She parked it outside the school yard fence and removed her valuables—a paper sack filled with cookies and a plastic bag containing my rubber thongs. Several men stood around the entrance, some just idle and starring, some pitching bottle caps.

"Please keep an eye on this," she boldly instructed the group. Most of the men ignored her, but one smiled and nodded. He was probably high on heroin, but he'd have to do.

Inside, my mother scanned the yard for the micro-demographic patterns, then headed toward the cluster of benches where the Black women were and sat down. It was an interesting spatial maneuver. From afar, it appeared that she was sitting among them. However, by using the bag of cookies as a border and shifting her body at a slight angle away from the group, she signaled that she had no intention of intruding on them. I stripped to my underwear and thongs. I hated that piece of rubber between my toes, but sprinklers were worth the suffering. I took off.

"Swimming" under a sprinkler is an acquired technique. The coveted spot is where the water rains heaviest. You have to push and shove your way there; invariably you get shoved out. At that point it may seem that another sprinkler is less crowded or less hostile, but it's a grave mistake to move, for it's only through persistence and seniority that you extend your time in the best spot. Unless of course some fat boy has sat himself down in the middle and appears prepared to slug anyone in the airspace above his head. Then you move.

Every so often, I'd glance in my mother's direction and see her reading or sunning. Once I saw that a woman with several children was standing in front of her and that they appeared to be chatting.

When I'd had enough water and shoving, I returned to the bench. She was alone again. She pulled out some cookies and told me to sit in the sun and dry off. I was thinking about my incompleted excavation to the devil and decided that I was ready to go home. I was also wanting to get the junk store over with. "Hey, Ma, let's go, OK?"

She felt my underwear; it was still damp. Past routine had it that my wet underwear would be removed and put in a plastic bag with the thongs, my shoes and socks would be put back on, and I would be allowed to wear my shorts and T-shirt home without anything under them. But this wasn't happening. My eyes darted to either side of her, searching for my clothes. They were gone.

"Where are my clothes?" I asked in consternation.

"I had to give them away," she replied. She immediately reached inside the sack of cookies and produced my shoes, a desperate effort to head off my worst fear—walking home with rubber between my toes. I grabbed the bag and looked inside.

"Where are my socks?" I yelled, hoping to justifiably escalate my rage.

"Gilda, just you take it easy now. A little while ago a mother passed by. She had four children who didn't have any clothes at all. You have lots more at home. And we'll be home very soon."

Did she actually think she could right the wrongs of this racist capitalist system by giving away a pair of my shorts and a T-shirt? But at four, I could not articulate the Marxist line. So I remained silent until we left the yard. Then, on the street, dread and embarrassment washed over me. The men were leering as I stood in my underwear. My mother started rolling her carriage, and I started to cry. We walked, and I whimpered, my tears fueled by every step as the leather backs of my shoes dug into my ankles.

When we passed by the junk store, she slowed down, peered into the doorway, and then glanced back at me. "Oh well," she muttered to herself, "another time."

★

From my father, I received a different, though not entirely contradictory, message. Following the clothes incident, I got into the habit of giving away my things to other kids—especially things I didn't much care for or that were a little broken. Clearly, I was hoping to head off the possibility of having something I did value "donated" to the cause of redistributing the wealth in America.

One Saturday afternoon, as my father stood in front of the candy store on the corner blowing rings of cigar smoke, I ran past him, clutching my battered fire truck. Pretending that his shoe was the curb, I stepped on it, leaving a big scuff mark. I intended to keep running, but he grabbed the back of my shirt and held me a few inches off the ground. My legs were still moving.

"Where the hell do you think you're going?" He puffed a cloud of smoke in my face.

"Around the block to play," I squealed, delighted to have provoked his attention.

Satisfied, he dropped me, and I scampered off. A short time later, I whizzed back around the corner, empty-handed. Again he tugged at my shirt, stopping me in my tracks.

"Where the hell is your truck?" he inquired.

"I gave it away to the kid around the corner," I answered.

"How come you did that?" He was truly perplexed.

"Because he's poor," I tooted.

My father laughed. "And what the hell do you think you are?"

My father loved to socialize, but guests rarely came to our apartment. Especially to our Jewish friends, my family was a reminder of their impoverished past as well the political ideals they had once held, which seemed to have vanished along the exit ramps of the Long Island Expressway. But my parents also discouraged visitors since preparation for company would precipitate the same argument:

"Bess, the apartment's filthy. When are you going to clean it?" my father would yell every Friday night.

"I'll clean it on Monday," my mother yelled back.

"You said that last Sunday," he retorted.

"I couldn't have said it last Sunday, Willy-boy. Last Sunday I wasn't talking to you." She laughed, amused at her own hostile wit.

"Bess, I'm serious. What about getting a cleaning lady?"

"A cleaning lady! A cleaning lady! I can't afford bus fare; how am I going to pay a cleaning lady?"

"Bess, you're exaggerating, Bess." Whenever my father was angry at someone, he'd say the name of the person at the beginning and end of the sentence. "I give you money. You have money for the bus. I'll pay for a woman," he tried to plead rationally with her.

"And what if Gilda gets sick tomorrow and there's a stack of doctor's bills. How will you feel if we spent the money on a cleaning lady?"

"Bess, I don't see the connection, Bess. Bess, get someone in here to clean or I'm moving out."

"Don't make promises you can't keep, Willy-boy." Again, her laughter.

At the beginning of the week, I watched as a line of young to middle-aged Black women queued up in the hallway. My mother graciously welcomed each applicant, sat her at the kitchen table, spread out the classified section of the paper, and asked in earnest, "Now, what do you want to be a cleaning lady for? I'm sure there are other, less degrading things you can do."

This "aspire higher" employment service for Negro women operated until the weekend. On Saturday afternoon when my father awoke from an all-night card game and steak breakfast at Bo's Bar, he noticed that not one speck of dirt had disappeared.

"Bess, what happened to the cleaning lady?" he asked.

"She left." Again that laugh.

"What are you talking about, Bess?" he persisted.

"I'm talking, Willy-boy, about this apartment. No one in their right mind is going to clean this place. And that includes me."

Between 1952 and 1963, my family moved five times. Twice to different apartments in the same tenement building, once to an apartment in the building across the street, once to a building around the block, and then back to the original building. These domestic disruptions were always initiated by my father. Crime, violence, and the rapid physical deterioration of Brownsville depressed him and made him nervous about keeping late hours at the bars. Then an incident would occur—a dead body left in the hallway or a rat in my bedroom—and he'd start pacing round and round my mother as she fussed in the kitchen.

"Bess, we have to get out of here, Bess." His arrogant tone would not mask the panic.

However, as soon as my mother heard the word "move," her fantasies catapulted only as far as the prospect of having more space to store her junk. The "compromise" they struck was always the same: a move to nowhere. A freshly painted, usually larger, apartment seemed to quell my father's dissatisfaction, at least temporarily. I guess he was resigned to the bottom line: leaving Brownsville was not on my mother's agenda—until 1964, when I graduated elementary school and the story changed.

A new junior high school was opening on Rockaway Avenue, the "border" dividing Brownsville and the adjacent neighborhood of East Flatbush. East Flatbush was inhabited primarily by lower-middle-class Jews, most of whom had grown up in Brownsville and could not afford the mortgages of homes in Levittown or even the rent in Queens. So beginning in the late 1940s, they had created an insulated enclave and did their best to simulate the lifestyle of suburbia.

The new school "zoned in" integration by dividing each neighborhood in half: 50 percent of the students would be white—mostly Jewish—and 50 percent Black. Black parents in Brownsville welcomed this plan; they understood that an integrated institution would provide more resources for their kids. But from the standpoint of the white residents of East Flatbush, the plan arbitrarily divided their community and condemned the children on the "wrong" side to a daily return trip to the ghetto they had fled and now feared. In an atmosphere of outrage, parents mobilized a boycott. Parent leaders of newly established East Flatbush Civic Association announced, "No child living in this community will attend the new school."

"Willy-boy, we're moving." My mother announced. "It's time to move to East Flatbush. White people, Willy. Jews. Dry cleaners. Waldbaums."

If we had stayed put, I would have attended the old, primarily Black junior high, thus continuing my unwitting role as leading lady in a life script written, produced, and directed by my mother and entitled "If the Negroes Go Back to Africa, My Daughter and I Are Going, Too." Instead, we moved—albeit temporarily—from a Black neighborhood to a white neighborhood so that I—in every sense the only child—could go back into the Black neighborhood that I had just left.

A summer Sunday afternoon at the home of my rich uncle Morty on Long Island was my only contrast to the dankness of Brownsville's tenements. Much later in life I learned that Morty was neither all that rich nor my uncle. My recollections of that house, a veritable study in the tasteless extravagance of the nouveau riche, are fixated on a statue posed on the bar in his "finished" basement: a male figurine that pissed Scotch in a thin stream and played Frank Sinatra tunes. Tacky as the place was, I hated to leave there. But my mother hated going in the first place: she was not amused by Scotch piss and loathed listening to tales of Morty's wife Rosetta's latest expedition to the shopping center. Barely an hour after arriving, I'd hear the introduction to our departure. "OK, party's over." Then she'd point to my father, relaxing in his seat and puffing away on his cigar. "You, up!" she'd command.

In the car ride home, my father would finish his cigar, my mother would scowl, and I'd stretch my head out the rear window, catching the wind and daydreaming that my parents had died and I was adopted by Rosetta and Uncle Morty. One Sunday in 1967, as we exited the Interboro Parkway, the ecstasy of this imagining was interrupted by an odor, a mingling of smoke and garbage that forced my head back into the car.

Ahead of us, down Pennsylvania Avenue, almost all the fire hydrants had been opened. Young, dark, wiry men with sticks were scaling up the street lamps and shattering the encasements and the bulbs.

"Look, look, look." For the first time that day my mother was animated, bouncing around in the front seat. "Close the windows, close the windows."

"Holy shit," my father laughed and jammed his foot on the accelerator. "Hold on." We sped through the gushing flood of water from below and the spray of shattering glass from above. I sat back and heard the swoosh under the tires and the rain of glass on the car roof and my parents squealing, "Weeee," as if they were riding on a roller coaster.

As we made a left turn, just a few feet short of home, my father slammed on the brakes. Police with sticks of their own were preparing to surround Pennsylvania Avenue. Their vehicles occupied the entire street. My father craned his neck out of the window and yelled at a pair of cops, "Hey, schmuck, you're in my parking spot." They glared at my father, and he glared back, fingering the scar on his cheek as they squared off. Then he put his car in gear, swerved around, pulled up on the sidewalk, and turned off the engine.

My parents punctuated this act of defiance with a handshake. At such moments, my mother could almost justify having married this man (although, in the larger scheme of things, she was never able to figure out why she had to marry at all).

"If you're staying outside," my mother said, turning to me in the back seat, "you need to wear a raincoat, the one with the hood. And you have to stay away from anyone who's carrying a stick."

"But, Ma," I said, "everybody is carrying sticks. I won't have anyone to play with."

"Then you'll just have to play with yourself," she retorted. My father hurled her a condemning look. She flashed a devilish smile back. I was left to decide on which corner I would watch the confrontation.

Throughout the 1950s and 1960s, the entire white population of Brownsville disappeared. Eventually, so did I. From time to time, my father would freak out about the crime, the deterioration, the desolation, and threaten to leave, too.

"Still making promises you can't keep, Willy-boy?" my mother would quip.

As the 1970s rolled over into the 1980s, my mother dug in her heels. A resistance movement unto herself.

The last time I saw my mother she was lying in a bed at Brookdale Hospital, the one and only health care facility in the war zone–like neighborhood. She was very sick and not at all afraid of dying. But she was upset about the impact of her death on the racial composition of the neighborhood. "Well," she sighed, "this old white lady is finally leaving Brownsville."

Days after her funeral, my father moved to Miami Beach. He quickly found an apartment, a girlfriend, a card game, a cigar store, and the dog races. "You don't mind closing things up, do you?" he asked as he practically galloped up the ramp into the airplane.

After forty years of accumulation, my parents' apartment had become one giant junk store. Just as there was no way to clean it, there was no way to close it. So I opened the door and invited the neighbors to come in and take anything they wanted. Everyone had known this white lady who roamed the streets in sneakers pushing a baby carriage filled with junk. People quietly rummaged and took whatever caught their eye. Some returned for a second look. Every so often, someone would walk out the door with an item that appeared to be of considerable value. I could hear my mother snickering, "You jerk. How can you let that go?"

It took less than three hours for everything to disappear. Only heaps of dust, a stray earring, and some pennies remained on the floor. "Did someone walk out of the apartment with the broom?" I was trying to remember.

Again, her voice crackled from the beyond. "You jerk. What broom? I've never owned a broom."

Just as some children derive comfort from spreading a parent's ashes back into nature, I had recycled my mother back into Brownsville. I closed the door, descended into the unlit, stale-smelling basement, and found her carriage. Like the driver of a caisson, I wheeled it through streets that held imprints of her feet and those wheels for eternity. I left it next to a thrift store on Sutter Avenue and walked west, along Hegeman Avenue, past the empty lots, past the Betsy Head pool, past the candy store and the junior high school to the elevated IRT, where I boarded the train back to Manhattan.

My mother died on the Tuesday before Thanksgiving in 1989. I did not go to work on Wednesday. In all my years of teaching at the State University College at Old Westbury, I had very rarely missed a class. In many ways, Old Westbury is an extension of my life script. Conceived as a college for the "educationally bypassed" student, it serves many Black, inner-city kids. They turn to Old Westbury with its residence halls as an alternative to going to a city college and living at home. Though built on a plush estate in one of the highest income areas of Long Island, the campus looks like a minimum security prison, with a cheaply made infrastructure, leaky pipes, and broken furniture. Students who live on campus leave these buildings only to board a rickety school bus that shuttles them to the local malls, where they work the 4–11 P.M. shift in banks, department stores, and gas stations, or to the Long Island Railroad, which transports them home, to addresses and tenements and lives I know very well. Nothing this society has done for them or to them and nothing I do with them adequately explains the internal combustion of raw intelligence, decency, resiliency, and humor that gets these kids from freshman English to senior seminar.

When I did not show up on that Wednesday, my secretary explained to the students that my mother had died. "Will she be back on Monday?" they queried.

"She didn't say anything about that. But I think in the Jewish religion they mourn for a whole week."

On Monday morning, my first class of students lingered outside the room, unsure whether I was going to show up. When I descended the staircase from my office, they followed me in and took their seats. There wasn't the usual rowdiness, partially as a show of respect for what had happened in my life the week before but also as an expression of confusion—perhaps condemnation—at the disrespect I was displaying for the Jewish tradition. I had never given them a reason to hold back their opinions, and one young woman immediately spoke up. "How come you're here today, Zwerman? We heard your mother passed last Tuesday. You're supposed to grieve for a week."

"You're right about that," I conceded. "I *am* breaking the rules of the tradition. I have to in order to obey the rules of my family. If my mother ever found out that I deprived you of one day of your education on her behalf," I swallowed back the tears, "she'd shoot me."

2
Political Trauma
as Personal History

Two Poems

Gene Dennis

Eugene Dennis, Jr., son of CP General Secretary Eugene Dennis and Party journalist Peggy Dennis, grew up in New York City. After graduating from the University of Wisconsin in 1964, Dennis moved to California, where he worked as a longshoreman while earning graduate degrees in history and archives management. Since 1987 Dennis has been the archivist and librarian for the International Longshore and Warehouse Union, and he currently directs the union's education program.

These two excerpts from a larger poetic autobiography explore fundamental red diaper themes: living with an ever-present sense of danger and coming to terms with one's political inheritance.

1952: Sanctuary

What nightmares
taunt this ten-year-old child,
he runs so fast feet stand still, Leaning
to leap the school stairs down,
Straining to escape the
footsteps sloshing blood and pain
pounding near.

The delicious fear fades with a rush,
Rescued by sunlight at the schoolhouse door,
Pursued by the rasping whisper of the
Creature screaming in frustration, Panting
the promise of tomorrow's torment.

Last Wednesday, no, the one before,
the creature crawled beneath
a federal agent's gray fedora,
dripping evil on the cop's
shiny black shoes: How about
an ice cream, kid? Let's take a walk
over to the park. Seen
any of your old man's
Commie friends around the house?

Run, run
Run into Thursday
When the creature lurked behind
the windshield of the dark sedan
doubleparked
outside the Downtown Y:
He stands on the frozen sidewalk,
Mouth open without sound, ready
to run again: muscles gripped
by a pulsating panic, skin
glazed by ice-bound sweat trapped
under blue wool coat. Crouch
to tie up the tornlaced
sneaker, hide the tension of
the sprinter's start, then off!
Schoolbooks dangling, flapping,
banging, braking the racing gait.
Turn the corner in a skidding jumble
with the echo of the awakening sedan.

Alone. Free. Look
to the end of the block, the bus stop:
The dark sedan watches, waiting.
Government tags glisten
on the license plate.

There is no truce in this terror,
no negotiations, Simply time
in the silent menacing canyon of
a cease-fire to race the dying dusk
to sanctuary.

Boris: Tired, clean-shaven, behind
the small soda fountain,
hands on the flip-top ice cream
freezer, Absently polishes
the chromed freezer lid reading
the *Daily News*. Quiet man, gentle man,
Proud of mixing the best egg creams
in town, of still selling
the *Daily Worker* from the secret place
under the counter
by the cash register.

So you want an egg cream
to spoil your supper? Maybe
a double-chocolate? So here,
I fix you another, but your
Momma shouldn't know. Take the
Worker for her. No, that's all right,
she pays me tomorrow. Here,
I fold it for you inside the *News*
so nobody sees.

Soda suds discolored by
milk foam and chocolate specks
fleck the empty glass. Squirm
and squeak the red leatherette
seat of the bar stool; Finger
the cream-colored veins
crossing the burnt gray marble
counter top. Tease drops of water
from the glass ring. Anything
to delay return to war. Sideways
stare at the finely sculpted
Continental slash of moustache
on Boris' lip. Wait for another
flash of smile: warm, protective,
wise, gently mocking. Tired.

Jump off the stool, clutch
the newspaper inside the no-
newspaper so no one can see

the secret. Thank the man
for the extra chocolate. Catch
his smile, take it and flaunt it
at the creature crouching
in the next doorway.

Courier child.
Proud coward child.
Too smart, too fast,
to be caught
This night.

Last Rites

My father
taught me to split wood
in a most spiritual
and efficient way: to rely
on a reading of strength
in the grain
and sever it
with a reverential swing
of the axe.

He taught me
to drive a car
with defensive skill
and techniques
to evade surveillance
and maintain traction
in the snow.

Yes, there were other lessons:
gentle parental persuasions to
Justice, Equality, and Peace. After all,
mom and dad were professional
revolutionaries, and often brought
their business home with them—but

there seemed to be a firm injunction
against even suggesting
I take up their line of work.

My father
shattered this protocol
six weeks before he died: Son,
he said (the pain in his chest
chopping his words), All I ask,
what
ever you do,
is that
you be
a good
Communist.

From *In My Mother's House*

Kim Chernin

Kim Chernin is a writer and a psychoanalytic consultant who lives in Berkeley, California. She is the author of twelve books, including *The Flame Bearers, Sex and Other Sacred Games,* and *Crossing the Border,* as well as other works of fiction, nonfiction, and poetry.

During the post–World War II domestic cold war known as the McCarthy era, Chernin's mother, a local CP leader, was arrested and jailed. Chernin was eleven years old. In this excerpt from her autobiography, *In My Mother's House* (Ticknor & Fields, 1983), Chernin describes her responses to the arrest, including an effort to protect her mother by hiding her fear and anger.

One night the telephone kept ringing. It was dark in the house, someone forgot to leave the light on in the hall. My whole room was dark. I heard [my parents] getting up, their bedroom door banged open. The light came on in the hall. I heard my mother's voice.

"Who? Don't tell me! Who? Where? Who else?"

I sat straight up in my bed. She put down the telephone. "Five people," she said to my father. He was tying the belt around his bathrobe. "David Hyun. Frank Carlson. Harry Carlyle . . . without bail, on Terminal Island."

. . . I slipped on my jeans and my Eisenhower jacket. I came back to watch them from my door. My father took my mother's hand. "What next?" he said.

"Deportations, Paul. Now already, it's deportations."

I went over to my closet. It was the only hiding place I could think of. I climbed up on the shelf, but I had to be quiet. The closet had a small inside window. It opened into another shelf, in my parent's closet, in the room next to mine. On my shelf there were extra blankets, for the winter. I tried hiding myself under them, piling them up on top of me.

My parents came back into their room. "The Party wants me to organize a defense. They want me to start an organization," my mother was saying. "I'm going to call a press conference in the morning."

My father sighed. "First they deport the foreign-born. And then?"

My mother's voice snapped, it was a whip. "Paul," she said, and she could have been talking through a microphone. "These people will not be deported. I'm telling you. We're going to fight."

The next day I was late for school. For weeks now I had been coming late so that I could miss Current Events. Usually, if I came too early I raised my hand and went out to the bathroom.

In Current Events they said there were prison camps in Russia.

In Current Events they said the reds were a menace. They said Communism was spreading out all over the world.

That day, in Current Events, they said that five Commies had been arrested. The teacher said it was a good thing. Now, she said, they could be deported.

One of those Commies she named was my friend. He was a Korean architect, he used to come over once a week in the late afternoon to give me art lessons. Sometimes, we went to his house for dinner. They served us spicy food in little bowls and David Hyun taught me how to eat with chopsticks. My mother had told me that if David and his wife were sent back to South Korea they would both be killed. I thought maybe I should raise my hand and say that to the class. But I looked around at them, these kids I'd gone to school with since the first grade. What difference would it make to them that David Hyun taught me to draw?

Tonio was another of my mother's comrades. He drove the Good Humor Truck. At home, we used to laugh with Tonio, at dinner. "The Communist Ice Cream Man," we called him. "Don't you give out propaganda with the ice cream, Tonio," my father would joke.

Tonio used to pick me up after school. I had a warm jacket and a thick scarf. Even on a cold day I could sit up front with Tonio, ringing the bell of the ice-cream truck. The kids came running after us, all over the neighborhood.

One night after dinner we saw Tonio coming up to the back door. He was wearing a police uniform. My mother wouldn't let me go out there. She wouldn't let me talk to Tonio. She wouldn't let me get anywhere near him.

"But why did he come here? Why did he come?" I yelled and yelled. I pounded on my bedroom door. I was furious at her because Tonio had betrayed her.

"He wanted me to give names," she said.

One day when I woke up in the morning a neighbor was standing next to my bed. I reached up to hug her. My mind raced. Our neighbor began to speak. I knew, even before she said a word to me. They had taken my mother. I was eleven years old.

It was summer, I put on my shorts. I got my bike and rode over to my friend's house. Her parents were Communists, we went to day camp together.

"Jessie, they arrested my mother. She didn't even get to say good-bye. No, I'm not kidding, are you kidding?"

Sara Kahen came out of the kitchen. "What are you whispering about?"

"They arrested my mother. This morning. I was asleep."

She got on the phone. "Sam? Rose was arrested. This morning. No, she's fine, she's not even crying."

Jessie and I got on our bicycles. Sara Kahen made us a big lunch. She chucked me under the chin. "What's the matter? You don't miss your mother?"

"I never cry."

In the afternoon the newspapers had the headline. Jessie and I saw it when we were riding home from camp. FIFTEEN COMMIE LEADERS ARREST-ED IN CALIFORNIA. There were names, pictures. I saw my mother, wear-ing my flannel shirt.

"Jesus, Jessie, look at that. They didn't even let her change her clothes."

Jessie Kahen used to call herself my cousin. We had known each other since grammar school, we were best friends. But the day after my mother was ar-rested, Jessie Kahen told all the kids at camp we weren't really cousins.

"The hell with her," I said to myself three times. Then, I rode home from camp alone, without crying. . . .

People kept coming to the house. Aunt Sara came, with a dish of stuffed cab-bage.

My father gave her a hug. "Thank you, Sara," he said, "but you'll under-stand. Tonight I'm not very hungry."

Sara was plump. She carried a red purse. When she came in the door you could go over and take a look into the purse. There was always something, a cookie wrapped in a napkin, some chocolate, a little game.

I loved Sara. She never forgot. "So come," she said, when she saw me look-ing. "You're too old all of a sudden to give a look in the purse?"

In Sara's arms, for the first time, I cried. With my father, alone, I wouldn't cry. "Tell me," he'd say. "Talk to me. Why should you have all this alone? Tell me, what are you feeling?"

"I'm all right," I'd say in a furious voice. . . . "Just leave me alone," I'd say, "I'm okay." Now he couldn't even keep my mother safe. Why should I talk to him?

One night he told me that bail for my mother and the other defendants was one hundred thousand dollars. He told me that meant they couldn't get out of jail. They had to stay there until the bail was reduced. He said, "How could we raise one hundred thousand dollars?"

"Well," I said, figuring quickly. "We'd have to divide it by fifteen, right? That means, for each one, less than seven thousand dollars. . . . Come on, Dad. You're making a big deal. You could get on the phone, start calling, you'll have the money like that." I snapped my fingers. I began to prance around.

"Listen, listen," he said, trying to grab me. "You don't understand."

"What? What?" I was scared now.

"One hundred thousand dollars each."

"Come on." I couldn't believe it. "Just come on. They couldn't do that. It's not fair."

"Ach, fair." He sat down at the table and looked tired. "A fair world we haven't yet been able to make."

I shook him by the shoulder. I didn't want to see him like that. . . .

"Goddamn it," I yelled and my voice thundered. "We won't let them get away with that." I was eleven years old, I knew something about the law. "It's unconstitutional," I screamed. "And we're going to fight it."

We fought. The hearings lasted six months. The lawyers also thought it was not constitutional. My father said, "In these times, who's going to protect the Constitution?"

"Daddy," I shouted at him. "We're going to protect it."

We were standing in the garage, stacking up newspapers for the school paper drive. "Daddy," I yelled, and I just kept on yelling. "We won't let them get away with that shit." He looked up startled. Then he smiled. That night, he talked to his brother Max on the telephone. "A fiery one," he said, and he had the same smile on his face. "Just like her mother."

I didn't tell him I hated going to school. I didn't tell him how one day, when I walked up to the school, I saw my friends gathered together, standing in a little group, whispering. When I came up there was a funny movement. Something that had been there disappeared. And now nobody had anything to say.

Then someone was talking. "Hey," he said to me, casual-like. "What's your mother's maiden name?"

My mother's maiden name?

The kids were all smiling. Then someone was holding the newspaper clipping in his hand. Oh yeah, of course, it had to happen. ROSE CHERNIN, COMMIE LEADER, ARRESTED IN LOS ANGELES. Sooner or later someone had to figure it out.

Who cares? I walked away, shrugging my shoulders. Then it came to me: now things were different. If I denied who we were, that was betrayal. It was not keeping her safe. I turned back. "Rose Chernin," I said. My voice was loud. "My mother's maiden name is Rose Chernin."

I never told anybody how much I hated going to school. Every day I passed through the front gate and my eyes itched. My mother said I was a fighter. I made a fist. The other kids, their gossip, that passed over. But my biggest fear was, I knew things I shouldn't know and I was afraid I might tell.

I knew the name of a man who had been deported. I knew he had come back secretly and was living in Los Angeles again. I heard them talking. He was underground, they said. If anyone found out, my mother said, he'd be sent back to South Korea. They kill Communists there.

There was a girl named Zoya Kozmodemyanskaya. I had a book about her. . . . Zoya was a partisan fighter in the Soviet Union during the war. The Germans caught her, they pulled out her nails, they put matches against her, and they hanged her. She was only thirteen years old. Later, her brother came with a tank battalion and found pictures of Zoya. Hanging. But she never told them, she never gave them a single name.

Would they torture my mother in jail? Would they torture me? Would I tell the names I knew? Would they put needles under my nails? Would they hold a burning match under my chin?

I knew the name of everybody who came to our house. I knew if you started talking you'd tell everything. "He sang his heart out," my mother had said one night at dinner before she was arrested. "Once he started, he never stopped. He gave even his wife's name. The name of his sister."

The fascists put children in gas ovens. They put children in cattle cars, separate from their mothers.

Once a week I wrote her a letter. "Dear Mama," I said. "Everything's just great here."

I didn't want my father to find out and tell her. I didn't want her to worry about me.

Mistaken Identities

David Wellman

David Wellman was born in New York City and raised in Detroit. A civil rights and antiwar activist in the Sixties, he teaches community studies at the University of California, Santa Cruz. He is the author of *Portraits of White Racism* and *The Union Makes Us Strong*, both published by Cambridge University Press.

Wellman was ten years old when his father, Michigan CP leader Saul Wellman, was sent into hiding by the Party; later, both parents were arrested. In his teens, aware that his family was under surveillance, Wellman worried that his behavior would be used by the authorities to discredit his parents. In this memoir, he describes what documents released under the Freedom of Information Act reveal about the focus of the Detroit police department's intelligence-gathering operations.

They showed up the first time in the summer of 1950. Two unmarked cars, parked in front of our apartment building. Inside each one sat two unremarkable white men in nondescript suits. They stayed there all day. And through the night.

Their arrival coincided with my father's departure. Saully was always gone somewhere, so I didn't pay much attention when he left early one June morning. But this time he stayed away. I sensed something wasn't right as we drove away from the house the next week. My mother was uncharacteristically nervous. Peggy's eyes darted back and forth between the road and the rearview mirror.

We were being followed.

It didn't take much to figure out that the vehicles behind us were connected to Saully's disappearance. I knew he wasn't coming home this time. I wondered when—if—I'd see him again.

"What's going on?" I asked Peggy.

"It's either the FBI or the Red Squad," she answered. "They're looking for Saully."

The opening moves of the Cold War were exploding in our lives. Saully was "underground" again. "Unavailable," Peggy called it. A leader of the Michigan Communist Party, he was expecting state repression and trying to avoid it. For the next two years the two ubiquitous cars with the two conspicuous men pretending to be inconspicuous were a permanent feature in our everyday lives. They followed my sister Vickie and me everywhere: to school, playmates' houses, sandlot baseball and football games, birthday parties, picnics. Trying to turn fear into fun, we made shaking them a game.

But when we got home, they were always across the street. Waiting for us. Smiling.

Saully surfaced two years later, in chains, escorted by marshals into the federal courthouse. He was charged with conspiring to teach and advocate the violent overthrow of the United States government. Two months later, while Vickie and I were in school, Peggy was arrested by agents from the Immigration and Naturalization Service. She was accused of entering the country illegally, violating the Walter-McCarran Act. Peggy and Saully now accounted for, the two cars ceased to be a regular presence.

Just when we thought we'd seen the last of them, however, they would reappear. Or friends would say they'd been "visited." And the two cars were always at communist gatherings. Abandoning all pretense of inconspicuousness, the occupants photographed comings and goings and wrote down license plate numbers. For the next ten years the Wellman family was the object of intense visible and invisible government scrutiny.

Because we were always being watched—and listened to by phone taps—we had no privacy. It felt as if the government penetrated the deepest recesses of our lives every minute of the day. I therefore fully expected to find Wellman dirty linen scattered throughout my Detroit police Red Squad file, which was released by court order in 1992.

Like most communist families of the time, the Wellmans devoted considerable energy to fitting in. We conformed to the cautious 1950s standards for appropriate personal behavior. Vickie and I were expected to be "respectful" around adults. We were supposed to be polite and not "talk back." We lived by implicit dress codes; haircuts were a constant source of tension. We were expected to look "good." Saully took pride in his expensive wool suits and carefully shined shoes. If Vickie or I tried to escape without combed hair, buttoned shirts—tucked in, of course—and shoes laced, we would be stopped at the door. Truth be told, the codes were quite conservative.

That was the family image we projected. So when Peggy and Saully were arrested and "defense" committees were organized, these groups produced literature that portrayed the Wellmans as a communist version of 1950s family values. The cover portrait of one brochure makes us look like a typical middle-class midwestern family. Vickie's hair is in pigtails. She has a shy smile on her lips. My hair is carefully groomed. We're looking very clean-cut and upstanding. Both of us are holding family pets. Saully is sitting behind Peggy, in charge—like fathers were supposed to be—his hands on her shoulders protectively. Peggy is at the center of the portrait, smiling, the proud, confident mother. "Stop this American family tragedy!" the leaflet insists.

Since patriotism was a Wellman family value, the white and blue were added to our Red politics. Saully was constructed as war hero. (He was. He had parachuted behind enemy lines in Holland, Belgium, and Germany in World War II. He almost died in Bastogne during the Battle of the Bulge and was awarded a Purple Heart.) Peggy was presented as a loyal, hardworking mother protecting her family while her husband was fighting fascism in Europe—a Red Rosie the Riveter. (She was.)

Peggy and Saully thought of themselves as American patriots. Communism, in their view, was as American as apple pie. Revolution was an American, not a Russian, invention. Communists were like the patriots at the Boston Tea Party. They invoked Jefferson, not Lenin, to legitimate their revolutionary ideals. They were offended when their loyalty was challenged. "I fought for my country!" Saully would proclaim proudly when the loyalty issue was raised.

They were proud when Vickie and I succeeded at conforming to 1950s citizenship codes. They made a big deal of my being appointed captain of the Brady Elementary Safety Patrol. When I was elected president of the Hutchins Junior High School Student Council, they told everyone and put that news in their defense bulletins. They were especially pleased when Vickie and I won American Legion Awards for "Americanism" at Hutchins.

The awards became national news. Media commentators obsessed over the irony, but Peggy and Saully insisted that communism and Americanism were perfectly consistent. The defense committees printed thousands of brochures reproducing the American Legion's stamp of approval on the Wellman kids.

I never felt that my parents' talk about patriotism and loyalty was a cynical strategy or an attempt to manipulate and dupe an innocent and gullible American public. I had the distinct impression that Peggy and Saully really *believed* it was important and honorable to be loyal Americans.

I couldn't understand why they felt that way.

THIS IS THE FAMILY THE GOVERNMENT IS TRYING TO DESTROY . . . WHY?

Above you see Peggy Wellman with her family.

Perhaps appearances are deceptive. Perhaps this normal, happy-seeming family is grouped around a mother who deserves to be deported as an "undesirable alien".

Undesirable?

Was Peggy Wellman undesirable when, single-handed, she raised and supported her two small children while their American paratrooper father lay in a far-away hospital, perhaps dying from the heart wound he had suffered in the Battle of the Bulge? Was she undesirable when she shared heartbreak and gnawing worry with tens of thousands of other American wives and mothers during the World War?

Was Peggy Wellman undesirable when she started work at 15, became active in trade unions, in movements for relief, unemployment insurance, the very right to live? The legal authorities did not regard her as undesirable. She was never arrested or jailed; and surely Americans would not accuse her of "guilt by association" because of her husband's conviction under the controversial Smith Act which is still under appeal and awaiting final judicial determination.

Or is her "undesirability" reflected perhaps in her main life work — her children?

No, despite the difficult war years, despite the arrest of both parents, Vickie and David, avoiding all pitfalls of delinquency, have emerged as a credit to their parents.

On Oct. 19th, David was elected president of the Student Council by a 3 to 1 majority.

STAR STUDENT DAVE WELLMAN
By FAY BRODY

Star Student! He sure is. In this story you'll find out why. When Dave Wellman came from Brady School to Hutchins he was recommended by the sponsor at Brady to be on the Hutchins Safety Patrol.

In June of 1953 he was sent by the school to Christmas Seal camp at Chelsea, Michigan for one week, to get officers training. When he returned he was made a lieutenant. Regularly you are supposed to be a lieutenant for one year. When the vacancy occurred, Dave measured up to the qualification and was appointed. That was only four months after he came back from the camp.

Dave has all the necessary requirements of a captain which are: Leadership, Reliability, Punctuality, Courtesy, Attendance, Respect, Attitude, will not exceed Authority, Interest in his Duties, Obedience.

Other than these a Captain must set a good example, he must be well liked, and he must be able to discipline.

Dave is also doing well in all his classes. He is one of the most highly praised pupils in his class. He has 12 honors, 3 in Service, 3 in Citizenship, 4 in Punctuality, 2 in Scholarship.

October will mark one year as Captain for Dave.

Yes, all in all Dave Wellman is very worthy of being named Star student of this issue.

Page of a leaflet circulated by the Peggy Wellman Defense Committee, about 1954. Courtesy of Linn Shapiro.

After all, wasn't the American government trying to deport Peggy and put Saully in prison? How could they be so foolishly forgiving? I was pissed off by their posture. I thought it made them look like "chumps." We were catching all this hell, and they were proclaiming the virtues of American loyalty.

The enormous energy we devoted to the rigid construction of a healthy, conformist, loyal American family was subverted by one fatal Wellman flaw: we didn't always measure up. Vickie and I weren't always perfect. In the 1950s, adolescent rebelliousness was not "normal." Conformity was normal. And for communist kids, whose parents were publicly identified as enemies of the state, minor transgressions could be cause for major alarm. I lived in mortal fear that, no matter how petty, my violations of 1950s morality would make me responsible for my mother being deported or my father going to jail.

I never stopped worrying that my failure to be a model little citizen would be used by the government against my parents. Mostly I feared we would be found out, that the FBI would discover we weren't the perfect all-American family. *That* was the family secret we worked hardest to hide. We didn't let *anybody* in on that one. Not even ourselves. So when my Detroit police Red Squad file arrived, my worst fear was that this secret would come out.

But it didn't. And that was the biggest surprise of all. The most interesting feature of the file is what was *not* in it.

No mention of visiting with Saully "underground." Lydia Mates, Peggy's dearest friend, would meet us after school unexpectedly. She would walk us to her apartment, where another family friend waited. (We knew better than to ask what was happening.) Then a ritual would start: into that person's car. Drive for a while in what seemed like circles. Stop at a gas station. Out of one car and into another. Drive some more. In and out of a couple of cars. Jump into one car, and there's Peggy. Keep on going. Into another car, and there's Saully in the back seat. Off to some place far from Detroit. A comrade's farm. A motel. I never knew where we were and never asked. We'd stay for a weekend and then the ritual would be reenacted, this time in reverse.

I can't imagine the police didn't know what we were doing. They knew exactly where Saully was when they wanted to arrest him. But none of this is in the file.

Neither is the time I smuggled a message out of the Milan Federal Penitentiary. Appealing his five-year-plus prison sentence, Saully was in Milan because he couldn't make bail. Unbeknownst to me, he was fighting with the Party over whether these days in prison would count toward his sentence or be "dead" time. He had to tell the court he wanted to serve time while on appeal or the time wouldn't count. Smith Act appeals were being denied by the Supreme Court; facing five years, Saully wanted to start serving his time. Party higher-ups, who were not behind bars, opposed the idea. It would look as if communists were admitting guilt if they agreed to serve while on appeal. So messages were being sent back and forth.

As one of our "contact" visits (we could touch) was winding down, Saully leaned over and, while kissing me on the cheek, whispered that he had a folded piece of paper in his hand. "I'll pass it to you when we shake hands," he said without giving me a chance to object. "Put it in your pocket and when you get outside, give it to Peggy." I was sure the guard sitting at the other end of the room, who was looking directly at us, would see the exchange. My worst fantasies would come true. Why was Saully doing this to me? Offered no options, and feeling somewhat honored and heroic, I accepted the assignment. Fatalistically.

I walked out imagining I was quite conspicuous, but nothing happened. I was certain the guard knew but chose to ignore this violation of state security. I fully expected the incident to be reported in my file. But it wasn't.

Nor was there any mention of me smoking pot with two classmates in the seventh grade. Or drag racing with Bobby Rowlson on Northwestern Highway. Vandalizing racist statues of Black boys dressed in jockey suits in wealthy suburbs like Bloomfield Hills or Grosse Pointe. Fighting after school. Violating Detroit's curfew law. Getting stopped by the cops in the high school parking lot for drinking alcohol. Having sex in garages and the back seats of cars. Nearly flunking out of high school. Being placed on academic probation. Cutting classes. Talking back to teachers. Being insolent to Peggy; getting so angry with her that I literally pulled a bathroom sink off the wall one Thanksgiving weekend.

Communists working hard to undermine the popular picture of them as disloyal aliens weren't very sympathetic to these expressions of adolescent rebellion. As a result, the communist kids I knew were a pretty conformist bunch. "Squares," I thought. But I also worried that my youthful transgressions would be grist for the government's mill, cause for public humiliation and ridicule, possible reasons for additional persecution of Peggy and Saully. If the government wanted to sabotage that all-American image, I certainly gave them lots of ammunition. But none of it appears in the Red Squad documents.

The file focuses on public events. It reproduces newspaper clippings and items generated by Peggy's defense committee. The people it names were open communists. It mostly reads like an inventory of perfectly legal and usually very boring left-wing activities over a ten-year period.

Some examples (with no apologies for the Red Squad's spelling and grammar):

1–29–54 Subject a spectator during the SA [Smith Act] trial. file 1480A2 for memo.

10–23–54 Subject attended a meeting and social at 1933 Hazelwood held in honor of his mother. Subject arrived in a car registerd to Martha Townsend 53 Chev cpe AD4073(54) with 4 other youths who did not enter meeting.

4–9–55 Subject attended a concert featuring Pete Seeger.

12–2–55 Memo. Subj present at meeting regarding Till Murder Case.

5–16–56 Memo. Subj attended wedding reception of Thomas X. and Stella Dombrowski.

5–16–59, Det. News art. in file 715, "Wayne Student Wins in Oratory Contest."

6–16–61, Det. Free Press and Det. News art. in file "6 TAKE 5TH 100 TIMES ON CUBA QUIZ and 6 DETROITERS TAKE THE 5TH IN CUBA FAIR PLAY QUIZ." Subj. refused to tell the committee whether he was the son of Saul and Mignon Wellman because he said the implication was "that my parents are communists." "I love and respect my parents dearly, but I have no choice as to their activities." He was a 5th. amendment witness.

The file reveals that the Detroit Red Squad was absolutely obsessed with race.

February 1, 1954 MEMO
Approximately 90 persons attended the affair of which 40% were negro and 65% were male.

February 18, 1955 SUMMARY MEMO
The hall was decorated with leaflets on the wall carrying the slogan "Stop Housing Segregation" and various other slogans with the same theme. The meeting opened with a Negro girl singer accompanied by a white girl on the piano. She sang a negro spiritual and a Russian Song.

September 4, 1957 MEMO
Among the early arrivals at the grounds were [a long list of names] and—
—and her Negro husband——.

There were no unusual incidents witnessed by the surveilling officers. This affair featured delicacies from various countries, interracial dancing, sports and various games and contests.

What were those unremarkable suits doing with all that time they spent following us? We lived in absolute terror of being overheard, being seen, being physically attacked by them. If we had something important to say, we went outside on the street to say it. I slept with a baseball bat under my bed. We were taught how to speak on the phone, how to recognize someone without verbally acknowledging them. We learned never to speak names on the phone. (I still don't.) We were told to distrust anyone we didn't know. (I still do.) We were not permitted to display emotions in public. (I still don't.) When we were too candid, or about to spill a secret, Peggy and Saully would put an index finger to their mouths signaling us to be quiet. "The walls have ears," they would say, gesturing about the room. We were experiencing and internalizing state terror, an American version of totalitarianism.

While they were totally obtrusive, these state voyeurs were not recording our lives totally. The documents don't show them to be the self-conscious terrorizers we experienced or the evil people we made them out to be.

Why the discrepancy between my experience and the state's written account of it? Could it be that the dirty linen wasn't revealed because the Red Squad was as wrapped up in 1950s culture as my parents? Could it be that they subscribed to the same family values as Peggy and Saully and felt that certain family secrets were actually "private"? Did they assume that even political outlaws had family business that was not fair game for state eyes?

The Red Squad file shows that Peggy and Saully were, uncharacteristically, wrong about one thing: the walls had no ears (or did and chose not to use them). The state's eyesight was pretty poor, too. So how to make sense of it? "Silly games," Peggy used to say. "Dirty tricks," friends thinking of Watergate explain, an abuse of power. "Police incompetence," theorize the sophisticated professionals at the university where I teach.

None of these accounts works for me. I think the Detroit Red Squad was practicing state terrorism. They were trying to put the fear of police power in the minds of the people they spied on.

To a large degree, it worked.

In the 1960s, a couple of my close friends were headed to Mississippi as field secretaries for the Student Nonviolent Coordinating Committee (SNCC). Neither of them were red diaper babies. We had serious discussions about whether or not I should volunteer. We feared that if I was discovered by Mississippi officials, the movement would be discredited. I didn't go. A couple of years later, when I became active in Berkeley's Free Speech Movement, Bobby Starobin (his father Joe had been foreign editor of the *Daily Worker*) and I spent many hours obsessing about whether we would jeopardize the movement by getting arrested. We worried that our open participation would be used to prove the authorities right: the FSM had been created by "outside agitators." (We still hadn't come to a conclusion when I was arrested in Sproul Hall.) I remember sharing my "secret" with close friends in SDS at every choice point throughout the Sixties, wondering if I should be discreet rather than publicly involved. I remember the ugly, self-defeating feeling of self-censorship. I still think twice (at least!) every time I decide to join a picket line or march in a demonstration. My stomach still churns into knots whenever a police car pulls up behind me—even when I know I've done nothing wrong.

I know I'm not the only one. With important exceptions, not too many red diaper babies who were raised in publicly identified families of Communist Party functionaries, people who routinely had run ins with the state, people whose parents were underground and in jail, played a very prominent role in the New Left. As I recall, a lot of these red diaper babies sat out the Sixties. In my view, many became carbon copies of their parent's tired, conformist, conservative, loyal-American, and irrelevant Old Left politics.

I wonder: Could it be true that the Soviet secret police were effective at surveillance but (as recent events suggest) failed at intimidation while the not-so-secret police in the United States, who were obviously unskilled at keeping tabs on the Old Left, were quite effective at intimidation?

Resuscitating Corpses:
Memories of Political Exile in Mexico

Diana Anhalt

Diana Anhalt, born in New York City in 1942, lives in Mexico City. She is writing a book on U.S. expatriates in Mexico during the Red Scare years, among them her parents.

Anhalt has said that her life is best described by the lyrics of an Argentinian ballad: "No soy de aquí, Ni soy de allá, No tengo edad, ni porvenir, Y ser feliz es mi color de identidad" ("I'm not from here, I'm not from there, I'm ageless and bereft of future, And finding happiness is the color of my identity"). In this memoir, she portrays the dilemmas and contradictions of life within the left-wing exile community.

According to Mexican tradition, once a year, on the Day of the Dead, the souls of our dear departed return to Earth and the living honor them with serenades, food, and merrymaking. We decorate their tombs, erect an altar in their memory, and prepare their favorite dishes. This has always struck me as a singularly practical arrangement and a civilized one. Imagine confronting one's dead with the eloquence and maturity provided us by the intervening years, telling them frankly—with no hairs on the tongue, as we say in Spanish—everything we feel and neglected to tell them when they were alive.

But this is no two-way street. We may answer their questions, but they will never answer ours.

My parents died a few years ago, before telling me whether they had ever been communists and before I had the courage to insist on an answer. In 1956, a fellow student at the American School in Mexico City told a group of classmates as we changed shoes after gym, "My parents say Diana's parents are communists." I was not terribly surprised. It helped explain why Belle and Mike Zykofsky, then in their early thirties, had left a secure if not prosperous life in the Bronx for an uncertain future in Mexico, taking me, aged eight, and my sister Judy, then five, along with them.

The FBI referred to us and to the additional fifty or sixty progressive American families who settled in Mexico during the '50s as the ACGM, the "American Communist Group in Mexico," and kept close tabs on our social lives, bank accounts, and border crossings. Among the earliest arrivals was 1969 Pulitzer Prize–winning poet George Oppen, who earned his living in Mexico as a furniture maker. The "Hollywood refugees" followed, including three of the Hollywood Ten—Ring Lardner Jr., Albert Maltz, and Dalton Trumbo—plus a producer, a director, a literary agent, a technician, and a number of screenwriters. Alfred Stern and his wife, Martha Dodd, a writer and the daughter of President Roosevelt's ambassador to Nazi Germany, came down shortly later. (Accused by the U.S. government of being Russian spies and fearing they might be kidnapped from Mexico in much the same fashion that Morton Sobell and Gus Hall had been years earlier, they left for Czechoslovakia.) Others included Bart VanderSchelling, who had been a professional opera singer prior to being seriously wounded in the Spanish Civil War; Fred Vanderbilt Field, an heir to the Vanderbilt fortune who had been imprisoned for contempt of Congress; and Cedric Belfrage, former editor of the left-wing newspaper the *National Guardian*. Several families from the Miami area arrived in 1954 following a series of investigations into alleged communist activities in the South. Some expatriates returned to the States within a year or two; others still live in Mexico.

Firmly convinced that it was simply a matter of time before the United States became another Nazi Germany, Belle and Mike chose to move to Mexico. Mexico was cheap, close, and simple: you could enter the country without a passport—which my parents and most of the others didn't have and perhaps even earn a living. My parents also believed, not altogether accurately, that the political climate in Mexico would be as temperate as the weather.

1950 was a good year to leave the United States if you'd been involved in left-wing politics, as my parents had been. My father had run for office on the American Labor Party ticket and had been involved in the labor movement. 1950 was the year the Korean War broke out and the McCarran Act was passed. Joseph McCarthy began gaining credibility, Alger Hiss was convicted of perjury, the Rosenbergs were charged with conspiracy to commit espionage, and Morton Sobell was kidnapped from Mexico to stand trial alongside the Rosenbergs. (Years later I questioned my parents' soundness of judgment in choosing Mexico as a refuge three months after the Sobell kidnapping, but soundness of judgment was not chief among their virtues.)

Despite our sudden departure, we managed to fill four suitcases, three pieces of hand luggage, and two boxes. My father insisted on packing his jazz and Burl Ives records. They took the typewriter, my uncle Herman's two oil paintings, the address of their old friend Theo, and their life savings of $1,000. My mother, whose culinary abilities rarely extended beyond opening a can of tuna fish, insisted on including her *Settlement Cookbook* and her knitting needles along with approximately three inches of blue knitted yarn, the result of her earlier attempts to knit a baby sweater when she was pregnant with my sister. (Shortly before my brother's birth in 1955 she pulled it out again. We discovered the same piece of knitting, still attached to the needles, stuck away in a lower drawer when she died.) I was allowed to bring my ice skates, a gray corduroy jumper with red hearts and flowers on it, and my Brownie camera.

No other trip I have taken in the past forty-four years is as closely inscribed in my memory as that first one. I followed the airline stewardess down the aisle of the DC-4 handing out chewing gum and chatting with passengers. She gave me an American Airlines junior stewardess pin, and a bald man asked me, "Where are you going, little girl?"

"I'm going to California," I replied.

"Well, if that's the case, you're on the wrong plane," he answered, "because this plane is going to Mexico."

I ran back to tell my parents, just in case they didn't know. California had been the only destination mentioned. However, they didn't seem terribly upset, and I had my junior hostess wings pinned above my heart. Although I'd decided by the time I was fourteen that I no longer wanted to be an airline stewardess, my passion for travel has never waned. Those wings have marked me. So have my parents' politics.

I still don't know if my parents ever were members of the CP. Someone once told me that ignorance was my way of defending myself from the truth, that I was afraid to discover they had been. The person who told me that was wrong. I was afraid to discover that they hadn't. If they were, I could forgive them—or at least understand—their taking me away from my home, my school, my country and for lying to me about our destination. That's when my anger began, although I didn't know it at the time, and it plagued me for years like a mosquito's buzz on a hot summer night.

Until we went to Mexico, the longest trip I had ever made was the drive from the Bronx to Jones Beach. When we arrived in Mexico, I was immediately aware of how far I was from the Bronx. The next morning I saw real palm trees for the first time. As we stepped out of the back entrance of "Shirley's Courts Motel," a boy wearing a red shirt whizzed by on a bicycle. On his head he balanced an enormous basket heaped high with rolls, and, for a moment, I caught the scent of freshly baked bread.

Mexico City hit me with an intensity that was physical, like an electric shock: squawking parrots in metal cages were hawked on street corners, beggars stretched out their hands for coins, packs of stray dogs followed me everywhere, and the colors were a continual surprise—blasts of pink, chartreuse, red-orange, lemon. Even the smells assaulted me: the pungent odors of diesel oil, sewage, freshly ground coffee and the fainter ones of dust and oranges.

On the Paseo de la Reforma, a wide, tree lined avenue said to resemble the Champs Elysées, a procession of scruffy burros loaded down with long wooden beams leisurely crossed the eight-lane boulevard against the light, led by several barefoot Indians wearing sombreros and dressed in white. As drivers leaned heavily on their horns and screamed obscenities out their car windows, two policemen slouched against the traffic light shaking with laughter.

It took no more than a few weeks for my parents to discover that there was a vast cultural gap—no, it was more like a gulch—separating them from the Mexican way of life. Theo, a former friend from the Bronx, attempted to bridge that gap. He was a Spanish Civil War vet and, as such, one of the few in our group who spoke Spanish. He and his wife, Betty, by virtue of having arrived five months earlier, were the acknowledged Mexican experts. They knew where you could subscribe to the Sunday *New York Times*, the only store in our neighborhood to sell Jewish rye bread, and which doctor to call for typhoid inoculations. Belle and Mike also consulted with them about hiring a maid, finding a place to live, and getting a job.

Within a few weeks, with Theo's help, my mother was employed, illegally—since she had no working papers—as a legal secretary in a large American law firm where no Spanish was required. My father, previously a salesman for a New York printing company, rented space in a small flower shop on the Avenida Juarez in order to sell the lamps he made out of colonial statuettes and pre-Columbian figures, purchased in small towns and markets throughout the country. He also sold "ex-votos" or "milagros" (miracles), thank-you notes to God crudely painted on pieces of tin salvaged from flattened-out cans. Hung in a church, they became visible expressions of gratitude for the making of such miracles as resuscitating corpses, impregnating sterile women, and restoring sight to the blind. (It would have been an even greater "milagro" if my father had been able to make a living at it.)

My parents warned me repeatedly never to discuss family secrets. (Children were regarded by the exile community as their Achilles heel.) But to my knowledge no secret was ever divulged, and thus even notoriety was denied me. Not only was I sworn to tell no one what I knew, I knew nothing. I used to think that if they'd been more overtly political my life would have been easier: I could have been openly disapproved of like the Trumbo and Lardner kids. Their parents' names were always appearing in the English-language newspaper. Then, I might even have had some secrets to divulge, and we too would have been looked up to as ACGM royalty.

Not even Theo's tutelage prepared me for the American School in Mexico City, an exclusive enclave of American citizens and a few well-heeled Mexicans. It boasted a football team, cheerleaders, twirlers, sororities, and homecoming queens—a far cry from P.S. 106. All the girls had names like Lindley, Kay Sandra, Betty Ann, and Leticia, wore crinolines to school, and ate lettuce and tomato sandwiches with the crusts cut off. Their mothers were Pink Ladies at the American British Cowdray Hospital or belonged to the Junior League and the Garden Club. Their fathers worked for the American Embassy, General Electric, General Motors, or the CIA. Among them were a select few descended from former plantation owners fleeing the United States—with their slaves—following the Civil War. These had inherited their ancestors' political proclivities and passed them on to the others, who came, for the most part, from Texas, hated Mexico, and couldn't wait until Daddy was transferred. The American Legion, the American Society, and the Republicans Abroad, in that order, were the most prestigious community organizations.

Then there were the rest of us, Americans who didn't follow the norm—politically motivated expatriates, an occasional Jew—outcasts. These included artists, writers, teachers, anthropologists, small shop owners, businessmen, a number of investors—particularly in construction and film—chicken farm owners, guest-house managers, a photographer, a dentist, a carpenter, and a piano tuner. They collected pre-Columbian pieces, read books, and listened to classical music. (Some of them even tried to learn Spanish.) I bent over backwards to compensate for my parents' inadequacies. I adopted the crinoline, joined the Girl Scouts on Foreign Soil and the high school sorority, but could never get my mother to cut the crusts off my sandwiches.

During the 1956 Stevenson-Eisenhower campaign, mock elections were held in each classroom. I was one of four in a class of twenty-five who campaigned for the Democrats. The other three were Jewish, children of the Left, or both. Despite the mighty tug of conformity it just wasn't in me to support Eisenhower. Even today I am incapable of voting Republican and would like to regard myself as a champion of the underdog—or at least a humanist. That was my parents' doing, and I am grateful. (Although I never gave them the satisfaction of telling them when they were alive.)

Our parents took a certain perverse pleasure in the fact that their kids were generally among the best in their classes and managed to win most of the prizes. (I was the exception.) In 1972, when my brother Paul, born in Mexico in 1955, won the much coveted Ambassador's Cup, awarded annually by the American Embassy to an outstanding graduate for "Upholding Truth, Wisdom, Service, and Citizenship," the irony was not lost on my family or on those expatriates who still remembered the '50s.

While the desire to fit in pulled me in one direction, I could also relish my ability to shake the pillars of the American community—no enormous challenge—by delivering a speech in favor of racial integration for the American Legion Oratory Contest or by wearing too much lipstick. At the same time I recited grace before meals at the homes of my conservative friends and marched in the Girl Scout Honor Guard at Camp Camahouila each year.

Although my social incursions into enemy territory were mildly successful, I never managed to free myself of guilt for "going over to the other side" or to overcome the sense that, no matter what I did, I was fooling no one. For my parents and others like them, the pitfalls were of greater consequence; they had to earn a living in a hostile environment. When, after six months, my father realized that there was no money to be had in the lamp and "miracle" business, he and my mother, with the economic backing of my uncle Benny, set up a sales representation firm specializing in TV components. They did well, and, although they may not have realized it at the time, were fortunate to be self-employed. Those who weren't, like the politically expatriated American School or Mexico City College teachers or some of the businessmen, were particularly vulnerable, and, sporadically, some would lose their jobs. This generally occurred immediately after *U.S. News & World Report, Time* magazine, or one of the local newspapers would run an article entitled "Underground Railway for Reds Begins at U.S. Border" or "Mexico Clamps Down on Stalin" detailing a communist conspiracy originating in Mexico, aimed at toppling the U.S. government. The names of the American "conspirators" would follow. Our name never appeared on any of these lists. (My parents claimed this was due to their discretion, but I believed it was because they'd never done anything important enough to warrant inclusion.)

I distinctly remember the September 1958 roundups when approximately ten Americans and thirty other foreign residents—Spaniards, Germans, Yugoslavs, and Poles—were arrested in a series of raids ordered by President Adolfo Ruiz

Cortines. We were still at the breakfast table when the phone rang, which is, perhaps, why I always associate this incident with the odor of burnt toast. I remember Belle in a tan sweater and slacks whispering surreptitiously into the receiver and then hanging up, but not before thanking the caller for having tipped them off. She and my father disappeared for two days. Her only instructions were: "If anyone asks for us, you don't know where we are." (We didn't.)

According to the expatriates, the roundup, which took place during a politically volatile period of labor agitation and teacher strikes, helped distract attention from the disturbances by pinpointing "foreign agitators" as the culprits. It may have resulted, as well, from pressure on Gobernación (the Department of the Interior) by the American Embassy, which would have liked to see Mexico take a tougher stance toward the political exiles. Following the roundups Belle and Mike distanced themselves from most of their progressive friends, convinced that at least one was an informer.

Throughout the '50s families continued to arrive as others dribbled back to the States, but by the early '60s the fiery rhetoric that characterized the witch-hunt era started to fizzle. McCarthy and the movement that bore his name had, for the most part, been discredited, the State Department could no longer deny passports arbitrarily, and the Hollywood blacklists were soon to become a thing of the past. Most of the Hollywood crowd had left, and the few political expatriates who remained in Mexico began to return to the United States.

Those, like my parents, who had established businesses and prospered stayed on. The years passed. Their children went to college, moved to the States. A few of their number died and were buried in Mexico. My parents retired.

Mexico City also changed. The nutty, small-time capital of 1950 had become an overgrown metropolis—surreal and slightly sinister—and the rapidly escalating population brought with it the attendant problems of pollution, traffic, and stress. No longer young, my parents worried about the altitude, the quality of medical attention, and finances.

In 1981, at the height of Reagan's popularity, my parents moved to San Francisco after having spent more than thirty years in Mexico. They returned to the United States with their Mexican paintings and furnishings; a taste for pre-Columbian art, spicy cuisine, and Mexican music; and enduring gratitude, respect, and affection for Mexico and the Mexican people for having taken them in.

Each year on November 2, the Day of the Dead, I have the same fantasy: I am seated at my kitchen table in Mexico City with Belle and Mike. We push aside the sugar

skulls, the cempasúchil flowers, and the special Day of the Dead bread. I serve Belle enchiladas and Mike lox and cream cheese on a toasted bagel—no onion. And then I say: "Hey, look. Don't you think it's about time you answered some of my questions?"

And, as we eat bagels and enchiladas, listen to some jazz—Sidney Bechet, maybe—they will do in death what they were incapable of doing in life. They will explain.

Growing Up in Exile

Ann Kimmage

Ann Kimmage was born in New York City in 1942 and grew up after the age of eight in Prague and Beijing. She teaches literature, English composition, and Russian at Plattsburgh State College in Plattsburgh, New York. One of the few U.S. red diaper babies with firsthand experience of everyday life in communist countries, Kimmage has published a memoir of her early years, *An Un-American Childhood* (University of Georgia Press, 1996).

   Here, Kimmage recounts her assimilation into Czech society, her growing doubts about the socialist ideology she embraced as a child, and her ultimate disillusionment with communism and the Left.

Just like a river,
I was deflected by my stalwart era.
They swapped my life: into a different valley,
Past different landscapes, it went rolling on.
And I don't know my banks or where they are.
ANNA AKHMATOVA, "Northern Elegies"

On a chilly, clear October day in 1963, the flight from Prague to London was ready for boarding. My parents had waited for this moment for thirteen years. For them it was a chance to resume their discontinued lives and to see family and friends from whom they had been separated for years. For me it was the last day in a country that from the age of eight had been my home.

   The sleepless nights and anxiety-filled days before our departure had drained me. My head was throbbing, and my stomach was in turmoil. A weakness in my legs and waves of nausea forced me to concentrate on my body rather than on the frightening panic running through my head. Once I boarded the aircraft, there would be just minutes, then seconds, left before the metal door would close, permanently separating me from my home. As the plane lifted, the last glimmer of the city's medieval skyline soon disappeared under the clouds.

I tried to close my eyelids, swollen from a night of crying, but a stream of tears made even this simple act impossible. My entire body resisted the inevitable motion of the airplane. I could not imagine a life for myself outside of Prague or Czechoslovakia. For me this departure was a funeral; for my parents it was a return from the dead, a resurrection.

The younger of two daughters, I was born in New York City in 1942 to Abe and Belle Chapman, American communists who were deeply involved in the Party and its activities. My mother was a neighborhood political organizer, and my father was a Party functionary in New York State and a prolific writer for communist publications. His special areas of interest were the nationalist communist-led movements in the Philippines and China. My parents invited to our small home in Queens their wide circle of like-minded friends, Blacks, whites, and Asians of many nationalities. I listened with curiosity to their intense debates about the future of America and absorbed their admiration for the Soviet Union and their dreams of remaking society according to the Soviet model.

My parents and their comrades cared deeply about unionization, the rights of working people, and the need to end discrimination. They made scenes in restaurants if their Black friends were denied service. They were proud to be alive at a time when the future was full of possibilities and eager to struggle for their vision of a better, perhaps even perfect, world. They lived life with passion and believed that communism would enable all people to live free and dignified lives.

Communist beliefs replaced the Orthodox Jewish upbringing that had lost its meaning for my parents. Their political convictions brought them into conflict with my grandparents and their religious way of life. In our home ideological discussions replaced prayers, while kosher food gave way to Chinese, Filipino, and other cuisines that broke all kosher dietary rules.

After the age of eight I never again heard my grandfather's Hebrew prayers or watched my grandmother light the Sabbath candles. In 1950, during the heyday of the McCarthy era, my parents, like a number of other American communists, went underground. Why they did so remains a mystery to me. They refused to discuss it, claiming it was for my own protection not to know. Now that my parents are no longer alive, I will never learn from them what happened to us that summer of 1950 when we left New York City in great haste and secrecy. I have discovered through my research that my father was involved with the Institute of Pacific Relations, that the Institute was implicated in passing information to the Soviet Union, and that my father was under subpoena to testify about the Institute in 1951 before the Senate Internal Security Subcommittee. By then, however, my parents had disappeared behind the Iron Curtain. A connection between their disappearance and the subpoena may exist but remains part of a murky past I will probably never be able to fully explain.

On a warm summer night, our family traveled by train from Grand Central Station in New York City on our way to Mexico, where we remained in hiding for several months. For me there were no explanations, no visible preparations, no warning. I was awakened during the night and told to slip on the dress I had chosen to wear the next day to my second grade class. My mother said we had to leave our apartment at once. I left my toys, books, and special treasures, assuming I would be returning shortly.

By the end of 1950 the Czech Communist Party, on Soviet instructions my father brought back after a lengthy stay in Moscow, provided a home for us in Prague, where we lived under new identities. We no longer used our original name, Chapman, but a newly created one, Čapek. As time went on I forgot my original name, which I never heard my parents mention again. My parents' silence about the life and family we left behind slowly placed images of America and my early childhood beyond the reach of my memory. In a few years I could no longer remember my grandmother's face or even her first name. The stories she used to tell me about her childhood and family life in the old country and on the Lower East Side lost their contours and color.

We lived in Prague on the top floor of a small villa surrounded by a sturdy fence. The villa had been a private home owned by a pilot who defected to the West in 1948, when the communist coup took place. My friends' names were no longer Susan, Rachel, or David, but Eva, Karel, Jitka, and Mařenka. The textbooks in my book bag were Czech grammar and literature, Soviet history and geography, and stories of Lenin, Stalin, and Gottwald (the Czech Party leader). I was creating a world of my own, a Czech world, one my parents never became part of. Abe and Belle refused to learn Czech, thus affirming their hope that the country would remain a temporary refuge.

By eleven I was more proficient in Czech than in English. I became a good student and a dedicated member of the Pioneers, a children's organization devoted to instilling communist political values. I wore my Pioneer uniform proudly. Its white shirt, dark skirt, and soft red tie meant I was on my way to becoming part of society's "vanguard." With my classmates I recited the Pioneer salute, "Ready for the Building and Defense of the Homeland, Always Ready." I greeted people with the slogan "Honor to Labor" and called everyone "comrade." Along with mastering Czech, I accepted new socialist realities for which I could no longer find the English words. I began to identify with the concept of the "new socialist person" I was being trained to become.

I was eleven when Stalin died in 1953, a day I remember to the smallest detail. I can still smell the cold wintry air and see the dim reflection of the sunlight on the cement walls around our house. I felt an overwhelming sadness, for I believed a great man had died. But by the time I became a teenager, Stalin, whose picture had hung in all my classrooms, had fallen far from his previous status.

During my teenage years I saw how former "truths" and heroes could be transformed into untruths and villains. At sixteen I could not accept every slogan or dogma as I had during my Pioneer days. I became skilled at separating my private realizations from the public performance that was expected of me without even being consciously aware of doing it.

The Slánský trial in 1952, the unpredictable and inefficient economy, the hardships of daily life, the lack of intellectual freedom, and the devastation of the Stalinist revelations made my parents seek a new horizon for their communist vision. They reasoned that there was nothing wrong with the communist ideology in and of itself, that the problem was the Stalinist model and its application in Czechoslovakia. They turned their hopes toward China.

In 1957 Mao's China was letting a "hundred flowers" bloom and a hundred schools of thought compete. My father, invited to speak at a conference on Benjamin Franklin in Beijing, fell in love with the possibility of an improved and superior version of communism. We moved to Beijing, where both parents worked at the Foreign Language Press.

In Beijing I was enrolled in a Russian school built for the children of Soviet engineers and technicians who were training the Chinese to use new technologies. Although I was excited about going to China, the move destroyed the stability of my life. I missed my friends, my school, and the cultural life of Prague. At sixteen I needed to assert some independence from my parents, which was quite impossible under the circumstances. The only circle of people I knew were my parents' comrades. I walked through the streets of Beijing thinking in Czech and reacting to everything as a Czech, feeling lonely and dislocated. The Chinese crowds around me only reminded me that I had no community of my own.

Within two years of our arrival in Beijing in 1958, the "hundred flowers" shriveled and were replaced by an anti-foreigner campaign that kept the Chinese away from us and us away from them. My parents' hope for a free and just communist future turned to ashes as several of their colleagues disappeared to the countryside to have their thinking corrected. My parents began to fear for their own safety as the atmosphere became more and more oppressive and dangerous. My mother persuaded Abe, who still maintained shreds of optimism in a rapidly deteriorating atmosphere, that we had to leave.

We returned to Prague in 1960, my parents' dream of helping to create a communist society shaken. The experience in Czechoslovakia, and then later in China, aged my parents physically and shattered their spirits. They resumed life in Prague but were frustrated knowing they were unable to return to the United States until illegalities connected with their departure could be resolved and until the Soviet, Czech, and American communist parties could reconstruct our previous identities with the proper papers. Their future depended on political forces they had no control over.

We did not discuss these painful issues in our family. My parents resumed their jobs, my father at the Czech Academy of Science and my mother at an international labor organization. I began to prepare for university exams, reestablished old friendships, and formed new ones. I also quickly resumed the hypocrisy of separating my private thoughts from what everyone was expected to say in public. Survival demanded that we pretend loyalty to a system we basically despised. Now eighteen years old, I was interested in boyfriends, my appearance, literature, and music, but not in politics. Just back from China, where the Party discouraged expressions of femininity as frivolous, I shed my baggy, dark blue Chinese clothes and cloth flat shoes for high heels, colorful dresses, and lipstick. During my stay in China my Prague girlfriends had started to attend dance classes and put on makeup and costume jewelry. I had much catching up to do.

My own process of disillusionment began with the myth of Pavlík Morozov. From early childhood we were taught to emulate this fourteen-year-old Soviet hero, after whom schools, parks, and streets had been named. A model of socialist morality, Morozov betrayed his parents because they had resisted farm collectivization. He was murdered in the woods by angry and desperate villagers for this betrayal, but Stalin made him a communist hero, a saint for communist youth. The message was clear: be vigilant even to the point of spying on your own parents and make commitment to the cause and the Party your highest priority.

By young adulthood I began to wonder about the significance of the myth of Pavlík Morozov and his kind of commitment. Would I turn against my parents if they refused to cooperate with the dictates of the state, or would my family loyalty be stronger than my commitment to the Party? Growing doubts about ideology, however, did not negate or shake my rootedness in Czech society and culture. If anything, my political alienation strengthened these ties; a connectedness to the Czechs became my new center as politics faded in significance. Feeling part of Czech society made it possible to cope with the hypocrisy that ruled our everyday lives. At twenty I thought I had my life under control, and I was excited about getting an education, working out personal relationships, and starting a career.

On a typical student day at Charles University, following a late afternoon lecture on Marxist dialectics during which two hundred students had been struggling to keep awake, I joined some friends at the university coffee shop. We talked about the latest issue of *Plamen* (*The Flame*), a new literary magazine that had published some daring short stories challenging the limits of censorship. Continuing our conversation at a nearby wine cellar, we talked about the importance of friendship and love and shared our intimate plans and dreams over glasses of wine.

On the tram ride home I thought about Bohouš, who had asked me out dancing that Saturday night and whose companionship I was beginning to depend on. He was kind, funny, sexy, and intelligent. We both loved wine, dancing, talking about books, and walking around Prague late at night. Whenever he looked into my eyes and held my hand, he called me "Anička," the intimate form of Anna in Czech.

The light in the living room told me my parents were waiting up for me. I feared something might have happened to Abe, who was still recuperating from three near-fatal heart attacks. When I entered the room, however, I heard my father's clear, strong voice: "Ann, sit down." My father looked animated in a way I had not seen in years. "We have just had word from the Party that we can start the process of negotiations to return home. I've been waiting for this news for so long I thought it might never happen in my lifetime. Imagine. We'll finally return home, back to the States . . ." His eyes shone in the dimly lit room, and with a trembling hand he caressed my stiff shoulder. My mother quietly smoked one cigarette after another.

I was speechless. The effects of the wine instantly evaporated; I felt complete panic. Slowly I got out the word "When?" My father, who could hardly contain his excitement, said, "Probably within a year. There is a lot of paperwork that needs to be done. It will be complicated, but it will happen," he said confidently.

I stumbled out of the room, feeling as if everything was crashing in on me, that I was about to lose everything and everybody important to me.

★

On a crisp fall day a year later my parents ushered me out of Czechoslovakia as if the last thirteen years had been a dream. I no longer felt like an American, and I had no ties to the country to which I was returning as an immigrant, exiled from my adopted homeland. On the plane I was not thinking of the changes that I would have to go through in resuming my life in the United States. I could only think of what I was losing; the sense of loss was overwhelming.

There is no denying that our lives were enriched and strengthened by our experiences in exile; at the same time, they were irrevocably altered and complicated. There were no magical resolutions for the problems we had been left with in the aftermath of a failed experiment. The loss of illusions and the years of dislocation left each member of our family with a void. We had to reconstruct our own identities and rebuild our individual lives.

My parents' faith in radical social change was shattered by the realities of communism, which contradicted and demystified the theories and ideals that they cherished. Once back in the United States, my father became a university professor and author of several literary anthologies, immersing himself in the world of literature and searching for life's deeper meaning in art rather than in a political ideology. My mother earned an undergraduate degree and became a librarian, learning at a late age how to compete in a different job market. In the end, although we all found a place in society, we could not escape the burdensome reminders of our past and how it distorted our lives, careers, and relationships.

As children of communists, we were supposed to be the progeny of a future, united international family. In reality, my sister and I had to find our own way without continuity of place or human relationships. My sister remained in England, never returning to America. We are separated by geography and lifestyles as well as accents. Returning to the U.S., I felt alienated and struggled painfully with an ambiguous identity that resulted from the decisions my parents had made. It has taken many years to overcome the rifts between us and between me and the country of my birth.

My parents were motivated by a dream of a better world. I lived my childhood between their dream and its failure, between two cultures and two identities. Yet, despite their loss of illusions and their guilt over the consequences of their actions, my parents' deep love for their daughters, passionate love of life, and profound concern for the plight of their fellow humans have been transcendent and more powerful than the painful memories. What I learned from this experience was that social change must be gradual and in keeping with the realities and capabilities of human nature. My parents' all-consuming faith in an untried future and their blind intoxication with goals that turned out to be based on imagined certainties have left me with more questions than answers.

Dead Men Tell No Tales

Ilana Girard Singer

Ilana Girard Singer was born in 1944 in Hollywood and grew up in San Francisco. A psychotherapist since 1973, she is director of the Women's Division at the Center for Counter-Conditioning Therapy® in Oakland, California.

Singer's father, an engineer and political activist, taught classes at the California Labor School, one of several left-wing adult education centers that flourished in the 1940s and 1950s. A sense of mystery pervades Singer's description of her father's early years in this country and his unexplained death.

My father lay in his coffin at San Francisco Sinai Chapel. He was only forty-three. My mother, her cheek bruised from the mysterious car accident that had killed him, stood at the podium reading one of her poems to the tearful crowd of hundreds: "Today we weep, tomorrow not; we'll be working for what he fought." A stoic brunette in a bright coral dress, my mother limped back to her seat. She, my little brother, and I had almost been killed on that rainy Memorial Day in 1954, the day that fractured our lives and deadened my ten-year-old heart.

Still dazed, my arm bandaged, I watched as, one by one, Communist Party and labor leaders, longshoremen, Jewish scholars, and Father's devoted students filed by his plain oak coffin. I saw Dr. Holland Roberts, a former Stanford University professor who'd given my father's eulogy. The FBI had labeled Dr. Roberts "the most active Communist in California." This dignified semantics scholar was now the director of the infamous California Labor School, where my father had taught many classes, from Marxist theory to calculus to Jewish literature.

Then I saw Romero, my father's Mexican friend from the Party cell. In a shaky voice, Romero told me that when he was chained and thrown into jail, my father brought food to his eight children. He and Father had illegally organized cotton pickers—Filipino, Japanese, Chinese, and Mexican—against the large farm owners in the Imperial Valley.

Many other mourners followed; some had worked with Father setting up reading and arithmetic programs for poor "Negro," Asian, and Mexican workers, a radical effort in those days of Jim Crow segregation. While we were grieving inside the chapel, FBI agents were outside copying down license plate numbers to add to their bulging files.

As the funeral parlor's limousine drove through the fog to Salem Cemetery, my mother pointed out the back window to the long trail of car headlights. All during their marriage, Mother had endured hardship and uncertainty— Father's long and sometimes sudden disappearances for "Party work," his cryptic phone calls and coded letters to her. He'd been followed and threatened for years. FBI agents had staked out our house, tapped our telephone. They had even contacted Father's boss at Bechtel Corporation, the giant engineering company that built the Bay Bridge and Hoover Dam and was quietly designing America's first nuclear reactor. Watching the car lights behind us, I remembered my father, wiry as his wire-framed glasses, setting traps at home for the FBI. He'd pluck a strand of his hair, then spit on it and "paste" it across a window or door. When we returned, if the hair seal was broken, he knew someone had entered the house.

I didn't even know my father's real name. Only years later did I discover that it was Joseph Levitin. I learned he was orphaned in Siberia and raised by relatives. They, like thousands of other Russian Jews, fled persecution and took my father to Harbin, China. When he was an adolescent, he managed to get passage on a boat from China to Seattle, where he enrolled at the University of Washington. But he was stateless, and when his student visa expired he disappeared into the throngs of transients who rode the rails looking for work during the Great Depression. Father worked his way down the Pacific Coast as a miner and a cowboy. That's when he saw the hunger and hopelessness of migrant workers and hobos and joined the communist cause. By the time he arrived in San Francisco, he'd lost his accent and his old identity. He was now Alfred A. Girard.

In San Francisco, Alfred A. Girard became a charismatic political activist, standing on soapboxes speaking to crowds of the unemployed. He went to breadlines, urging the hungry to demand unemployment insurance and Social Security. Then he met my mother, a quiet Canadian nursing student, also here illegally. While he crusaded on street corners, she stood guard, looking out for the city's "Red Squad" that attacked crowds with billy clubs and tear gas. They married, and soon after, my sister was born. Four years later, the Alien Registration Act of 1940 made membership in the Communist Party illegal, and undocumented immigrants like my parents had to register and be fingerprinted to get their "green cards." Fearing arrest because of their leftist politics, my parents fled. Mother took my sister and stayed with her own mother in Vancouver. Stateless, without a passport, Father was barred from Canada. Friends helped him slip into Mexico. Three years later, my parents finally reunited in the village of Tecate, Mexico. By this time my father was speaking fluent Spanish and working as a beer taster at Tecate Brewery.

In 1944, my pregnant mother sneaked from Tecate across the border to Los Angeles so I could be born an American citizen. Soon after, Father was caught crossing into California and arrested. For months, Mother didn't know where he'd gone. She frantically searched for him and, penniless, had to place my big sister and me in foster homes. Finally, she found him in an immigration prison in Arizona. Eight months later, Father was released into the U.S. army and sent to Japan with the occupation forces. That's how he finally got his U.S. citizenship.

After World War II, my parents reunited in San Francisco. Like many returning veterans, Father went to school on the GI bill; he became an electrical engineer, worked for Bechtel Corporation, and resumed his radical politics. But, by the early '50s, the nation's anticommunist witch-hunt had intensified. The House Un-American Activities Committee (HUAC) hearings came to San Francisco in December 1953. Two months later, my father was fired. Three months later he was dead.

The fog was still heavy when the funeral limousine pulled into the cemetery. I saw Father's friends huddling together. There were so many people who loved him. I overheard a woman whisper, "Too suspicious." The long-faced man next to me nodded and said, "Too many comrades silenced by so-called accidents."

The accident . . . We were driving through the rain when I last heard my father's voice. He was telling my favorite story, Robin Hood, how the merry outlaw who stole from the rich and gave to the poor outwitted the nasty Sheriff. Suddenly, our Studebaker began spinning and then flipped over three times. Everything blurred, and I blacked out. When I awoke, I was upside down, trapped between twisted metal and shattered glass. I climbed through a broken window and saw my mother and father lying in the mud . . .

I stood as close as I could to his grave while our friends tossed handfuls of damp soil into the open pit. I clutched in my hand the Robin Hood hat Father had given me. I pulled off the yellow feather and watched it float onto his coffin.

★

My father taught me how to spot the FBI. They were so obvious in their snap-brimmed Fedoras and grey flannel suits. They looked like Fuller Brush sales-men, without the sample cases. One day, when I was eight years old, while Father was at Bechtel and Mother was in the backyard hanging out the wash, I heard the doorbell. Two stiff-looking men asked to see my mother. I knew who they were and tried to close the door, just as my parents had taught me; one of them stuck his boot in the door and blocked my effort.

Just then, Mother came in and saw me struggling. She nudged me aside, but I hid behind our bookcases, listening to their interrogation. "Give us names of your friends and we'll help you," said one of the men. "We know you're not a citizen." Her voice trembled as she told them no. Although she was a permanent resident and now a legal alien, Mother was still a Canadian citizen and afraid of deportation. After the FBI men drove away, she left me alone in the house and rushed out to a pay phone to call her attorney. She couldn't use our own telephone because it was tapped.

I remember other run-ins with the FBI. One night after a hootenanny at the California Labor School, my father was driving us home. We were all sing-ing Woody Guthrie's "Union Maid": "I never was afraid of goons and ginks and company finks." Suddenly, my parents stopped singing. My father kept glancing at the rearview mirror and said sharply to my mother, "I'll pull over and park. I'll tell them I know they're FBI." Mother, sounding nervous, urged him to keep driving, to lose them in the hills. Father zigzagged through the dark, narrow roads but never lost those headlights piercing the veil of fog behind us. They wanted us to know they were there, my father explained. They wanted to intimidate us.

Despite my bravado, I was always afraid. I was even afraid on Sunday nights when my family sat around the RCA console, the living room centerpiece. My parents sat together on the worn couch while my sister, our little broth-er, and I sprawled on the Mexican rug. We were listening to Berkeley's KPFA radio, America's first member-sponsored station and rumored to be run by subversives. One Sunday, an announcer reported that the FBI had nabbed my father's friend, Bill, on Market Street and deported him back to Finland with-out telling his family. My stomach knotted as I looked at my parents' drawn faces. I worried, could this happen to them?

I remember another night at the radio. We heard that Julius and Ethel Rosenberg, convicted of espionage, had been executed. I imagined I was one of the two Rosenberg sons. I was in the death chamber of Sing Sing prison trying to unstrap my parents from the electric chair. But it was too late . . .

I was very sad for their sons, Robby and Michael, but I also worried: Who would take care of me, my brother, and sister if *our* parents were electrocuted?

At my elementary school, no one ever mentioned the Rosenbergs, and I never dared say a word. The class bullies already picked on me. They pointed at the mismatched skirts and blouses my mother bought at rummage sales to benefit the *People's World* newspaper. We didn't have a television, and one day, when I asked who Buffalo Bob and Claribelle the Clown were, the bullies pulled my braids until I cried. Father refused to buy a TV, not just because money was scarce but because he didn't want us to sit passively riveted to a flickering box that, he said, sterilized and distorted information while hypnotizing its viewers.

Each morning, I recited the Pledge of Allegiance just like the other kids. But in 1954, the Pledge changed; the words "under God" were added. From then on, I did as my parents instructed me. I placed my hand over my heart but refused to say, "One nation, under God." Just before my father was killed he explained to me that the United States of America was a special country because, unlike the czar's Russia where he was born, America separated church and state.

All the kids in my class hated bomb drills. When the sirens whined, our teacher barked, "Drop. Cover up and shut your eyes!" I scrunched underneath my desk, my back to the windows. Miss Meadows told us the windows were reinforced with chicken wire to protect us from flying glass when the Russian bombs exploded.

"Who drops these bombs?" one boy called out. Another answered, "The Reds. The Jews. The commies!" I looked around. Who were they accusing? Did they know about my father and our family's secret? I pictured the Rosenbergs' electrocution and the three jolts it took to kill Ethel. I thought about their young sons, and I vomited on the polished linoleum floor.

Garden Village Elementary was in the San Francisco suburbs. Our family friend Malvina Reynolds wrote the song "Little Boxes" about our neighborhood, Daly City: "Little boxes, on the hillside, little boxes made of ticky tacky . . . and they all look just the same."

Each Saturday, the neighborhood kids went to matinees at the Serra Theater. I wanted to go with them, but Father said that serials like "Flash Gordon" and newsreels about the Korean War were propaganda. Instead, I read. Father gave me books about real people, *Sacco and Vanzetti* by Howard Fast and stories about children in the Warsaw Ghetto.

I helped my father build the pine bookcases in our living room. They were jammed with books by authors whose radical writings had been purged from library shelves across the nation: Thomas Paine, Upton Sinclair, Emile Zola, even Dante. My beloved *Robin Hood* had been banished from some school libraries because Senator Joe McCarthy called it "communist doctrine."

I followed my parents' strict rule not to let neighbors into the house, not only because they'd see our banned books and newspapers but because in those days Americans were suspicious of anyone who read "too much." A 1951 bestseller, *Washington Confidential*, captured the sentiment of the times: "Where you find an intellectual, you will probably find a Red."

My best school friend, Patti, lived in one of the pastel "little boxes" on our block. But the inside of hers was different from ours. She didn't have any books, except her Bible and her catechism reader. Over her bed she had pictures of Jesus with long hair. Patti often wore yellow because, she said, it brought her closer to Him. Patti could never figure out why I didn't go to church.

I loved Patti's front room with its picture of pink flamingoes hanging over the couch and plastic flowers on the blond coffee table. Best of all, there was an Admiral TV. I loved watching it on school holidays, especially "Queen for a Day." Patti's mother watched it, too; she looked just like Doris Day and wore red nail polish. She also sang "Oh My Papa" with the "Hit Parade" and sometimes served us a real treat, TV dinners—turkey, sweet potatoes, and peas wrapped in aluminum! One morning I went to Patti's house to play. Her mother came to the door but her voice was not friendly. She told me Patti wasn't home. Then she asked me, "Aren't your parents foreign born? What nationality are you?"

"I'm American," I answered warily, remembering that my parents had warned me about hidden loyalty questions. And then Patti's mother asked me outright if my father was a communist. I felt as though I'd been stabbed and could only stammer, "No. He's a progressive." I got away as fast as I could, confused and afraid I'd given away The Secret. (It's no wonder I was scared all the time. In 1954, 78 percent of Americans polled in a national survey thought it a good idea to report to the FBI any relatives or acquaintances they suspected of being communists.)

When I ran into the living room, my father was in his overstuffed chair reading the *People's World*. "Are you a communist?" I asked him. He didn't answer. He just kissed me softly on my forehead as I told him what had happened.

He never did answer that question directly, but now that I reflect, I realize, he told me in his own way. He took me to "The Thinker," a statue by Rodin, at the Legion of Honor near Golden Gate Park. We sat on the base of it and talked and talked. He told me why he loved this statue: "Just like 'The Thinker,'" he said, "your thoughts are free." Those words, he explained, were also the meaning of "Die Gedanken sind frei," a nineteenth-century German song we often sang at the California Labor School. His message is in the lyrics: "I think as I please. . . . This right I must treasure."

I loved going to the California Labor School with Father, not only because he taught there but because I fit in and escaped from local bullies and nosy neighbors. In this amazing school there were so many busy classrooms, from ceramics to modern dance to graphic arts. Great thinkers taught there, such as historian W. E. B. Du Bois, America's foremost black sociologist and a founder of the NAACP; Frank Lloyd Wright, the maverick architect; Harry Bridges, president of the International Longshoremen's and Warehousemen's Union (ILWU). Langston Hughes, the blacklisted revolutionary writer, came to read his poetry during Negro History Week.

At the Labor School I heard *our* music, not the soppy "Hit Parade" songs like "How Much Is That Doggy in the Window?" I loved when people overflowed the huge auditorium to hear concerts by Paul Robeson, Leadbelly, and Josh White. Most of all I loved belting out songs with hundreds of adults and other children at Pete Seeger's hootenannies, songs like "Last Night I Had the Strangest Dream" and the Communist Youth League's "World Youth Song."

While the kids from my elementary school were at the Serra Theater watching *The Thing from Another World*, I went to the Labor School to see *our* movies. One special evening, Father and I set up chairs in the back room to see *Salt of the Earth*, the banned movie about Mexican American miners striking against unsafe working conditions. I liked the miners' gutsy wives, who were demanding sanitation for their desert shanty town and equality with their "macho" husbands. It reminded me that my family had lived in Tecate and that my father had worked in the California mines. We learned that vigilantes in New Mexico had attacked the mining families who were acting themselves in the film and that Howard Hughes, the movie producer, sabotaged its printing and distribution. Despite the censors' hand, millions saw this workers' film, winner of France's International Grand Prize for Best Film in 1955.

Each night after working at Bechtel, Father taught adult classes at the Labor School in which he discussed authors ranging from Thomas Paine and Thomas Jefferson to Hegel and Shalom Aleichem. On Sunday mornings, he was headmaster of Die Kindershule (the Children's School). I took his classes and learned about the three hundred years of Jewish history in America, about Harriet Tubman and the Underground Railroad, and about the plight of migrant workers—people I heard nothing of at Garden Village Elementary.

When the California Labor School opened in 1942, it became a vital hub of San Francisco culture. The President's Commission for Fair Employment Practices commended the school in 1946 for "making America a place where all groups can live together in harmony." Some of San Francisco's biggest business names—including the Magnins and the Gumps—and politicians and university professors served on the board of directors, donated money, and taught classes. By 1951, about fifty thousand students, many returning WWII vets subsidized by the GI Bill, had taken classes at the school in San Francisco and at its satellite classrooms that stretched from Eureka in the north to San Diego eight hundred miles to the south.

But by 1951, the school had changed drastically. Because of America's political climate, San Francisco dignitaries and business leaders abandoned the school. Enrollment dropped. Then in December 1953, HUAC held hearings in San Francisco and a former student, Charles Blodgett, became a "friendly witness"; he accused some teachers, like my father, of being communists. The school was hounded by the IRS and hit with enormous court expenses. My father and his colleagues had been trying to save the school, but in 1957, it was padlocked.

My father didn't live to see his beloved California Labor School closed.

Forty years after his death, I returned to 321 Divisadero Street, the old site. I found the padlock gone, replaced by a metal security gate that guards its current tenants, a yoga center and a pornographic studio, from the street people below. My father was only forty-three the last time he taught about social injustice in this dilapidated building. For years I've been trying to obtain my father's 500-page FBI file under the Freedom of Information Act. So far, nothing. The FBI claims it's still under review, subject to national security codes.

One recent afternoon I stopped at the San Francisco Museum of Modern Art to see an exhibit by Dorothea Lange, the pioneer photographer who chronicled the social breakdown of America during the '30s and '40s. When I entered the gallery, I gasped. There on the wall in front of me was a black and white photograph of a fiery organizer at a microphone, the *People's World* newspaper in his pocket. He was addressing a crowd at the San Francisco General Strike of 1934 that closed down the city and other Pacific Coast ports. The photo was titled "Man at Mike." The man was my father at age twenty-three.

From *Loyalties: A Son's Memoir*

Carl Bernstein

Carl Bernstein, born in 1944, grew up in the Washington, D.C., area. He and Bob Woodward are widely known as the *Washington Post* reporters who investigated the abuse of presidential power known as Watergate. Bernstein has served as Washington bureau chief and senior correspondent for ABC News and has coauthored two best-sellers, *The Final Days* and *All the President's Men*.

In this excerpt from *Loyalties: A Son's Memoir* (Simon & Schuster, 1989), Bernstein relates how his adolescent rebellion took the form of embracing Jewish religious practice.

To the best of my knowledge, I had never heard the term "Bar Mitzvah" before we moved to Harvey Road. It certainly was never mentioned at the *shule*. There the conception of Jewishness was a secular one. And that was the tradition of my mother. Her grandmother, Bubba, had left religion behind in Russia and didn't get it again until toward the end, which was why she moved to Fifth and Jefferson, to be within easier walking distance of the synagogue.

My father, always rational, was an atheist by the time he was in college. His religious upbringing had been traditional: His own father was what was known as a "two-day-a-year man," religious in the sense that he observed the High Holidays. The family belonged to a Conservative congregation, called the Hebrew Tabernacle, at 160th Street, in Washington Heights. "Once in a while we'd go to synagogue on a Friday night," my father recalls, "but it wasn't really ly part of the pattern of living. Religion wasn't important. Still, when he was eleven, a tutor in Hebrew started coming to the house; there was never any question but that he would be Bar Mitzvahed. . . .

After we moved, I began agitating for a Bar Mitzvah almost immediately.

Every boy my age on the block took Hebrew lessons, and the rewards of a religious life, spiritual and material, seemed worthwhile. My parents were opposed. Almost every Friday night and Saturday morning somebody's brother or cousin or best friend was getting Bar Mitzvahed. There would be a huge party afterward. . . . Thus, beginning with Friday-night Sabbath services and extending through Saturday-midnight breakfast, my weekends were largely occupied by devotion and celebration.

Even on Saturdays when I did not know anybody being Bar Mitzvahed, I often went to services. Returning in the afternoon from synagogue, I would reopen the dispute. "You won't let me do anything. You won't join a country club, you won't let me be Jewish." Sometimes I screamed. And then I wrote my parents a note saying that they were atheistic Jewish Communists and that that was why they didn't want me Bar Mitzvahed.

I hated what I had done—so much that I forgot about it for years, until my Aunt Rose reminded me of it. She had found the note on the mantelpiece and intercepted it. But I had begun saying pretty much the same thing aloud: "You don't want me to be Jewish. This has to do with your politics. And it's not right. And you don't really believe in freedom. It's Communism. . . ."

Instead of a Bar Mitzvah, my father offered a trip across the country. "We'll send you to San Francisco."

"Nothing doing," I said. "I want to be Bar Mitzvahed."

Finally they relented. I was twelve. We joined MCJC, the Montgomery County Jewish Center, and became part of the flock of Rabbi Tzvi Porath, who agreed to forgo the usual requirements of lengthy study in anticipation of a contribution to the building fund. I was signed up with a tutor, in Riggs Park, whom I went to see two evenings a week to learn Hebrew. Of the traditions and philosophy of Judaism I learned nothing, except what I picked up in the synagogue.

The articles of my faith were stored next to my bed in a deep-purple velvet case emblazoned with a yellow Star of David: the *Siddur* (prayer book); *tefillen* (phylacteries, like the ones my great-uncle Itzel's ancient father had gone into the basement to put on, wrapping the thongs around his head and attaching the little box to his forehead so it looked like a light on a miner's hat); *tallis* (the prayer shawl that I insisted the maid iron every week); *yarmulke*. This little packet of plush velvet became the symbol of my rebellion; if I knew my parents were having their friends over, I would slip it onto the ledge in the entryway so it could not be missed when the front door opened.

We now owned a '51 Chevy with power glide, gray, with four doors, as the

FBI files note. On Sundays my mother would take the wheel, and my sisters and I would be ferried across the South Capitol Street Bridge (the Frederick Douglass Bridge, it has since been named by Congress), to Trenton Terrace. Years later my sister Mary asked my mother whether the Communist Party held its meetings every Sunday at Trenton Terrace, and was that why we went there. I must admit the same thought had crossed my mind. Even today, when I encounter a reference to Communist Party "cells" in those volumes published by the Government Printing Office, I imagine the dining room in Annie Stein's apartment—below ground, bare except for a table and a few chairs, the walls painted institutional green. I still get uncomfortable driving across the South Capitol Street Bridge. No, my mother had said to my sister, with what sounded like equal parts of amusement and chagrin. "We went there to be with friends—just to have a little fun." Or, as my father put it, "We all hobbled together."

Then one Sunday we were bundled into the car in a hurry. The telephone had been ringing a lot. We got into the car so fast that my sister Laura had only one shoe. Recently, she asked me whether I was going to write about that day. She had been eight at the time. "I was barefoot," she said.

We had just about enough money for tolls and gas to New York. Twenty dollars. I remember my mother and father counting in the car. When we got to the Jersey Turnpike we stopped to go inside a restaurant, and Laura started crying because the pavement was cold on her feet. My father carried her. Inside we didn't have sufficient money to get enough to eat and be sure we'd make all the tolls. My mother went to a pay phone and called the Gellers, collect; they had just moved to New York, to Queens. We would be staying at their house, she said afterward. We would go sight-seeing in New York. It would be fun. She didn't say why we were going to New York, but I knew that this too had something to do with the troubles.

In fact, the phone calls that morning had been from friends, operating a primitive kind of early-warning system. A subpoena server had shown up in Langley Park, at Ethel Weichbrod's, about ten minutes by car from our house. The subpoena commanded her to appear the next day before the House Committee on Un-American Activities, for an unannounced hearing to investigate the Rosenberg Defense Committee. . . . The alarm had gone out immediately from Ethel Weichbrod. . . . In Silver Spring, our phone rang with reports of the subpoena server's progress. When he got to Tahona Drive on the edge of Langley Park we lit out. . . .

We stayed in New York for a week, until the Un-American Committee had finished its hearings.

My father and I went to a fleabag hotel somewhere in Queens, the Franklin Park Hotel. For seven nights we slept together in a big double bed, sitting up and talking until late in the night. I think it was the only time I had ever been with him that long, without my mother and sisters. It was the best time.

My Bar Mitzvah came and went. I sat in a chair that resembled a throne, elevated from the congregation, among them the pillars of Washington radicalism, most of them, like my own parents, Jews who weren't religious. I sang my *haftorah* satisfactorily; the Torah I read from was blessed, in Hebrew, by my Uncle Itzel, by Joe Forer, and by my father, each of whom, according to ritual, brought the strands of the *tallis* to his lips and kissed it before touching the corner to the holy scroll itself. At the time my mother said the whole experience was probably more humiliating for my grandfather than for anyone else; his abhorrence of religion was deep, he was fierce in his disbelief, and I could not persuade him even to wear a *tallis* during the ceremony. Yet my memory of the occasion, and indeed the spirit of the entire affair, is quite happy, not just from the point of view of my own satisfaction, but from what I remember as a kind of transition, an easy mixing of my parents and their old friends with our new neighbors, of my Gentile schoolmates and kids from the block, of the disparate elements of my mother's family. . . .

The reception was held in our living room; Sligo Creek Park was blanketed with snow.

The FBI was across the street, taking down license numbers, which is how they picked up my Uncle Itzel's Dodge. For months afterward they followed him off and on, cataloguing the addresses and doorways where he would linger for a minute or two. They must not have realized that Uncle Itzel, though in his seventies, was still the circulation manager for the *Forvitz*, the *Jewish Daily Forward*; he was still making his rounds, collecting subscription money from those few Yiddish-speaking Jews left in Washington who took the paper.

For my Bar Mitzvah my father gave me the cufflinks he had worn at *his* Bar Mitzvah—a gift from his family: gold, with the initials "A.B." scrolled in script so florid that the letters twined and danced.

Those cufflinks from my father and a ring, also from his boyhood, were both lost. I lost the ring when I was with my grandparents at the beach, and I remember digging frantically at the water's edge, the feel of sand and grit and tiny stones under my fingernails. Even more painful was the feeling of panic when I first realized that it had slipped from my finger.

A Poisoned Childhood

Miriam Zahler

Miriam Zahler, born in 1944 in Detroit, lived in Michigan most of her life. From the mid-1970s until shortly before her death from kidney cancer in 1995, she worked as a freelance writer, taught English as a second language, and was active in local organizations working for social justice.

In this account of a childhood steeped in sadness and fear, Zahler writes about the importance of a warmhearted and seemingly fearless family friend in whose presence she felt supported and safe.

Legal challenges by Detroit-area activists have resulted in unprecedented access to FBI and police files. Like David Wellman, Zahler documents childhood memories with information from her family's files. In them, Zahler found corroboration of her sense of external threat.

When I was seven, I discovered the crawlspace in the attic of our house and, in it, evidence of the danger that would soon begin to terrorize me. I found the opening to the crawlspace at the back of a closet, covered with a board. Curious about what was behind it, I removed the board and crawled through the opening.

I found an empty, unfinished place behind the wall. In it was a big cardboard box filled with Marxist classics and other books by or about communists, socialists, and union organizers.

My mother had acquired those books in the thirties—which was probably when she became a member of the Communist Party—and the early forties. She was a full-time homemaker by the time I was born, but during the Depression she had worked outside the home as a presser in dry cleaning plants, a waitress, and a seamstress and had been a shop steward of the Amalgamated Clothing Workers of America.

My father also had low-paid jobs, including assembly line work at auto plants before they were unionized. He was unemployed during some of the Depression and didn't become an electrician until the forties. My father was never a member of the Communist Party, but he was sympathetic to its aspirations for American workers.

Despite the hardships, there was, I think, something dynamic and hopeful on the Left during the thirties and early forties. I, however, not having been born until the mid-forties, was a red diaper child of an entirely different milieu. For me, growing up in a communist home during McCarthyism was a vastly debilitating experience. By the '50s, there was no longer a mass movement and, as far as I can tell, not much remained of a sense of hope or solidarity on the Left. Instead, fear and despair prevailed; at least that's what I remember. The political events of the period disrupted my childhood as forcefully as if Joseph McCarthy had been camped on our doorstep.

Once, when I was about eight, I answered the telephone to hear, over the voice of the caller, the voice of my mother, who was right in the next room. I told her that something was wrong with the phone, and she came and listened. She seemed disturbed but didn't explain what it was—a previously taped phone conversation mysteriously being played back. Yet I understood it was a phone tap. As I had when I discovered the books in the attic, I felt there was something menacing our home, something that could even invade it.

When I was nine or ten, the FBI came to the house. I was standing next to my mother at the back of the kitchen, directly opposite the front hallway, when the doorbell rang. My father, who had just gotten home from work, opened the door. I saw two tall, unsmiling men, wearing the fabled FBI trench coats, standing on the porch. They addressed my father by name, identified themselves as FBI agents, and said they would like to come in and ask some questions.

I stood rooted to my spot, paralyzed by the fear that they would come in and then something unimaginable and terrible would happen. My father hesitated and seemed to stand aside for them to enter. But my mother looked up from the stove and told them not to bother her. She didn't want to talk to them and she was sick, she said. (She was recovering from a bursitis attack and had gotten out of bed only to prepare my father's dinner.) To my relief, the FBI agents left. My mother did not seem particularly affected by the encounter; I could see that my father was frightened.

I didn't learn until years later that the FBI made numerous return visits. Nor did I know of the letter in the early '50s from the Immigration and Naturalization Service (INS) directing my mother, who had been born in Poland, to appear for a hearing on her citizenship status. I later found the letter among her papers, with a copy of her reply. She wrote back that as she had been a naturalized American citizen for many years, the INS had no grounds for reviewing her status and she would not appear.

My mother knew that she was under surveillance—though I doubt she could have imagined how extensive it was—because of her CP membership and her political work in the early fifties, mainly efforts on behalf of victims of McCarthyism. Most conspicuously, by early 1952 she had become deeply involved in the defense of Ethel and Julius Rosenberg and Morton Sobell.

Some of the surveillance of my mother seemed deliberately blatant. In February 1953, my mother and three other members of the Detroit Committee to Secure Justice in the Rosenberg Case had made an appointment to meet with Mayor Albert Cobo about the Rosenbergs. An execution date had been set, and the Detroit committee hoped to persuade the mayor to publicly support the international campaign for clemency. When the delegation entered his office, Mayor Cobo had FBI agents waiting there to take photographs. The mayor then refused to talk with them.

I heard such stories from my mother and some of her friends only years later. My mother must have thought she was shielding me from fear by keeping silent. But the unspoken and unexplained anxiety in our house was actually as harrowing as FBI agents at the door. In that pinched atmosphere, I had a sense of some unidentified, very grave, lurking peril, a feeling that took on a horrifying reality when the Rosenbergs were executed.

Perhaps ironically, my knowledge of the government's surveillance of my family has come from two official sources—an incomplete copy of my mother's Detroit police Red Squad file, which I obtained in 1991, and my brother's FBI file, which he requested in 1978 under the Freedom of Information Act.

My brother's file is surprisingly thick for a person who has never been politically active or subscribed to particularly leftist views. My brother, a physician, was denied a commission in the Public Health Service in 1960, and he always suspected that the otherwise inexplicable rejection was based on our mother's political history. Eighteen years later, he requested his FBI file to see if the contents bore out his suspicion. We think they do.

The files corroborate my childhood impression that my home and family were under siege. The volume of detail is astonishing. Included are lists four and five pages long of "individuals identified" at meetings and of cars "seen entering the area" or "parked in the immediate vicinity." One document contains a list of subscribers to the *Michigan Worker* newspaper; another is a two-page report on the February 1953 funeral of a woman who had been active on the Left. The report names the individuals who gave the eulogies and those whom the agent or informer identified among the mourners. Each of the thirty-eight cars in the funeral procession is identified by license plate number, model, year, and name and address of the registered owner. The report concludes, "Also available is a photostatic copy of register of persons paying last respects to the deceased."

The Red Squad file contains copies of my mother's letters to the editor published in the *Detroit Free Press* in the 1950s and pictures of her taken at demonstrations and picket lines. According to the file, she saw the movie *Salt of the Earth* in 1954, attended concerts by Paul Robeson between 1953 and 1958, and went to the *Michigan Worker's* Christmas Bazaar in 1953, at which, the report notes, "Approximately 35% of those in attendance were Negroes."

If there is anything heartening in the files, it is the FBI interviews with our neighbors during the fifties. My brother's file contains the address of every place my mother lived and summaries of FBI interviews with her neighbors. The names are blacked out so I can only speculate about who at the height of McCarthyism made such statements as this to the FBI: "Yes, we've heard that Mrs. ——— is a communist, but she's a very good neighbor."

My mother did not tell me her feelings about the McCarthyite onslaught, but in the ways that children have of acquiring such information, I received a filtered version of her perceptions. What came through settled around me in heavy layers of sadness and fear.

My worst nightmare when I was seven and eight was that my mother would be taken away, as Morton Sobell had been from his children and the Rosenbergs had been from theirs. Ethel and Julius were at the very center of my terror. I wasn't told much about them. What I knew was that they were innocent, they were facing death, and they had two children. I wondered who was taking care of Michael and Robby. I worried about what would happen to them. I asked my mother why the Rosenbergs were in jail. For passing out some leaflets, she said; I concluded that if the Rosenbergs were in jail because they passed out leaflets, my mother, who also passed out leaflets, might be arrested, too.

According to her Red Squad file, my mother arranged the hall rental and distributed literature announcing the Detroit mobilization meeting for a June 14, 1953, Washington, D.C., demonstration to urge clemency for the Rosenbergs. She also had been "active in the drive to secure signatures on [clemency] petitions which will be sent to President Eisenhower."

I was overcome with fear that my mother would not return from the June 14 demonstration. I went into her bedroom closet and stood among her clothes and cried. I felt bitterly angry and confused. I couldn't put my fear into words, and I couldn't understand why I was suffering so. My father tried to persuade me to come out, but I stood in the closet and wailed that I wanted my mother back—as if she had gone to meet the fate of the Rosenbergs, who were, in fact, electrocuted within the week.

My mother must have felt that in working to save the Rosenbergs she was in some way fighting for her own life and family, her own future. She knew that if people like the Rosenbergs could be framed and murdered, so could anyone else on the Left. Certainly those were *my* secret feelings; I felt our survival and well-being somehow depended on Ethel and Julius's. For me as well as for my mother, their death was devastating. An unspeakable horror.

I remember the day they died as vividly as I remember anything in my life. I was eight years old. My parents were in our little kitchen, and I was in the adjoining living room watching television. Suddenly the program was interrupted for a news bulletin. My mother came into the living room and stood still in front of the TV. A man on the screen said that the Rosenbergs were dead.

There were seconds of leaden silence. Then my mother ran out of the room. My father and I followed her to the bedroom, where she lay on the bed sobbing. I had never seen her cry. I stood at the doorway and watched in horror. "We tried so hard, we tried so hard," she sobbed. "We tried so hard to save them." My father went over to her and spoke to her, but she didn't talk. She continued crying, I don't know for how long.

During the rest of the summer, the air in the house felt choked and thick. Grief over the Rosenbergs lingered; for some years after 1953, our lives were overlaid with sadness.

My mother left the Communist Party in 1956, but throughout the decade the FBI kept track of her contributions to Michael and Robby's trust fund and of her work on the Committee to Secure Justice for Morton Sobell and the Committee for Justice in the Rosenberg Case.

The McCarthy period might have been unremitting in its psychological horror if not for Bob Travis. Bob was a well-known figure on the Left, particularly in the Left labor movement. He had been one of the leaders of the 1936–37 Flint sitdown strike, the decisive union battle that resulted in General Motors' recognition of the UAW and the eventual unionization of the American auto industry. For a couple of years in the early 1950s, he was active in my mother's political circle in Detroit.

Bob Travis was an enormously charming and kind man, and I adored him. One of the things that most endeared him to me was his apparent fearlessness. He seemed unfazed by the FBI and took great satisfaction in their inability to rattle him. He was a wonderful storyteller; my favorite of his many FBI stories was about a trip to California that he and his wife, Helen, took one summer in the mid-'50s. They were followed by FBI agents every mile of the way. Bob described the FBI agents' checking into the same motels and parking their car next to the Travises' to make sure they knew they were being followed.

Bob's dismissive attitude impressed me more than the government's attempt at harassment. He described the FBI's absurdly elaborate surveillance with such amusement and disdain that he counteracted some of my fearfulness. Because he seemed impervious to their antics, I felt protected from the FBI when he was around.

While the other adults around me were uniformly guarded and grim, Bob smiled, was expansive, and radiated confidence and warmth. In the darkness of the McCarthy years, Bob Travis absolutely sparkled. When I was seven or eight, he would take me on occasional Saturday afternoon outings during which I felt extremely happy and safe. Bob might have thought of our outings as a favor to my mother, knowing she would appreciate having that free time. Perhaps he saw in me a confused, frightened child whom he wanted to try to help. I prefer this explanation; it's consistent with my belief that he was an exceptionally sensitive and compassionate human being. I suppose it's possible that he gave me that special attention simply because he liked children and saw that I was fond of him. Whatever the reason, I have always been grateful to him. During a time of intense suffering, he provided love and reassurance of the most real and precious kind.

I would like to be able to end an account of the '50s differently. I deeply admire those whom I knew on the Left; I salute them for their courage and sacrifices and their uncompromising fight for decency during an indecent and ghastly time. But I know that my torment could have been alleviated only by them, and except for Bob Travis, it wasn't. I absorbed a great deal of poison from an environment that reeked of fear, danger, death, and grief, and I sustained some emotional injuries that took many years to heal. While the adults were preoccupied fighting McCarthyism, they ignored its devastating effects on a defenseless child.

Carry It Forward and Pass It On

Robert Meeropol

Robert Meeropol earned undergraduate and graduate degrees in anthropology from the University of Michigan and a law degree from Western New England College School of Law. Married, with two grown children, Meeropol lives in Easthampton, Massachusetts. He is the founder and executive director of the Rosenberg Fund for Children.

On June 19, 1953, Meeropol's parents, Ethel and Julius Rosenberg, were put to death in the electric chair. This essay is based on a speech Meeropol delivered at Town Hall in New York City on the eve of the fortieth anniversary of his parents' execution.

What I remember of my first three years was ordinary. I lived with my parents and my older brother Michael in a small apartment on New York City's Lower East Side until June 1950, when my personal nightmare began. First my father and then, a month later, my mother were arrested by the FBI and charged with conspiracy to commit espionage—more specifically, stealing the secret of the atomic bomb and transmitting it to the Soviet Union.

The next four years were hellish. My brother and I were placed in an orphanage by relatives, denied the right to attend public school in New Jersey, and seized by New York City police after we started living with Abel and Anne Meeropol in 1954. We were returned to live permanently with the Meeropols in late 1954; our names were changed, and we dropped from public view for the next eighteen years.

My childhood encompassed the worst and the best of what it meant to be a red diaper baby. The worst included our family being torn apart by the United States government, relatives refusing to come to our aid, and those who rallied to our defense being unable to adequately protect us. The best included those who came forward to help and adopt us despite great risk to themselves and the thousands of generous individuals who raised a trust fund that enabled us to obtain counseling and attend schools and summer camps where progressive values were appreciated.

Despite the public nature of my childhood, the public knew almost nothing about my life. The images presented by the mainstream media were false.

In a scene from the movie adaptation of E. L. Doctorow's *The Book of Daniel*, a novel inspired by my parents' case, the two small children of the couple who have been condemned to death for stealing the secret of the atomic bomb are brought to a huge clemency rally. The throng is so tightly packed that the children can't be brought to the front, so they are lifted up and passed from person to person over the crowd and deposited on stage while thousands chant, "The children, the children." The children are, of course, traumatized. Nothing like this ever happened to Michael and me.

In *Daniel*, Hollywood indulged in the stereotype that progressives sacrificed their families for their causes. The film portrayed those who fought to save our parents as pathetic people who succeeded only in destroying their children. In actuality, those people protected us.

In fact, it was the right-wing-dominated Society for the Prevention of Cruelty to Children that traumatized us. The Society filed a child abuse petition in New York family court just a few weeks after we started living with Abel and Anne Meeropol. It claimed we were being abused for political purposes, that we were being exploited by those who were raising a trust fund for our benefit. These claims were not true, but the judge issued the order, and we were seized by the New York City police and removed to an orphanage.

Many who had fought to save our parents now rallied to our support, and we won the ensuing custody battle. Those who filed the petition were not content with killing our parents; they wanted to kill their legacy as well! They wanted us to forget our parents or grow up reviling them. But the movement that tried to save my parents nurtured and protected Michael and me for many years afterward. It kept the spark of our parents' resistance from being extinguished. We became the children of that movement, and my contact with many wonderful people in it is why I grew up with a positive attitude toward people and life. That movement also empowered us to reopen our parents' case in the 1970s and ultimately, in 1990, enabled me to create a new organization, the Rosenberg Fund for Children.

I have come to believe that working with groups that engage in community organizing efforts is necessary, but not sufficient, to sustaining long-term progressive activism. My life has demonstrated that building a community of support for individual activists is also necessary. That is why I am devoting

The Rosenberg children and their grandmother are joined by supporters in Washington, D.C., as they attempt to deliver a letter from Michael to President Eisenhower asking for clemency, 1953. Courtesy World Wide Photo, Inc.

myself to an organization that supports individual activists by directly providing help to their families in times of need. The Rosenberg Fund for Children provides grants to the children of targeted activists to enable them to benefit from the essential building blocks of these communities of support: alternative institutions such as schools, camps, and after-school cultural programs. By channeling its grants through alternative institutions whenever possible, the Rosenberg Fund for Children also helps to strengthen progressive community by supporting family-oriented programs that help convey progressive values from one generation to the next.

Experience has taught me that we must link our politics to our community and our families and we must build bridges across racial, cultural, issue-oriented, and age boundaries so that progressive inspiration will be transmitted to future generations. The resistance of Ethel and Julius Rosenberg is one with many others today, including that of imprisoned American Indian Movement leader Leonard Peltier and Mumia Abu Jamal, the first political prisoner in this country to face execution since my parents.

Through the Rosenberg Fund for Children I seek to transform the destruction visited upon my family in the 1950s into something positive in the 1990s. Bringing out the truth of their frame-up is no longer sufficient for me. I wish to draw upon the power generated by their resistance to inspire the activism that will defeat the forces that murdered them and oppress so many today. I work to pass the spark of Ethel and Julius Rosenberg's resistance on to the next generation and the generations that follow.

My parents were not powerful people—until they resisted. The myth that they organized a communist spy ring that stole the secret of the atomic bomb was used to sell the Cold War to the American public. The power their resistance generated threatened the basis of domestic Cold War ideology, making them very dangerous. The cold warriors fought back with every weapon in their arsenal. They used the press to portray my parents as fanatics who would sacrifice their children if they had to. Those who worked to save them were tarnished with the same lie.

And it was a lie. The Rosenberg family was functional and loving. The Meeropols, the progressive schools we attended, the progressive camps where we spent our summers provided us with a healthy, positive environment after my birth parents' death. Those institutions and that environment worked for Michael and me and for hundreds of other children scarred by the McCarthy witch-hunts. My wife, Elli, our daughters, Jenn and Rachel, and so many others are living testimony to the fact that political activism is not incompatible with building loving and nurturing families and communities.

My parents wrote that they were comforted in the sure knowledge that others would carry on after them. They were right.

The Rehabilitation
of Howard Bruchner

Sharon Temple Lieberman

Sharon Temple Lieberman's father, the prototype for this story, passed on
to her "a love of history, a discipline whose intricacies he thought he had
mastered." Inspired by him, she earned a doctorate in medieval history
from the University of London. Lieberman lives in Ann Arbor, Michigan,
where she writes poetry and fiction.

The strains of preteen friendship form the backdrop for Lieberman's
exploration of how death, religion, and communism affected a marriage
and of a daughter's attempts to make sense of the discord between her
parents.

1962. "Love, love me do." The Beatles send their love across the Atlantic.
It bottoms out off the coast of Cuba. The missile crisis is in full swing. We
are on the brink of nuclear war. My friends' fathers are building underground shelters; their mothers are stockpiling canned goods. And my father is laughing.

"The Soviet Union is the best friend we have. They know what it's like to
lose life. Twenty million died in World War II. They're not crazy."

The United States is trying to provoke them, my father explains, but Khrushchev won't fall for it.

My father has an insider's knowledge. He is a communist. His best friend is
high up in the national Party leadership, in close contact with Soviet sources.
My mother is also a communist, although her fervor cannot match my father's.
They met at a Communist Party meeting in 1937. My mother was recording
secretary. My father, a disaffected Zionist Socialist, came to observe. That night
he fell in love with an ideology and a woman. He has remained faithful to both.

★

"Love, love me do." I am singing at full volume as I walk home from school
with my best friend, Marlene. At twelve she is fully developed. She has spit
curls, full bangs, and a bouffant flip. A year younger, I am flat-chested. My
mother cuts my hair in a Buster Brown pageboy, bangs sheared unevenly. She
makes me wear leggings under my skirts. Fashion is not in my mother's vocabulary. I gain cachet by having Marlene as best friend.

We descend the six-block steep incline, street after street of brick row houses
with one exception—my house. Detached, perched atop three artificial ter-
races, it gives an illusion of grandeur that diffuses the closer you come. We
scale the three flights of stairs, past the cherry and plum trees, past the aza-
leas and ivy. My father's shingle hangs from a post at the summit—Howard
Bruchner, Attorney-at-Law. I am proud of this sign; it lends me authority in
this lower-middle-class neighborhood.

Marlene and I are standing at the front door. Above the knocker broods an
oversized, gilded American eagle. My mother sees no contradiction between
being a communist and being patriotic. But just in case the neighbors are in
any doubt, she has hammered the bird to the door.

Through the window, I see my mother, still in her nightgown. She rarely
dresses, prefers to let her body breathe. Marlene's mother is always dressed.
She wears curlers and watches soap operas while she irons, an activity that my
mother has banished from her repertoire.

My mother shouts out, "Is anybody with you?"

"Marlene," I answer.

"Wait a minute. I have to find my wig."

Since my grandfather died two months ago, my mother has worn a wig, or
as she calls it, a *sheitel*. It symbolizes her newfound adherence to orthodox
Judaism, a *volte-face* that has stunned my father.

"Papa would have wanted it," my mother tells him.

"Your father didn't have a religious bone in his body," my father retorts.

"You don't know what you're talking about," she screams.

My father does not argue. When my mother performs the Friday night
rituals, he leaves the small dinette, retreats to his study. I watch from the living room; she does not expect me to join her. Yet I cannot walk off, as my father
has done. She stands over candles, does swimming strokes mid-air, cups her
hands over her brow, and chants in Hebrew.

My father says that my mother has retreated to the Middle Ages.

My mother says Marxism is my father's religion.

My father says my mother will come to her senses. "We have to be patient. She's in mourning."

In my mother's closet hang the remains of her father—two coarse, gray suits and three sets of long johns. She sits beside a row of his black leather high-top lace-up boots. Her face is pressed to the hem of his trousers. The cuff of his jacket brushes her head. His long johns, ghosts on metal hangers, dance, rocking, chanting the Kaddish for the dead. A house of *shiva*, mourners closeted together.

In my mother's kitchen sits my grandmother, four feet, ten inches tall, her feet not touching the ground. She wears slippers with stockings rolled down to her ankles. She fingers a large bump on the bridge of her nose, inflicted when a pot fell off a shelf. Over three years my grandmother has worried it into a large knot.

"Papa was a saint," my mother tells her mother. "And look what's left," my mother whispers to me, looking at her mother. Aloud she adds, "He wasn't a greenhorn."

My grandmother is hardly responsible for her place of birth. Nor is it her fault that she has outlived her husband. Yet my mother holds her liable on both counts.

My mother finally opens the door. With or without her wig, she is beautiful. Her eyes, almond-shaped, like teardrops turned sideways, hold me in their gaze, frantic and sorrowing. It is not only my grandfather's death that consumes her. She thrives on melancholy; it is an occupational hazard. She is a poet. "Why do you think so many of the greatest poets lived in England? The climate. All that rain."

Marlene and I stampede through the open door.

"What's the hurry?" my mother asks.

Our club is meeting at my house. Marlene and I go into the basement. My father's books line stucco walls. A battered sofa, metal folding chairs, an old upright piano, two bicycles, and piles of newspapers compete for limited floor space. We set up a card table, go upstairs into the galley kitchen, make some Kool-Aid and onion dip, grab a bag of potato chips, and run back down the stairs.

Marlene curls a finger through the dip. Then she tells me, *sotto voce*, that the other members of the club are going to introduce a motion to oust me. I am a charter member of our club and have been president for both years of its existence. I recruited all the members.

There are seven of us: Marlene Rubin, whose father is a shoe salesman; Mandy Rudner, whose father is a CPA; Rita Weinstock, whose father was a

Kosher butcher until he was caught selling commercial-brand chickens as certified kosher ones; Robin Spalding, whose father works in a department store; Arnita Schiller, whose father is dead; and Rochelle Pavoni, whose father doesn't tell her what he does. (Several years later he will be arrested for dealing in child pornography. The police will remove crates of literature from his attic.)

"Why? What did I do?"

"They say your father is a communist. We made a pact. If we talk to your dad, we have to go home and wash out our mouths with soap."

"My father is not a communist," I lie. I am not ashamed of my father's politics. But I know we live in dangerous times.

"Mandy's mother says your father was on television for being a communist. She saw him."

The Cuban missile crisis is to blame. It has rekindled fears, revived memories of HUAC's visit to Baltimore five years earlier.

I was six when my father appeared on television to answer the charges leveled by the House Committee on Un-American Activities. I remember my mother hurrying home from shopping to watch the televised hearings. The committee would not say when my father would be called. We were there in front of the television at the start of each day's telecast, and when my father finally appeared, I watched my mother watch my father. I try to remember that face, like St. Theresa in ecstasy.

My father was heroic. He delivered a lecture on the history of the Fifth Amendment. He accused the government interrogator of "hamming it up for the television." Threatened repeatedly with contempt of court if he continued to obstruct the government's line of questioning, he persisted. I had never seen my father lose his temper. Suddenly he was thumping the tabletop with his fist.

Contrary to our expectations, my father was not charged with membership in the Communist Party. But he was worried that media exposure would damage his practice. Eager to make a public demonstration of prosperity, he bought a Cadillac, navy blue, sleek, fin-tailed, with a leather interior. A tactical maneuver, to be sure, since he had always driven a Chevrolet.

Every night after dinner we would go driving through the more affluent middle-class neighborhoods in Baltimore. We would cruise the streets slowly, stop on sighting a familiar face, roll down the automatic windows, and exchange pleasantries. Nothing more; the car spoke for us.

It spoke a different language to the poor. I often went with my father to visit his clients in the slums of south and east Baltimore. I remember living rooms with no furniture except a television on a wooden crate, floors covered in linoleum, walls papered in newsprint, staircases so steep and shallow I would hold on to my father's hand as I mounted them. We never drove our Cadillac to these houses. We parked blocks away. I recall trudging behind my father and asking why we had to hide our car. "These people have so little," my father told me.

The HUAC hearings, far from damaging my father, galvanized his career. Within weeks of his televised appearance, my father was a celebrity. Clients called to ask if he would defend them with the same ferocity he had displayed on television. We traded in the Caddy for a new Chevy. My father once again became a private citizen.

Now, after five years of relative peace and obscurity, I have to deal with his notoriety again. The girls arrive. They are cold to me and standoffish. I take my seat at the table. Robin sits next to me. The girls slide into their chairs. They sit opposite, solemn, prim. I see them passing notes, sharing knowing glances. I call the meeting to order. Robin reads the minutes from the last meeting. We move on to new business. Mandy Rudner raises her hand.

"I make a motion that we have new elections."

Several of the girls nod their heads, but no one else says a word.

"But we just had elections," I reply. "We have rules."

Robin puts down her pen. "The same people keep getting the best places. We need new people."

"It's kind of hard to have all new people," I say. Now I am exasperated. With four posts and only seven club members, someone is bound to serve consecutive terms. If they want me out, they will have to say so.

Mandy blurts out, "Why should you always be president?"

"Because I'm elected. Fair is fair."

"Why not vote for new people? Let's say you can't be voted to the same office for more than two terms. Like the president." Mandy turns red.

"Sure," I say. "It's a free country."

We write our choices on scraps of paper, deposit them in a shoe box. Arnita reads the returns. Rita is our new president. I am elected treasurer, a demotion that I accept with studied nonchalance.

My father arrives halfway through the meeting. He greets each girl by name. They are sullen, poker-faced, muster anemic, monosyllabic responses. When he walks out of the room, they start whispering. When they see me looking, they lower their eyes and cast conspiratorial sideways glances.

My father has been good to these girls. He chauffeurs us everywhere—to Louisa's Pizza, to Carvel Ice Cream, to the bowling alley and movie theater. He has helped them with papers. He has given free legal advice to their parents.

Marlene later tells me that the girls keep their pact. All except Marlene go home and wash out their mouths with soap. Ignorance is its own reward? No, I want revenge. I tell my mother.

My mother says that she is going to call "every damned one of those ignoramuses." I instantly regret confiding in her. My mother and the telephone have a history. In collusion with her Aunt Dena, my grandfather's sister, she calls her enemies, real or imagined, and when they answer, she hangs up. She does this all day. When she tires, Aunt Dena relieves her for two- or three-hour stints. If the enemies retaliate, for a week or so the lines are congested until the passion is spent. I foresee weeks of telephone wars.

My mother picks up the phone. I can't bear to stay in the same room but remain within earshot in the hall next to her bedroom.

She is polite, warmly familiar. "Patricia came to me very upset. She says the girls are saying things against her father. You know how girls are about their daddies. They're saying my husband is a communist. It's absolutely ridiculous. He loves this country. He is a loyal, patriotic American."

My mother's mixture of indignation and assurances is convincing. I know this because within a week every member of the club calls me to apologize. Arnita stammers that it wasn't her idea. She claims Mandy was the mastermind. Mandy's apology is perfunctory. "Just wanted to say, 'Sorry.'" Rita calls and assures me that she knew it was a lie. "You're father doesn't look anything like a communist." Robin assures me that she knew my father couldn't be a communist all along. "He's so nice," she explains. At our next meeting, new elections are held, and I am restored to president.

Is my father a loyal, patriotic American? I am not altogether clear on this. He prefers the system in the Soviet Union. But he loves his country. He doesn't want to leave it; he wants to transform it. But I am not immune to school propaganda. I share my friends' fears. Part of me believes that communists are not like the rest of us; they are subhuman, a threat to civilization. What is civilization? The opposite of chaos. The opposite of my family. I am ashamed and proud to be different. I am confused.

Yet I am my father's mouthpiece. I tell my class that the United States has ringed the Soviet Union with missiles and that the Russians have as much right to put missiles in Cuba as we have to put them in Turkey. I tell them that our president needs an issue, that he is a "warmonger." When I say this, there is a sharp intake of breath. Even the big talkers are silent. My teacher, Miss Sloan, has lost her smile. Through tight lips she asks me where I get my information.

"My father told me," I say with less than complete conviction. When the lunch bell rings, my friends slink away. I do not even look for them in the cafeteria.

When I recount the incident to my father, he laughs. "Don't worry about it," he tells me. "In the future just be careful what you say."

It is a hard lesson to distinguish between what I can and cannot say. But if I am in any doubt as to the need for discretion, I have only to recall my father's friends, many of whom went to jail. One close friend, soon after being called to testify before HUAC, collapsed on the tennis courts and died at forty of a heart attack. These men sat in our living room over coffee. They stood around the battered piano in the basement and sang "Old Man River" and "Joe Hill." Jacob Mazarov drank too much and did the *kazatzke* while everyone clapped encouragement. There was an air of manic festivity, as if these comrades sensed that theirs was a dance of death. I was wary of my father's friends. And guilty for harboring these feelings.

1962 is not a good year for me: My lone voice warning classmates that their Cold War hysteria is so much hot air. My temporary demotion in the club. My mother in the closet. My mother, born-again Jew. And now my mother completes her metamorphosis. She quits the Party.

I have seen it coming. Contrary to my father's assurances, my mother does not recover from her father's death. Her grief intensifies, as if she has to prove her devotion to her father, as if no one believes her. She is suddenly angry with everyone. She wants to cut ties, break with all her friends, with her past. She wants to hurt my father.

My mother offers copious reasons for her defection. Her comrades are petty and backbiting: "I feel like I'm in a sorority." The men are dry, unimaginative, unreflective. Men who still believe in Stalin, men who cannot tolerate even a joke at the great man's expense. "They've gone stale."

She has been a member of the club for too long, heard the same slogans too many times. "They're kidding themselves if they think Russia is any better. Let them go there and see how they like it." I have heard this challenge, standard retort to any criticism of our system of government, many times. But never from my mother.

"Power corrupts. Don't you see that?" she says to my father. "The Soviet Union is no different from the United States. They have no morals, no scruples. You're kidding yourself. When are you going to grow up?"

When will he agree with her? Mourning has isolated my mother. She needs an ally. I think that if my mother could have detached my father from the Party, she would have been restored to us. But it is a price that my father is not prepared to pay. His identity is too closely tied to his communism. My mother recognizes this as well. She has declared war.

It is early evening. My father is surveying his library in the basement. Among his prized collections is a complete set, from 1936 on, of a Marxist publication, *Science and Society.*

I see my father standing before the bare shelves, and I can only guess what he is thinking.

"How could she do such a thing?" He turns to me, shakes his head. "I don't understand your mother," he says.

My father leaves, disappears for two days, and then returns. I do not question his departure, but I cannot understand why he returns. I think perhaps he does this for me. Maybe he does it for her.

I ask my father, "Do you think Mommy's crazy?"

His lips compress; his brow puckers. The world's problems aren't enough. He has to carry my mother on his back.

I lie in bed and listen to my mother's fusillade. My family does not feed merely on global tensions. We have our own underground springs.

My father's life and the Russian Revolution were virtually coterminous. My father was born in 1916, the Russian revolution a year later. In 1962 my father could look at his world and be proud of what revolutionary ardor had won. "When I was born, not one country was communist, and now look. One-third of humankind."

I am looking. My father died in 1987. He predeceased Soviet communism by three years. If he had believed in God, this would have been the moment to thank Him. My father was spared the shock of seeing the system that he spent a lifetime defending fall to pieces. He left with his convictions in place. Gorbachev was the best thing that ever happened to the Soviet Union, said the man who had once thrown a woman out of his house for insulting Stalin.

"Your father was a wonderful man in every way," my mother says to me as she approaches her eightieth birthday. She is bent on tidying her own house, anticipating her departure from this world. She wants to rewrite history, the way Stalin and Khrushchev doctored the record, the way Nixon and Reagan and North shredded it.

"I'm going to write a story called 'The Rehabilitation of Howard Bruchner,'" I tell her. "I'll have to interview you."

She is embarrassed. "Couldn't we talk about something else?" she asks me.

I persist. "Tell me about your joining the Communist Party."

"What do you want to know about that?" She laughs a girlish, self-conscious laugh.

"Why did you join?"

"It was a nice group of people."

"How many? Do you remember their names?"

"No, I really don't." she says. She has spent a lifetime forgetting.

"What did you do at your meetings?"

"I can't remember."

"But you were recording secretary. You kept the minutes." I regret calling attention to her memory lapse. For two or three years her mind has been falling away, breaking into pieces. She sifts through the rubble.

She can't remember what she did or said five minutes earlier. But incidents from the past survive haphazardly. She can tell me how on their first date the shadows cast by leaves of a beech tree played on the shoulders of my father's white jacket. She recalls reciting Poe in unison with my father: "For we loved with a love that was more than a love."

"He memorized a dozen poems to impress me," she tells me. She has remembered something else. It is offered by way of proof that her commitment to communism was always equivocal. "You know that poem I wrote to Lenin? The one published in the *New Masses?* I wrote it for Roosevelt. Just changed the names to get it published."

As I press her about the Party, she scavenges in the recesses and comes up empty. "It's not important. It's history. Part of the record. You don't need me for the answers."

"Tell me about the Smith Act trials. Why wasn't Daddy ever tried?"

"Don't think they didn't want to get him. They went after him. I can't remember the year."

"There were many years. He was before HUAC in 1948, 1951, 1952, and 1957. How did he escape?"

"Do you really want to do this?"

"I want to know about my father, and you."

"There was a lawyer, state's attorney, Merrill, I think. He once said to me, 'I'm against everything your husband stands for, everything he represents, but he is a great lawyer.'"

"You mean he was too smart?" I know it isn't that simple. Many intelligent people went to jail.

"He didn't have to advertise. He didn't show off. Some people wanted to be heroes. Make a name for themselves. They got caught."

Once my father told me that he knew that there was an informer in the

Party. He knew the man could have fingered him. "Never understood why he kept quiet," my father said.

"Maybe he was just lucky," I suggest to my mother.

"Maybe so," she says.

"I remember an incident," I tell her. "We were in front of the White House. Don't know what we were doing there. You spotted an American Nazi Party member, a tall man with a swastika on his armband. You pulled me across the street, walked up to him, and yelled, 'Our boys died fighting you bastards. How dare you show your face in public?'"

I remember my mother's head pitched forward, the vessels in her neck straining, and the shrill, hysterical tone of her voice. I was afraid of the man; I was afraid of my mother. And then I saw my father running toward us. He wrapped an arm around my mother, took my hand, and shepherded us back across the street to the line of march. Now I ask my mother, "Did it have anything to do with the Rosenbergs?"

My mother says, "The Rosenbergs? I don't recall. Who were they?"

At first I think that she is joking, but I am mistaken. She is embarrassed that she can't remember. She wants to help me and offers to go to the library to look at back issues of the papers from the time. "Maybe that would bring it back to me."

"It's not important," I tell her. "You stood up to that Nazi. It took a lot of guts."

"Tell me again what I said," she asks. She laughs when I am finished and says, "Well, that sounds like me."

She is silent for a few seconds. I suggest that we continue another day. She wants to talk.

"Years ago I inscribed some lines on the back of a photograph of your father. From *Julius Caesar*. 'His life was gentle, and the elements so mixed in him that nature might stand up and say to all the world, this was a man.'" She pauses. "I lost it. Looked everywhere. It'll turn up when I'm dead and gone."

It shames me, but I do not tell my mother that I know the photograph she is talking about, that I have it in my possession. It is my small revenge. For her defection. Not from the Party. That is not mine to judge. From my father. From me.

Born Underground

Anna L. Kaplan

Anna L. Kaplan, born in New York City, was raised in Los Angeles and lives in Southern California. After practicing medicine for twelve years, she now works as a mother and writer.

With the intensification of the Cold War and legal attacks by the federal government on the CP in the late 1940s, Party leaders came to believe that the organization would soon be declared illegal. To ensure the CP's continued operation, many cadre went into hiding, or "underground." Little has been written about their experiences or the effects on their children. Here Kaplan describes a family history in which the underground played a pivotal role.

I was ten years old in 1964 when I discovered that my parents had been members of the Communist Party from the early 1930s until 1958. In a newspaper, I read a remark supposedly referring to my mother's communist activities. (In fact, the article confused my mother with someone else of the same name.) Only when faced with my questions about the article did my parents realize that I did not already know about their Party membership. They had not made any conscious decision to withhold information from me, and I never suspected their involvement. I knew that they and their friends talked about world events, politics, and solving problems in a way different from my school friends' parents or my teachers. Thinking back on it, I assume that they must have talked about "the Party" or the "Movement," which could have meant anything, including the student movement, the civil rights movement, or the labor movement. When they said "the Left," to me it meant they were more radical than the average person. I found myself, suddenly, as it seemed to me, in the midst of ex-communists. Other family members and most of my parents' friends, just about all of the adults I knew and loved, had been Communist Party members.

My teachers at school taught us that the communists were evil Red devils trying to overthrow the government by force. We had "yellow alert" drills, during which we practiced going home by the most direct route to await a nuclear attack by the communists. We learned to "duck and cover" if a bomb dropped suddenly. Finding out my parents had been communists frightened me at first, but then I asked myself, "My parents?" and realized that my teachers had to be wrong.

While my parents never seemed average to me, I had little suspected the extraordinary events of their lives. As I learned more about those events, I came to respect my parents as American heroes committed to helping individuals in society as well as to improving conditions in general, doing this with an enduring faith in the American people and government that far surpasses my own. I wanted to go to school, announce my discovery to my entire class, and correct the other children's misconceptions. But I felt my parents' need to keep this information private, so I only shared the treasured secret with my best friend. Over the years, I told other close friends, all of whom accepted it without trouble and only thought more highly of my parents. My parents' reticence to discuss openly their time with the Communist Party persisted. Only as I passed my fortieth birthday did I see a change.

In the early 1950s the national Communist Party leadership decided to send some Party leaders into hiding. Although my parents did not believe, as did some others, that the United States was about to become a fascist state, they did what they were asked to do. My father was labor secretary of the Communist Party in San Francisco. My mother was state education director. They were ideal choices for the underground. Then in their late thirties, they had been married for many years but remained childless, although not by choice. In the underground, they established new lives, sometimes together, more often alone. Initially, my father worked his trade as a machinist, and my mother waited tables. After the arrest of California Party leaders in 1951, my parents were told to separate. My father was placed in charge of the California underground, while my mother was sent to Chicago. They were contacted either by people already known to them or by individuals using code and other identification. My mother lost her contact for a time, checked into the local Y.W.C.A., and supported herself by waiting tables until she served food to a Communist Party leader who recognized her.

After two years of separation, my parents "got word" that they could vacation together. They were to meet at street corner "A" on Monday, Wednesday, or Friday or at nearby corner "B" on Tuesday or Thursday. However, on Monday, Wednesday, and Friday, my father was sent to A, while my mother was sent to B. After two days, they both thought this might have happened and met midway, each walking to the other corner. They had become quite skilled at these maneuvers and knew that they would somehow find each other. They spent their time together in a tent in King's Canyon, California. Then my father went back to his work, my mother to Chicago.

My mother never suspected she was pregnant until her third or fourth month. Married for twelve years, she and my father had been evaluated and treated for infertility as far as was possible at the time. Pregnancy was the last thing on their minds. Finally my mother got suspicious and went to a doctor. She told her contact at their next meeting and sent a message to my father, but the people with her message were picked up by the FBI. Word finally reached my father that he was needed in New York. Having no idea why he was needed, he sent someone else. This poor man burst into tears when he arrived in New York and found out why my father had been summoned. Finally, the same trusted friend who had arranged my parents' vacation was sent to get my father, who could hardly believe the news and was seen counting the months since their vacation on his fingers.

A month before the due date, my mother developed potentially devastating bleeding. She needed an emergency Caesarean section to save both her life and mine. The operation was performed by a politically friendly physician, under spinal anesthesia so that my mother wouldn't "talk." My mother assumed her doctor was a communist but says that no one in the underground ever directly asked a host or helper. I cannot imagine what she could have revealed in an anesthesia delirium, but they probably thought it better for her to have all her wits about her. We both did fine, although we were in the hospital for a long time.

Since my mother still did not think that fascists were going to take over the government, she put my father's real name on my birth certificate. She slightly altered her own name, giving it as Celia instead of Celeste, and used her mother's maiden name. Years later, she requested a correction, saying that the information had been obtained during an emergency and the resulting confusion.

My mother was visited in the hospital by a "friend," a previously unknown contact, who arranged to have flowers delivered "from her husband" who was "out of town." When we left the hospital, my mother followed her new instructions. Much to his consternation, the taxi driver left us in the middle of a snowy New York street. My mother went inside an office building to be met by her next helpers, and we started our lives together. My father didn't arrive until I was a month old. He was able to visit us only once more during the next year and a half. During this time my mother raised me on her own, not an easy task for a thirty-nine-year-old with no family to help her. She wrote some, having been assigned the job of underground educational director, but spent most of her time with me, learning about babies in general, with help from Dr. Spock, and me in particular. My mother could not contact her family, and, of course, being separated from my father was very hard on her. Crying, she used to sing me a lullaby that her mother had sung to her: "Daddy will come to his babe in the nest. Silver sails across the West. Blow him again to me, while my little one, while my pretty one sleeps." Hearing that song still fills me with sadness. I did not realize when I was a small child why the song upset me; later my mother and I deciphered this wordless infant memory, my only memory of the underground.

During this time my father's mother died. Being underground, he did not find out until afterward and never got the chance to see her. In 1955 my father moved us from New York to Los Angeles, close to the remaining family. The McCarthy period was drawing to an end, and it was time for all of us to leave the underground.

My father found work as a machinist, although he lost some jobs because the FBI followed him and scared his employers. I've been told that I sat on his shoulders at Party meetings and listened to my mother speak, but I do not remember. By 1958, when I was four years old, my parents left the Communist Party. They had, for years, been questioning the role of the Party in the United States and felt it could not offer viable solutions or be a viable political force. They could not abandon the Party while in the underground during the worst of times. Now in the open, they made the difficult and painful decision, surrounded by loving friends and family, many of whom were making the same transition. My mother went back to graduate school to get a degree in social work. My father's job situations got progressively better.

By the time I reached twelve or thirteen I started endless discussions with my parents because I thought that they were naively optimistic about the nature of human beings. We still don't agree about that. They allowed me to travel to the U.S.S.R. at age sixteen to see things for myself. I never needed to rebel, and I never experienced a "generation gap" with my parents or their friends.

I am my parents' daughter. But what they passed on to me has been filtered through my forty years of experience. My ideas would be considered way to the left of center, although I don't think that terminology has much meaning now. I have opinions about everything, which I freely express, but the most political thing I do is vote. I have been a card-carrying ACLU member, a supporter of Greenpeace and of my local public television station. I have always been a registered Democrat, but when voting over these many years I have often felt like a lemming going to the sea.

The most important thing to me is my family, which in addition to my parents includes my husband and our son, born in 1989. My husband and I are both physicians, board certified in family practice. I face some of the same challenges my parents did at my age, but I could never have their courage, commitment, strength, and belief, which keep them fighting to make things at least a little better. I do not believe that I can change the world.

As I look back, I think that after leaving the Party my parents split the world up into small pieces that they could try to improve. My mother worked with individual children and their families for ten years, then became executive director of her agency, piloting it through a transition to serving a broad multiethnic group of children all over Los Angeles. After retiring, she helped found and then chaired the Los Angeles Roundtable for Children, which brought together top public and private leaders to assess and make recommendations to improve the welfare of the children of Los Angeles County. My father eventually finished his college education, long before interrupted by the Depression, and spent time with his beloved violin. He became an activist again, as an advocate for senior citizens and an expert on Social Security and Medicare. He has been a member of the California Commission on Aging and a presidential appointee to the White House Conference on Aging. I am exceptionally proud of my parents. I wish everyone would understand what people like them have done for our country.

As I started to write about these memories I received a personal invitation to join the Republican Presidential Roundtable, a select group of four hundred dedicated to promoting Republican candidates and regaining the White House. Am I on the wrong list!

3
Claiming Our Heritage

Photo on preceding page: Young Communists march in New York City, probably during a May Day parade, late 1930s. Courtesy of the Tamiment Institute Library, New York University, John Albok Collection. Photograph by John Albok.

The Life and Times of an Elderly Red Diaper Baby

Ruth Pinkson

Ruth Pinkson was born in Harlem in 1913 in a fifth-floor walk-up, cold-water tenement flat. Involved in left-wing political and cultural activities since childhood, Pinkson has been a CIO organizer, an assistant to presidential candidate Henry Wallace and to physicist Leo Szilard, a Hollywood public relations copywriter, and a civil rights and peace activist. In this series of vignettes, Pinkson recounts her progression from youthful to adult activism.

Among my early memories is our family being plagued by what was then my personal bogeyman—strike or slack. When I heard my parents discussing this, I knew there would be little food, no rent money, and lots of problems.

My father, a needle trades worker and militant trade unionist, had fled czarist Russia with my mother and come to America to seek a better life. As teenagers in Russia, they had joined the Jewish Labor Bund. When they settled in Harlem, my mother became a suffragist and an admirer of Emma Goldman and Margaret Sanger. Both my parents became socialists. I well recall the heated discussions my parents, aunts, uncles, and their friends had about the Russian Revolution and the establishment of the Soviet Union. The confrontations between my parents on the socialist Left and my aunts and uncles on the socialist Right became increasingly acrimonious and passionate, and before we kids knew what was happening, our family split in two. I did not see my cousins, with whom I had been very close, for many years; this was quite traumatic for my brothers and me. All we knew was that my folks became *linke*—left-wing—and the rest of the family were *rechte*—right-wing.

While my friends and schoolmates went to vaudeville shows, my parents took us to Madison Square Garden to hear Eugene Debs, who had been imprisoned for his opposition to World War I. When Debs approached the podium, the crowd of twenty thousand rose to its feet as one and applauded, shouting and cheering endlessly. My brothers and I couldn't fully understand why all these people enthusiastically greeted a man who had just been released from prison. Yet the event made a deep impression on me. When I told some of my friends at school about it, they didn't know who Debs was or what I was talking about.

My parents were intensely interested in passing on their Jewish and working-class heritage to my brothers and me and in imbuing us with a social consciousness. They enrolled us in a *shule*, which aimed not only to acquaint children with Yiddish language and literature and Jewish history but to cultivate in us an affinity for the socialist ideals of our parents. We grew up bilingual in Yiddish and English.

Marching in New York City's annual May Day Parade with our friends and teachers was the highlight of our *shule* experience. For us, May 1st was a great event. My parents stayed home from work and kept us out of school so we could attend the huge demonstration. We arose early in the morning, dressed in special attire, and got into a spirit that none of the other holidays evoked.

When I was about five years old, we left Harlem for the Bronx, moving from one tenement to another in various neighborhoods. We finally ended up at the Workers Cooperative Colony, known as the Coops. Two huge red brick buildings covering two square blocks in the far reaches of the East Bronx, the Coops comprised a unique community. A couple of thousand people, including hundreds of children of all ages, lived there as one great family. The concerns of the Coops residents mirrored the concerns and ideals of my parents. Being part of this community gave us a sense of security, of oneness in our outlook and our activities. Everybody knew everybody else and had each other's support. Coops residents created cultural and sports centers within the houses; a huge library that featured symposia, lectures, and book reviews; and an auditorium for tenants' meetings, concerts, choral groups, and celebrations.

Internally a self-sustaining community, the Coops functioned also as the heart of neighborhood rent strikes and demonstrations. We were involved in all the events and issues of the day, from freeing the Scottsboro Boys and Tom Mooney to helping organize the neighborhood into tenants' unions. How well I remember our battles led by the Unemployed Councils during the Depression to put back the furniture of evicted families in the blocks surrounding the Coops. These struggles of the Unemployed Councils were a training ground for those of us who later became trade union organizers for the AFL-CIO.

During World War II, my young brother, a flight officer based in England, was missing in action for almost a year. When we finally learned that he had been killed in action, almost all the Coopniks helped to sustain our family. Hundreds of people came to his memorial, filling the large meeting hall and spilling out into the corridors and street.

During the Great Depression, no one else in our family could find work, and I became the breadwinner. After graduating from high school, I relinquished a music scholarship to work as a secretary and attend City College at night. As soon as I got my first job, my father informed me that I had to join the union in my field. I looked up the Office Workers Union and became a member. No sooner did you open your mouth at a meeting than you became an officer of the union. Growing up as a red diaper baby had an impact on my readiness to speak up at union meetings. My experiences as a child of progressives and trade unionists prepared me to become a committed trade unionist.

Before I knew it, I was editor of the *Office Worker* and on the organizing committee that conducted one of New York City's first big white-collar strikes, at Ohrbach's and Klein's. Thus started my career as a union organizer. Along with this came my involvement with our justice system, when I, among many hundreds, was arrested and spent time in jail for union activities.

When the United Office and Professional Workers of America was formed and granted a charter by the CIO in 1937, women rose to positions of leadership. I was sent out to become West Coast organizer. After almost two years, I was burned out. Returning to New York City for R & R, I met and started working for John Strachey, a noted British author and Labor member of Parliament, who had come to the U.S. to study the Roosevelt administration and write a book on the philosophy of the New Deal.

I married a veteran of the Spanish Civil War, who had served in the medical corps of the Abraham Lincoln Brigade. After the birth of our first child, I went to work as secretary and assistant to Henry Wallace when he became editor of the *New Republic.* I continued in that capacity through Wallace's 1948 Progressive Party campaign for president, remaining active in the union all that time. After my second child was born, I reluctantly left the employ of one of the finest persons I have ever worked with.

Following the death of my husband from a brain embolism, I was left with a nine-month-old baby girl and a not-quite-four-year-old son. I went to Los Angeles to join my parents. I found work with a Hollywood public relations agency, where, among other duties, I wrote spots for CARE and helped in Helen Gahagan Douglas's 1950 campaign for the Senate against Richard Nixon.

I enrolled my young son in a *shule* similar to the one I had attended as a youngster. Living with my radical parents and being part of the discussions

Do You Want

Equal rights and laws that fit the special needs of women?

Full equal rights for Negro women?

Full political and civil rights?

Full opportunity for active trade union membership?

Full opportunity for education and advancement?

Equal pay for equal work?

Full opportunity for work without discrimination because of sex or color?

Safeguarding of motherhood by a real system of maternity insurance?

An adequate system of social insurance?

Day nurseries, playgrounds, and better schools?

Decent housing?

Education, vocational training and jobs for the youth?

Abolition of child labor?

Comfort for yourself, your children, your family?

A world free from control by monopolies and trusts?

A world free from fascist rule?

A world free from unemployment, crises and war?

THEN THE PROGRAM OF THE
COMMUNIST PARTY IS YOUR PROGRAM

Join the Communist Party Today

UNITE IN ACTION AGAINST FASCISM
AND WAR

CP leaflet, about 1939. Courtesy of Linn Shapiro.

we had nightly at the dinner table about the events of the times, the beginnings of McCarthyism, my son was initiated into an atmosphere of politics, social action, and unionism, particularly when my dad went out on strike in the needle trades.

Eventually, I met and married my present husband, Ray Pinkson, who was also a lifetime activist for progressive social causes, and moved to a suburb of Washington, D.C. After the birth of another daughter, with three youngsters at home, I became a homemaker. My new career involved being a Boy Scout den mother, a Girl Scout Brownie leader, and a teacher at the Cooperative Jewish Children's School of Washington, D.C., which was fashioned along the lines of the *shules*.

Among our *shule* activities was an annual Brotherhood Program in collaboration with several Black and white churches. The older children and their parents picketed Woolworth's in Washington, D.C., to help integrate the store and collected money for civil rights struggles in the South. We also demonstrated at Fort Detrick in Maryland, the nation's major research center for biological warfare. Our kids not only became aware of the social issues of the times but became involved in them.

We got our baptism by fire in 1954 when my husband, who had been president of a progressive bookshop in Washington, D.C., testified as an "unfriendly" witness before HUAC. The story in the *Washington Post* went into great detail about the hearings, and we became persona non grata in our neighborhood and in our town. I was immediately removed as editor of our Democratic Party precinct newsletter and lost my position in the Girl Scouts. For two to three weeks we found four flat tires on our car every morning. A friend of my three-year-old daughter was yanked out of our backyard sandbox by her father, who shouted, "I told you not to play with that commie kid." My son, scheduled to go to a two-week neighborhood summer camp, became the target of attack by some parents who wanted to withdraw their sons if "that commie Pinkson kid" was going to attend. He went nevertheless, thanks to the principled position of the owner of the camp, who refused to be intimidated. A number of years later, we tried to integrate our neighborhood by selling our house to a Black family. Once again, we were shunned and castigated by neighbors and so-called friends. These were difficult times for our children as well as for us, but they learned firsthand what it meant to live by and act on your principles.

On November 1, 1961, I joined thousands of women from sixty cities who came out of their kitchens to march in front of the White House to "Stop the Arms Race, Not the Human Race." This event marked the birth of Women Strike for Peace (WSP). I was among the founders and remain active to this day, still working for peace and disarmament. For several years, I was coeditor of our local WSP newsletter, and my husband and children became adept at collating, stamping, and mailing. We participated in the peace movement as a family; our kids became veteran marchers. At one anti–Vietnam War demonstration in Washington, three generations of our family marched together: my Gold Star mother, my husband and myself, and our kids.

In early 1962 I started working with the eminent scientist and peace activist Dr. Leo Szilard. He had helped to draft Einstein's famous 1939 letter to President Franklin Roosevelt urging the president to start a program to produce a nuclear bomb and had helped to design the first atomic reactor. After Hiroshima, Szilard was appalled at the fearful implications of nuclear war and became a crusader for peace. He founded the Council to Abolish War, which became the Council for a Liveable World. I worked first as his secretary; as the Council grew rapidly, I became the office and personnel manager.

These are some vignettes of a life of activities and involvement to better the human condition, a tradition inherited from my parents and passed on to our children and to their children. Already our two older granddaughters have become a fourth generation of activists.

The grandchildren speak: "Our parents and grandparents filled our hearts and minds with a social conscience. Our participation with them in various demonstrations and actions for peace, for a healthy environment, etc., attending the annual meetings of the Abraham Lincoln Brigade in San Francisco, and similar events have given us an understanding of progressive history. We are proud of the heritage of our grandparents and our parents. For their teachings and inspiration, we are eternally grateful, and we hope to continue our family tradition of activism with our own children." Kimberly and Nicole Pinkson, aged twenty-four and twenty-one.

Why Didn't I Question?

Don Amter

Born in 1916, Don Amter grew up in a prominent CP family in which both parents were Party leaders. Daily life was organized around political activity; for the young Amter, "class struggle" was not a rhetorical phrase but a fact of life. Here, Amter confronts a question often asked of CP members: how could he not have known about the abuses of power in the Soviet Union? He candidly describes the process of moving from a certainty that communist ideology could explain all aspects of reality to a questioning of long-held beliefs.

After serving in the Army during World War II, Amter worked as an industrial designer and a college sociology professor. In recent years his activities have focused on the politics of environmental pollution.

I was in the army in northern Italy in the spring of 1945 when I learned about the letter that Jacques Duclos of the French Communist Party had sent to the American Communist Party decrying its direction under the leadership of General Secretary Earl Browder. As the culmination of an opening up process, Browder had changed the Party into the Communist Political Association. Eventually, in response to overseas criticism, the association was changed back into a party, Browder was expelled, and William Z. Foster regained leadership.

I thought that Browder had done a great job of modernizing and Americanizing the Party, which had grown tremendously in numbers and influence under his leadership. It had become much easier to approach people and talk to them about our ideas. I thrilled to his pronouncement that "Communism is Twentieth-Century Americanism." My personal opinion was that destroying all those achievements constituted a wrong turn. Yet I said nothing and did nothing. Looking back I do not feel that I could have done anything differently. To explain why requires exploring my personal history.

★

My parents, Israel and Sadie Van Veen Amter, were members of the Socialist Party when the Russian Revolution of 1917 exploded on the world scene. In 1919, together with thousands of others, they broke away from the Socialist Party to form the Communist Party.

That same year, Attorney General Palmer launched his "Red raids," unleashing his young bulldog assistant, J. Edgar Hoover. My father, one of the leaders of the fledgling party, had to go underground. I was left for several months with the family of Elizabeth Gurley Flynn, who would later become an important Party leader. I remember walking with my mother one night when she stopped to talk to a man. I looked up at them towering over me and realized with a start that the man behind a mustache was my father. Being only three, I had no idea what was going on.

In the years that followed, I was left with one family after another while my parents were busy. They believed that the revolution in Russia would soon be followed by one here, and so the frenetic activity. It was only when we went to Ohio when I was ten that our family came back together.

Around that time, my mother, who had dramatic and artistic talents, wrote a poem to me, the last line of which was, "I dedicate you to the revolution."

My mother and father had gotten married at the turn of the century. During a pre-wedding gathering at my socialist grandfather's house in Denver, Eugene V. Debs, the featured guest, put his hands on the shoulders of my parents-to-be and said, "My children, you are the hope of the future." Shortly thereafter my parents took off for Germany, he to study at the Leipzig Conservatory of Music and she to study at the Leipzig Conservatory of Art. When they returned to the States in 1913 my father soon gave up piano and composition (he had written an opera) and turned his total attention to the struggle for socialism. My mother, on the other hand, could never give up her artistic sensibilities. My earliest remembrance of what politics meant was watching her draw an illustration of a little American girl giving a loaf of bread to a little Russian girl. She explained its meaning to me. The drawing was done to support famine relief for the Soviet Union.

I grew up with the increasing understanding that what was happening in the newly born Soviet Union was, with variations, the model for the rest of the world. This understanding wasn't just academic. It shaped our lives.

When they returned from Germany my parents settled in a little colony, mostly anarchist, in Stelton, New Jersey. Feeling the need to break away from "bourgeois" ways of living, they became "free thinkers." They lived a Spartan lifestyle, became vegetarians and naturists. They did not take note of such "bourgeois" occasions as holidays or even birthdays and bought no toys for my sister and me.

My sister Nell, who was seven years older than I, was annoyed with having to take care of me. Perhaps because of the age difference, we had little in common. Nell turned out like our father in character and interests, including playing piano. I turned out more like my mother, with many disparate pursuits, especially art.

My father was sent to Ohio in 1926 to be the Party organizer. Early on I became involved. By eleven years old, I was selling the *Daily Worker* at the gates of giant factories such as Fisher Body. I accompanied my mother to southern Ohio, where she was organizing coal miners. I stayed with miners' families, including a Black family with a boy my age. I spent most of the time playing with him and felt at home there.

In Cleveland, where we lived, the Black population centered in the Central Avenue neighborhood. I remember going with my mother to a community center, where I looked around curiously while my mother engaged in "political talk." While she said nothing to me about it, I was vaguely aware that she was making contact with this section of Cleveland's population.

The following year there was a meeting of the League of Nations in Cleveland's largest central auditorium. The Party organized a group to disrupt the proceedings by calling for the admission of Soviet Russia. My mother had taken me up to a balcony seat when suddenly we heard someone shouting, "Admit Soviet Russia to the League!" My mother stood up and added her voice to the fray. People in adjoining seats shrunk away from us as if we were some kind of poisonous snakes. Police came and dragged us down the stairs and out of the hall, just in time to see my father held between two large policemen, his face covered with blood, being thrown into a police van.

I was very upset. Internally, I was in turmoil. But I was not surprised. After all, I knew we were in a "war," as I had begun to perceive it, and casualties were to be expected. I must have picked this attitude up from my parents' cues. We were, I realized, different; that awareness was always with me. I felt a constant anxiety that something bad could happen at any time. I feared that in school or in the neighborhood I might suddenly be unmasked as a "lousy commie," turning others against me.

So for me there were internal costs, anxieties, and fearfulness about the future, which shaped my behavior and modified my actions. My parents never overtly pressured me as to what was expected of me. The straight and narrow political path we trod together was pressure enough.

An incident that helped shape my attitudes stands out in my memory. As a kid, I was always making things, but I did not have the money to buy the tools

I needed. One day, with another boy my age, I went to the local Woolworth's five-and-dime store. I pocketed a couple of tools worth ten cents each. When we got home I showed them to my parents. There were no arguments, no recriminations, no punishment. My mother took me aside and told me that they certainly had no sympathy for a giant company like Woolworth. "But," she said, "think of what this would do to the important political work your father is doing if it came out publicly that his son was a thief!" That was all she had to say. I would never do anything to discredit my family and the whole movement. That lesson has been with me for the rest of my life.

By the time I was twelve, I had a general understanding of what our movement meant. I began to see that there was a "big picture" in which all things were interconnected and, therefore, I had to care, to be concerned. Poverty was an issue that affected us directly. It was all around us. One day while I was playing ball in the street, a pale, skinny man came out of a house and asked me if I would go to the corner store for him. I did so, and when I gave him the bag, he tried to give me a dime. I refused it. When he asked me why, I blurted out very undiplomatically, "Because you are too poor!" Honesty, not diplomacy, had been stressed in my family, as I found out on too many other painful occasions!

In 1928 growing unemployment signaled the coming economic crash. The Party organized a mass meeting, and demonstrations were held in Cleveland's Public Square. At the age of twelve, I painted my first posters and was arrested for the first time as I carried a poster around the square. My mother was arrested because, with her flair for the dramatic, she grabbed an unemployed man, took him up on the speakers' platform, and offered to sell him to any employer for nothing but food. She was charged with selling a person under an obscure anti-slaving act.

Those were rough times economically. The Party was just about broke, and so was my family. My sister Nell was told she would have to stop school and piano lessons, both of which she loved, and go to work in a factory. My parents moved me out of academic schoolwork and into industrial shop courses so I would be able to go to work early, which I soon did. My parents had a scornful attitude toward "bourgeois" education, an attitude I carried with me until I left the Party. I went to college when I was in my forties and found that, yes, my informal education was in some ways superior but also very narrow and limiting because it excluded the ideas of some of history's greatest minds. (In fact, some of our best leaders in the Party had formal educations. But this was always played down.)

We returned to New York, where my father became national secretary of the Unemployed Councils. Now the economic crash was felt with a vengeance. On March 6, 1930, the Unemployed Councils held a huge demonstration in Union Square. My father, Robert Minor, William Z. Foster, and Harry Raymond were beaten up and thrown into jail.

These experiences reinforced the ideas I grew up with and confirmed that our direction was valid. We were fighting to help ourselves, the poor, and all the oppressed people the world over. I was surrounded by an ideological framework that explained all. The people we knew, the conversations we had, the activities we participated in wove a total approach to life, a philosophy and a practice that constantly reinforced our beliefs.

I had great faith in my parents. They were adults; I was a child. What they knew, what they did, what the Party (and by extension the worldwide communist movement) did, the struggles of colonial peoples provided a seamless web of justification for all they and I believed. For me, my parents were superior beings. I was very proud of them.

For every question, there was always an answer and an argument that seemed to prove the correctness of our movement and its politics. It was a comforting feeling to know that we were always right! It also gave me a feeling of superiority. So what if the rest of society shunned and maligned us? We knew that we were right, that history would go our way, and that we would win out in the end!

Surrounded by our culture, our own little world, we formed a sub-society, particularly in New York, with its many left-wing organizations, art and music groups, unions, local clubs and centers, and a thousand personal connections. It occurred to me with a shock one day that I could go from group to group and never come in contact with the "ordinary" citizens of New York! But our world was rich in meaning, commitment, and positive works.

If there was something I did not understand, at least my parents did. It followed that I would accept as correct what they said and did. All this fit with the logic of the Soviet Union as the model for the future; I thought Soviet-style communism would solve all problems. My red diaper baby status gave me a long-range perspective from which to view political ideas that some others, thrown into the hot crucible of immediate struggles, could not so easily achieve.

As I got older, I began to see little things that bothered me. I was troubled by our attitude toward people who disagreed with us politically. It seemed that there was no such thing as an honest political difference. Persons who differed from us were attacked ferociously and mercilessly. We were told that Trotskyists were murderers and wreckers and enemies of the revolution. They were so vilified that I came to believe that they practically had horns! Once Maurice, a member of my Young Communist League club, came into a meeting with a pamphlet handed to him in the street. It turned out to be a "Trotsky-ite" (that's what we called them) publication. Club leaders told Maurice that he could not read the pamphlet. He demurred, the leaders held a trial, and he was expelled. I felt it was wrong, but I said nothing. Why?

I thought that the Party leaders knew more than I did. (They certainly did.) I thought that maybe the "Trotskyites" were wreckers and enemies in ways I could not see because I did not have the facts with which to fill in the whole picture. After all, the only "facts" I knew came from Party literature and hundreds of meetings and conversations. Firsthand experience for most of us was limited to the small corner in which we lived and labored. I knew the Trotsky-ists opposed many of our activities. As for what they did in the Soviet Union and elsewhere, I had to take the word of the Party leaders and of the printed statements. Much later it occurred to me that our leaders, who told us what the Trotskyists wrote and said, must have read their literature; otherwise how could they quote and refute them?

Another area that troubled me was how the Party conducted its fight against racism, which we called white chauvinism. The Party had done yeoman service in raising this issue, working for equality. The slogan was "Black and White—Unite and Fight!" In the early '30s the Party took up the defense of the Scottsboro Boys. Ruby Bates, one of the young women who the Southern bigots had hoped would testify against the Scottsboro defendants, refused to do so. She was brought north to speak for the defense committee and spent some time at our house. But during the early 1950s the legitimate fight against racism had a tendency to turn into a witch-hunt against our own people. White comrades had to be very careful because an inadvertent act or statement could be construed as racist. You could be hauled before an investigating commission and be disciplined or expelled.

Because I was an Amter, a name much revered in the Party, I had a little more maneuvering space than some. But I was not immune from attacks. I had been teaching at the Jefferson School of Social Science, set up by the Party as the successor to the old Workers' School. I was also organizing classes for our local Party group, and I was going to handle one on the "Negro Question" myself. A young white comrade who was married to Jesús Colon, a Puerto Rican writer for the *Daily Worker,* exclaimed that I—a white person—could not teach such a class. Only a Black person could understand the "Question."

When the news broke to the world in 1956 that Khrushchev had exposed what we came to know as the crimes of Stalinism, the young students in one of my classes asked me what I thought. I said that the news was shocking and I was not in a position to make any statement. One student suggested that we call in Doxey Wilkerson, one of the school's directors, to talk about the event.

I said that I doubted he knew any more about the new situation than I did. The students wanted to bring me up on charges of chauvinism because I said that Wilkerson, a Black man, didn't know any more about a subject than I did! Later Doxey and I had a good laugh about it. But it had become evident that the anti–white chauvinism campaign had, in fact, gone overboard. The top leadership of the Party had to call a halt, saying that the fight against racism was better conducted in practical struggles to fight discrimination in the workplace and the community rather than by examining each other with a microscope.

For me personally this was very dangerous territory. I saw what happened to individuals who crossed the line and could be humiliated or expelled. Expulsion would be the ultimate punishment. I'd feel like a man without a country. My family, my friends, my political home, my philosophy and activities would all be gone. I trod fearfully; a mistake could destroy all that I had lived for. I had seen families torn apart by sharp political differences.

Stalin died on March 5, 1953. In the fall of 1953 my father died of Parkinson's disease. They were the two most important men in my life, and I experienced their loss as extremely painful. In 1956 the Khrushchev revelations burst on us like a bomb, exposing the crimes that we had spent a life denying as capitalist propaganda or the work of disgruntled opportunists. Suddenly we were being told that it was all true. It was a long time before I could bring myself to actually read the Khrushchev report. Just to follow the stories in the news was enough to make me sick at heart. Were all our leaders, even my parents, complicit in these crimes? No, I could not believe that my parents knew. I saw my parents as completely honest, committed, self-sacrificing, working hard for a better future they believed was coming.

My shock was deep and total, my mind numbed and pained. It was impossible for me to think about these revelations clearly for a long time. How could all this have taken place without our knowing it? Did any of our people know the truth? If our leaders didn't know, did they have the responsibility to find out the facts? Did this mean that all we believed in was a lie? I realized that sooner or later I and all of our comrades would have to sift through everything we knew and believed in to understand exactly what had happened.

I began to be critical of what we were doing politically. Previously, I had not been able to criticize, believing that maybe the Party had been wrong on some things but those would be corrected in time. Marx had said that the new society would be created out of the old, that the new would have many of the characteristics of the old—warts and all. I knew that my parents had some minor differences with Party policy but believed changes would take place eventually. For instance, they felt Browder's direction had been mostly a good one and were a little disturbed with the turn back to Party from Association and all this implied for our political work. But democratic centralism was interpreted to mean that while you might have differences, you didn't discuss them because that could be seen as opposing the party line, and that in turn could be construed as factionalism—grounds for expulsion.

After the Khrushchev report the American Party prepared for its 1957 national convention. John Gates, a Spanish Civil War veteran and editor of the *Daily Worker,* threw the paper's pages open to critical viewpoints, which had never been done before. It produced a torrent of new ideas and debate. The preconvention discussion bulletin printed my statement of eight basic criticisms of our past policies and practices, which I had raised in local discussions. Comrades were becoming critical and thinking independently for the first time. In the convention the Gates faction won a majority of the delegates, but because of the changing attitude, many voted with their feet and left the Party altogether. The Foster faction inherited the splinter of the once sizeable Party.

I left the Party after the turmoil and debacle of the convention. Now I started to question everything, as Marx had once instructed us. I decided to go to college so that I could become a teacher. I felt that the Marxist method of analysis was a good basic tool for explaining the underlying dynamics of political and social life. Indeed, I found out that the prevailing philosophies left a lot to be desired. After getting my B.A. and M.A., I taught in many of the New York City colleges while going on for my Ph.D. in sociology. In my classes, I never privileged my ideas of socialism, but I did encourage students to analyze social structures and social relations in a way that would give them some real understanding of underlying causes and dynamics. I enjoyed teaching. My greatest reward would come when students would suddenly see a connection or a formerly hidden explanation and their eyes would light up at the revelation.

In the 1970s, I joined a group called Viewpoints that was influenced by Eurocommunism. In 1980, when the group disbanded, I joined the newly formed Democratic Socialists of America. Now I am also a member of the Committees of Correspondence, a group made up predominately of former members of the Communist Party, which aims to find new directions for the socialist project.

In a way I feel like Adam after he was expelled from the garden of Eden. The sense of loss is always with me. I have a strong sense of shame at the lies, the bloody past, the terrible acts done in our name. My only excuse is that I really did not know. And that I did what I thought was right. I have to be a little more humble in view of our terrible blunders.

I feel as my friend Al Prago, a Spanish Civil War veteran and educator, once said to me: "What I am left with is the Marxist way of analyzing society." But the world is changing, and we will have to change with it or be left on the sidelines. My activities these days are directed toward the ecological. This is not an attempt to run away from politics but to make evident the important links between the two. I have joined a number of environmental organizations, and I write and speak on this subject. My goal is to make whatever small contribution I can. And I still believe that the reorganization of society is the only hope.

Three Generations of Activists

Ethel Panken

Ethel Panken, born in Philadelphia in 1917, graduated from college with a B.A. in education and taught in an elementary school before marrying. She and her husband raised three children in a suburb of New York City. Panken has been active in the Women's International League for Peace and Freedom (WILPF) and since the mid-1970s has served as one of WILPF's representatives at the United Nations.

Strong female role models—mothers, aunts, grandmothers, and family friends—have played an important role in the lives of many red diaper babies. Decades before the concept of supermom gained currency, Panken's mother raised children, managed a household, and found fulfillment in a job outside the home while actively participating in left-wing politics. Despite her mother's occasional arrests, Panken describes a relatively untroubled childhood. As an adult she, too, has combined parenting with employment and activism. Panken's children have taken different political paths, not unusual in left-wing families.

My parents were Jewish immigrants who left their homelands because of anti-Semitism. My father was born in Odessa, Russia, in 1888, and my mother in Kremnitz, Poland, in 1896. Both arrived in the U.S. in 1910, although my father first stopped in Liverpool, England, where he stayed a few years to study cabinetmaking.

My parents met in Philadelphia at night school, where they were learning English. Within a few years they were married. Both joined the Socialist Party but left it to join the Communist Party, which they believed to be the true Marxist party. For the rest of their lives they remained supporters of the Communist Party and the Soviet Union.

We lived in a middle-class neighborhood. During the Depression, many poor people, usually white and male, went door-to-door asking for handouts. As each person appeared, my mother would invite him in, ask him to wash his hands, and then give him breakfast. At the same time, she would lecture him on the advantages of socialism over capitalism.

I was a teenager during the Depression, and although I knew that my mother was different from other mothers, I had great respect for her. I felt that her life was more meaningful than the lives of my friends' mothers, who spent their time playing cards and shopping. There were mornings when my mother was up at 5:00 A.M. to help an evicted family move back into their house. She was a member of the Unemployed Council, participated in hunger marches, and was active in the campaign for Social Security. She also supported the campaign for the Scottsboro Boys.

When I was about ten years old, I was hospitalized for typhoid fever. My mother and her friend visited me on the day Sacco and Vanzetti were executed. Both women had been actively involved in the case and cried most of the day. It was a sad day for me also, since I knew they were innocent of the crime.

Politics was the main subject in our house. I remember many nights when my parents' socialist friends visited and the yelling and screaming kept me awake. My father was considered a brilliant Marxist, and I used to joke that he rarely talked to me until I was old enough to understand Marxism. Then there were always political discussions with my brother and me and our friends.

My mother did not believe in disrupting the lives of her children, so we were rarely taken to demonstrations or meetings when we were young. However, as teenagers, we did attend special events. I particularly remember a big meeting for Earl Browder, and we participated in annual May Day celebrations.

Because we lived in a big house, my mother often invited visitors to stay with us. The most colorful person was Aunt Molly Jackson, who was a miner's wife. She sat in a rocking chair all day, smoked her corncob pipe, and sang folk songs.

When I was thirteen years old and my brother fifteen, my mother felt we could take care of ourselves and she could again be a working woman. She returned to her former job as a seamstress in a men's shirt factory. These were the happiest years in her life, working side by side with other women, active in the ILGWU, and financially independent. She gave us chores to do, but she still had the main responsibility in running the house.

Several times my mother was arrested but not charged because the assistant district attorney's father was a business friend of my father. Both men had woodworking factories, and my father often used his friend's facilities. I no longer remember why my mother was arrested, but I do recall that one such incident occurred on the day of my graduation from elementary school. That was quite traumatic for me, but luckily my favorite aunt attended in my mother's place. After graduation, we all went to the jail, and she was released. Fortunately for me, we had neighborhood friends who were also radicals, so I did not have to be ashamed of my mother being arrested.

Across the street from us lived the head of the local American Legion. One day he came to our house to tell my mother that he had just been visited by the FBI for information about her. He said he had been pleased to tell them she was a wonderful person, a very good neighbor, and helpful in the community. We were shocked to hear that his politics did not interfere in his assessment of my mother; we never knew he felt that way.

Many years later, after I was married, we moved from the city to the suburbs. There I became active in peace and social justice organizations. As a member of the local civil rights group, I was chosen to announce at a public meeting that we were calling for open housing in our town. The community was not at all receptive to this!

Soon after this event, I was napping when my seven-year-old daughter awakened me and said, "There are two robbers outside who want to talk to you." I opened the door and there stood two men wearing hats—FBI, of course! Since I refused to talk with them I never knew exactly what they wanted. My daughter was not able to articulate why she thought they were robbers.

My mother died in 1960 at the age of sixty-four. Of my three children, it was the oldest daughter who chose to follow the legacy left by her grandmother. In college, she joined the anti–Vietnam War movement; she then devoted many years to working for the elimination of racism and for social justice. We are very fortunate to have had such a remarkable mother and grandmother as our model.

A Child of the Old, Old Left

Amy Swerdlow

From the ages of four to eighteen, Amy Swerdlow lived in the Workers Cooperative Colony in the Bronx except for the two years she and her parents spent at the Jewish communist camp Nitgedaiget, which her father managed. Swerdlow was a Young Pioneer by family choice and on her own became an active member of the American Student Union and later a founder of Women Strike for Peace. In 1994 she retired as professor emerita from Sarah Lawrence College, where she taught U.S. history and directed the Women's Studies Program. Swerdlow is the author of *Women Strike for Peace: Traditional Motherhood and Radical Politics in the 1960s* (University of Chicago Press, 1994).

British Marxist feminist Sheila Rowbotham recalls that the lives of kings and queens made up her childhood view of history. For most American children of my generation it was the Boston Tea Party, George Washington and the cherry tree, as well as the ride of Paul Revere. But not for me. For me, it was the story of *Our Lenin*, my favorite childhood book, which had a red cover. I mourned the sad fate of the Paris Commune, the tragedy of the Triangle Fire, the Haymarket martyrs, and Joe Hill. I celebrated socialism in one country. That was my historical heritage. Other mothers sang "Lullaby and good night" to their kids; my mother sang "The worker's flag is deepest red, It shrouded oft our martyred dead," and she wiped her eyes as she sang.

I was born into a doctrinaire Communist Party family of the 1920s. At least my father was doctrinaire; my mother was skeptical, more a utopian anarchist than communist. In the 1930s, as leading members of the CP would enter our apartment for meetings, be they Earl Browder, the head of the Party, or Pop Mindell, the director of Party training schools, my mother would ask, "Und vemen hut er geshusen?" which meant, whom did he shoot? That cynical question harked back to her romantic memories of Russia in 1905 and to her anarchist leanings. She preferred brave utopian revolutionaries to party bureaucrats.

A favorite childhood story for me was how my mother had led a strike in the shop where she worked as a waistmaker. As she told it, she had pulled the power, cut off the electricity, stopped the machines—just like Norma Rae (how I cried when I saw that scene in the movie)—and called on everybody to leave the premises. As she took first place descending the dark stairway, she was hit on the head by a scab—a dreaded word in my world—carrying a lady's handbag filled with lead. She attributed her constant headaches to this assault. It was not until Katherine Hepburn became a famous movie star that my mother told me of marching in suffrage parades in Hartford led by Katherine Hepburn Senior. Feminism and suffrage were not my mother's causes during the Depression and the rise of fascism.

My parents did not marry legally until I was seventeen. They explained that they refused marriage as a protest against the bourgeois state but finally had to marry during World War II because my mother became an enemy alien when the Germans captured the part of Russia she came from. She would have been forced to register with the government, and that was even worse than legal marriage. So she reluctantly agreed to accept citizenship through my father. U.S. citizenship was something my mother had never sought, as she was loyal only to the international working class.

I can tell dozens of stories about events in my childhood that marked me as different, a political child. When only ten or maybe twelve I was already a member of the Supreme Soviet . . . at Camp Kinderland, where for one week of a memorable summer I earned the privilege of standing at attention, raising the red flag, saluting, and pledging my loyalty to the cause of the working class in its struggle for freedom. From the age of six, I would have to stand up in class at my parents' behest and tell the teacher that I would be out of school on May Day because it was a workers' holiday. The teacher would be irritated, and the other children, except those who came from families like mine, would be bored. I remember the truant officer coming each May Day and my father dramatically expelling him from the apartment, shouting indignantly, "Take me to court! This is a holiday as sacred to workers as Christmas and Easter." In the eighth grade my stomach churned and I thought I would faint as I had to stand up on the auditorium stage and refuse a bronze medal for coming in third in a potato race with the statement "I cannot accept a medal from William Randolph Hearst." Fortunately there were a few other children also refusing, some with more politically profound statements—and gold medals to boot.

Amy Swerdlow at about age six, wearing her "best attire," a Russian peasant blouse and skirt. Courtesy of Amy Swerdlow.

At an early age I heard my parents argue about Leon Trotsky and about Jay Lovestone and Ben Gitlow, two dissidents who were expelled from the CP. There were endless discussions of the various factions and fractions to which my father belonged or that he hated. I am told that when I was six or seven, I would ask my mother, "Did Daddy go to a faction or fraction meeting?"

My father indoctrinated me into the theory of surplus value when I was six years old. He used a child's primer translated from the Russian, which was about Mr. Knox, Mr. Box, and Mr. Fox, all fat-bellied capitalists with leering faces similar to those in William Gropper's painting of the Senate. Knox and

Box and Fox employed workers to make hats, but these bad men paid only for part of the commodity the workers produced. The other part they kept for themselves; that part, I was informed, was surplus value. Because the workers were only paid for a portion of the commodity they produced, they never had enough money to buy it back. This led to overproduction (never called underconsumption), bare heads, and the depression that my father and all the Jewish communists I knew seemed to call the "crizzis."

As a child of the '30s I was convinced that capitalism was bad. I lived the Depression among unemployed garment workers in a housing development called the Coops, short for the Workers Cooperative Colony, and we all suffered. The cooperative colony lost its building after the stock market crash of 1929, my father was blacklisted by his union for communist activities, and we were threatened with eviction. My parents were in constant conflict with each other, a situation my father attributed to the miseries of the capitalist system. He never tired of explaining to me that under socialism there were no such things as unemployment, injustice, or deprivation—thus, I concluded, no fighting parents.

My father's vision of the Soviet Union was so ecstatic and utopian that I was anxious to see it. When he explained to me that the world revolved around its axis every twenty-four hours, I suspected that we who were in the U.S. during the day would be where Russia was at night. For months I tried to wake up in the middle of the night to see the Soviet Union, but I constantly overslept. When I finally made it and ran to my window, all I could see was the corner of Allerton Avenue and Bronx Park East on which a grim, gray building, the Hebrew Home for the Incurables, still stood.

As a child, I often resented my father's stern political lectures because I experienced them as dismissive of my feelings and needs, but I never questioned his fanatical hatred of capitalism and his belief in a proletarian utopia. His vision of a socialist world without class conflict or war promised the harmony I yearned for within my own home. When I noticed discrepancies between the Party line and what I thought of as real life, or that my father talked about the working class incessantly while he was not a laborer but a union official and later a Party functionary, I was afraid to dig deeply because he would become indignant and warn that any deviation from loyalty to the dictatorship of the proletariat, which meant the U.S.S.R., would sink me into the dangerous degradation of Trotskyism. Eventually, in the late 1950s, my father became disillusioned with the Soviet Union and denounced it as vociferously as he had praised it, but he never gave up his Marxism or his hatred of capitalism.

Much later, when my father was close to his death, he told my son, his grandson, that there was only one thing he wanted him to remember, that the history of civilization was the history of class struggle. I had heard that pronouncement all my life. Accepting that assumption, there was little reason for me to study history, especially as it was taught in high school. Instead I turned to Popular Front politics. I believed passionately in the Loyalist cause in Spain. Trembling with shyness, I would stand in subway cars at the age of fourteen pleading for contributions to medical aid for Republican Spain. Even while striking for peace in high school, I admired and supported the young men who joined the Lincoln Brigade to fight with guns for the Republican cause in Spain.

At fifteen, I picketed at dawn on 42nd Street in support of "collective security" as the lights atop the *New York Times* building flashed the news that Neville Chamberlain had signed the Munich pact. I wept because I understood that fascism and war had prevailed. I believed in "collective security," something the Soviet Union and my father seemed to support, which I interpreted as the military cooperation of the good guys to isolate and defeat the bad. I had no trouble including the Soviet Union among the good people and was not put off by the influence of the young communists in the leadership of the American Student Union (ASU). In fact, I admired them. When the ASU decided to drop the Oxford Oath in support of the Loyalist cause in Spain, I concurred.

In 1940 I served on the ASU staff as national high school secretary. We campaigned actively against the Selective Training and Service Act of 1940 and continued through 1941 to oppose American involvement in what we were told was a phony war. Eileen Eagan, in her book *Class, Culture, and the Classroom: The Student Peace Movement of the 1930s*, reports that after the Germans invaded the Soviet Union, the ASU's "Yanks Are Not Coming" poster was put aside for "All Out Aid to the Allies." I don't remember that, but I know I was demoralized when the ASU voted to disband itself at its annual conference in December 1941 after the Japanese attack on Pearl Harbor. I was in a painful muddle. I wanted desperately to see Germany and Japan defeated but at the same time felt that I was betraying my antimilitarist principles.

By the late 1940s and through the 1950s I lost all interest in politics, in part because I could not express my deepening distrust of Soviet domestic and foreign policies for fear it would place me on the side of the red-baiters and cold warriors who seemed determined to overturn progressive public policy gains and repress all radical dissent.

In 1961 I was totally alienated from politics, scornful of Cold War liberalism, McCarthyism, and the Old Left. I was a suburban housewife who had gone back to school to take an M.A. in art history. But I was alarmed by the Berlin Wall crisis, the threat of radioactive fallout in my children's milk, and inspired by the Civil Rights Movement, Bertrand Russell, and the antinuclear Aldermarston marchers in London. On November 1, I responded to a call transmitted by a neighbor in Great Neck, Long Island, to join a demonstration at the United Nations to protest both Soviet and U.S. nuclear policies. There, and later in Washington, I met a group of nonideological, pragmatic, and politically creative women who were the brightest and bravest I had ever known. For the first time I began to work in a separatist women's movement, where my voice and feelings were heard. I found Women Strike for Peace (WSP) to be a magnificent outlet for my indignation at doctrinaire theorists out of touch with life. I had already thought the unthinkable, that the survival of the planet was as important as class struggle. Now I could act on that conviction.

My years working and marching with WSP—writing fliers, policy statements, and press releases; editing its national publication; demonstrating; chaining myself to the White House fence; traveling to Hanoi in the midst of the war in Vietnam and to Cuba, East Berlin, the Soviet Union—were years of challenge, excitement, and growth.

My rising feminist consciousness finally convinced me that I was too ignorant of historical process to go on as a political activist. My father had been wrong, I concluded triumphantly. The superstructure had a life independent of the base. There was more than class struggle; there was gender struggle. As well as production, there was reproduction. I began to feel my ignorance of women's history or of any understanding of why women were politically disempowered forty years after suffrage.

One incident still haunts me. When WSP went to Geneva in 1962 to lobby the disarmament conference, I was in charge of arrangements. I contacted the Women's International League for Peace and Freedom (WILPF) office in Geneva for logistical information and advice. The office was run by a formidable older woman, Gertrude Baehr. She was difficult and cranky—a cold warrior, it seemed to me, because she kept inquiring about the political credentials of the WSP leadership, meaning were there any communists in the movement. I gave her short shrift and refused to take her advice, which I saw as outdated and conservative, only to learn later that she had played an important role at the International Conference of Women at The Hague in 1915 and was the person who had called upon Jane Addams and WILPF to oppose the Versailles Treaty's treatment of Germany. Gertrude Baehr was an international pacifist and feminist of distinction, and I did not know enough to ask her to address the women of WSP, who were latecomers to the Geneva disarmament scene and knew nothing of their feminist pacifist foremothers.

In the late 1960s, as WSP shuttled from one peace demonstration to another and as I traveled all over the world on peace missions to Sweden, Cuba,

Hanoi like a visiting firefighter, I began to realize that I was not quite grasping where the fire was located. In addition, I thought back to the fact that my parents spoke of Alice Paul and Carrie Chapman Catt with disdain while they loved Ella Reeve Bloor and admired Elizabeth Gurley Flynn, both CP "holies." History had never attracted me as a field of study. I hated the way my father debunked the grand events of the past from a Marxist point of view. Moses did not part the waters, I was informed; he just knew the tides better than the Egyptians. The Civil War was not fought to free the slaves but was really a competition between northern capitalism and the slavocracy for economic power. I hated that explanation, as I wanted some American heroes of my own and I loved Honest Abe. My father had a materialist class-conscious answer for everything, but in those answers I had always found my feelings and my yearnings demolished.

Most radicals who come to the study of history come desiring to find patterns and evolve theories. I came looking for anomaly and ambiguity. I had had enough of my father's version of theory. I wanted to flesh out the details, to understand people's everyday lives in addition to strikes and revolutions. I still believed in class struggle, but I wanted to understand it in nondogmatic reality. I wanted to learn my own roots as a radical woman, to find my own and my mother's foremothers, to understand the intersection of gender and class, a phrase that has since become a cliché.

I decided in 1972 to enter a graduate program in women's history. I thought I just wanted to illuminate the dark corners of my brain by getting a handle on historical process, social interaction, and gender ideology. In my second year I was hired to teach a course at Sarah Lawrence called "Women Organizing Women." I found myself challenged by students who were even more nontraditional than I was, more radical and feminist. We struggled together to determine what was historically significant for them and for me, and in the process I found that I loved the challenge of teaching. I also found that once a political activist, always an agitator and proselytizer. Everything I learned I immediately rushed back to tell my sisters in the peace movement. I had them reading Eleanor Flexner's *Century of Struggle* and discussing Lucretia Mott, Julia Ward Howe, Jane Addams, and Emily Balch, women none of us had ever heard of in our active days in WSP.

While I was working on my master's essay on the New York City Ladies' Anti-Slavery Societies, my father, then in his eighties, questioned me in detail. I told him about the evangelical moral reformers whose agenda formed the basis for abolitionist politics. He then asked the inevitable: "How did they fit into the class struggle?" I became apoplectic and retorted indignantly that I was not writing for the *Daily Worker*. But his question stuck with me. Of course those women were responding to class tensions in Jacksonian America. In fact, it was their fear of the immigrant laboring poor and of class conflict that led them to benevolent moral reform. They wanted to remake all New Yorkers in their own pious, hierarchical image. To put it simply, slavery collided with the bourgeois Protestant ethic. I then wrote a paper entitled "Anti-Slavery's Conservative Sisters," which has been recognized as one of the first histories of female abolitionism to deal with class issues. That recognition, I say humbly, should go to my father.

In fact, I owe much to both my parents' political visions. The utopian element in my communist upbringing gave me my sense of fair play and my belief in human possibility. My father's ideological rigidity, against which I had to rebel to survive with brain and ego intact, gave me the courage to think critically and, I hope, with some flexibility about social issues and the movements for social transformation in which I have participated. My parents' pride in their outsider status as Jewish communist bohemians in WASP bourgeois America, their interest in the arts and literature, their disdain for material profit—sometimes carried to extremes that made us poor and me uncomfortable—gave me the sense that I was entitled to be different, even from them. Their legacy of struggle and commitment to a world of justice, peace, and joy inspires me to "keep on keeping on" even in bad times such as these, and it is something that I pass on to my children and grandchildren with pride and hope.

Touch Red

Dick Levins

Dick Levins, born in 1930, grew up in Brooklyn, New York. He has been
active in the radical science, Puerto Rican independence, Latin American
solidarity, organic agriculture, and environmental movements. A Marxist
ecologist, he teaches at Harvard University and the New York Marxist
School.

Levins describes a childhood in which every aspect of life was analyzed
from a left-wing political perspective and being outside the mainstream was
viewed as both desirable and inevitable. Raised to see the world in terms of
a clash between those who understood the truth embodied in Marxist dialectics and others who were less enlightened, Levins continues to view a
commitment to revolutionary change as a "permanent way of life."

My earliest memory is of the acquittal of Dimitrov at the end of the Reich-
stag Trial in 1933. They tell me I asked, "What about Torgler [another de-
fendant]?" I was three at the time.

I grew up saturated with political news and discussions. Around then my
Uncle Lou taught me to recite the preface to the *Communist Manifesto* from
memory in order to trot me out, snap his fingers, and have me amaze his friend
Toop with "A specter is haunting Europe . . ."

We were a Red household, immersed in the political and cultural life of the
Left. Being Red defined the environment within which we moved, the challenges to our thinking, the agenda for thought and feeling.

It began over a hundred years ago when Dukirova, the *rebbetzin* in Kremenchug, Ukraine, broke with the Jewish religion over sexism. She was a far better biblical scholar than her husband but was not allowed to take on students
or preach. She complained that the rules of orthodoxy, from shaven heads to
segregated seating, were stacked against women. Told it was the word of God,

she responded, "Your God is a man!" and gave up religion intellectually and emotionally.

The *rebbetzin*'s granddaughter was my maternal grandmother, Leah Sackman. She was at the fringes of the socialist movement in her farming community near Elizavetagrad and participated in the three-cornered debates between Zionists, socialists, and orthodox believers about the appropriate way of life for Jews: Can we work with Russians and Ukrainians and even Cossacks? Should we use Hebrew or Yiddish? Is our struggle here or in Palestine?

Leah and my grandfather came to America because he was threatened with conscription during the Russo-Japanese War. Unwilling to fight for the czar, he left first, later sending for Leah and my mother. In America, Leah was an organizer of unemployed women and was active in the big garment district strike in the 1930s. At that time, in one of his flips and flops across the border between skilled worker and petty entrepreneur, my grandfather was a small subcontractor in the garment industry. I remember my grandmother coming home from canvassing unemployed women with stories of her adventures. Once, she was leafleting an apartment house and was greeted with hostility by a woman on the first floor. But that same woman stopped her on the way downstairs, having read the leaflet, wanting to talk about the ideas. She often equipped me with *pishkes*, collection cans to raise funds for various good causes, and I could report back my own adventures. It was from her that I got the notion that the struggle was a permanent way of life and that maybe my grandchildren would live to see the better world we fought for. Even in the Sixties I never expected an imminent revolution or wondered about my own role in it, and our defeats did not lead me to despair.

My grandmother told me of listening to Emma Goldman on the Lower East Side. She had frequented Margaret Sanger's first family planning clinic, and her heroines were Ella Reeve "Mother" Bloor, Rosa Luxemburg, and Rose Schneiderman.

She did not approve of pets. She was offended by the care lavished on dogs and cats while starving people were looked on with indifference by the affluent. In practice this meant that all the stray cats that were in residence in our home were defined as transients "until the winter is over."

Because of my grandfather's anger at the czar, my grandparents dropped the use of Russian when they arrived in this country. They preferred Yiddish. But for my Aunt Betty the revolution pardoned past sins; she and my uncle kept up Russian for household use.

Some relatives were strongly connected to Left Jewish culture. My father was the one member of the family who moved freely into the gentile world. He never read Yiddish or spoke it, except by necessity. He organized the Bay-

Beach Fellowship jointly with a Protestant minister to combat incidents of anti-Semitism in our area of Brooklyn. But for most of the family, only in the Communist Party and its organizations did we get to know and marry non-Jews. That is how I eventually met and married Rosario Morales and spent nearly a dozen years in Puerto Rico.

My father was the first in his family to become a socialist, joining YPSL, the Young People's Socialist League, in the Brownsville neighborhood of Brooklyn. He chaired the meeting in which their local chapter voted to secede and join the YCL, the Young Communist League. He led his younger sister into the Communist Party. His own view of the struggle frowned on the flamboyant flouting of bourgeois respectability in favor of a more conservative style that avoided offending custom where it didn't seem politically necessary and emphasized a goal of meeting people on terms they could relate to. My parents married conventionally, whereas others chose to live together monogamously without marriage, and still other communist subcultures interpreted "free love" to mean a casual sexuality.

My grandfather, with three years of formal schooling, was self-educated in Russian, Yiddish, and English. He believed that, at a minimum, a socialist worker needed to know history, evolution, and cosmology. Before I could read, he read to me "Bad Bishop" Brown's *Science and History for Girls and Boys*. The author, an Episcopalian bishop, had been excommunicated for heresy and published a quarterly journal entitled *Heresy*. One of his pamphlets was around the house for years: *The Science of Moscow and the Superstition of Rome*. By the time we finished the book, I knew that science and politics were one and that I wanted to do both. The first book I remember reading for myself was Paul de Kruif's *Microbe Hunters*, which decided me on being a biologist.

My friend Spencer was also a Red. His great grandmother was a comrade of my grandmother. He always gave me books as birthday presents. *Bows Against the Barons* retold the Robin Hood story from a class perspective. "Norman and Saxon workers, unite!" shouted the shoemaker-organizer in Nottingham. *Soldier of the Sun* was the story of an Inca boy who fought the *conquistadores* and after defeat ended up fleeing into the jungles to continue the struggle.

We Reds were contemptuous of comic books (but I also read some!) and rejected the superheroes as Aryan vigilantes. I didn't read the daily comic strips because they were reactionary propaganda: the pro-capitalism of Little Orphan Annie, the imperialist racism of Terry and the Pirates, the many adventures aimed at stealing the valuable gems adorning the religious treasures ("idols") of their rightful but dark-skinned owners. Anyway, comics were not carried in the newspapers delivered daily to our home, the *Daily Worker,* the *New York Times,* and the *Freheit.* Of course the police, whom we called "Cossacks," were the enemy, attacking demonstrations, beating strikers, assaulting Negroes. I never had the sense of safety that a policeman was supposed to inspire in children. But a friend of my grandmother's whose husband was a policeman warned us when the demonstrators would be roughed up.

Our health care was guided by Dr. Benzion Liber, who was also the physician for the Coops, the left-run cooperative housing project in the Bronx. A strong advocate of preventive medicine and self care, Dr. Liber taught people how to read thermometers, use fasting, dieting, exercise, baths, and compresses, and to keep windows open. (In those days you could still think of the city atmosphere as "fresh air.") His advice combined physical and mental health. He used to say, "You want to make a revolution? You have to make a revolution in yourself!" We were sympathetic to naturopathy and were vegetarians on and off. He encouraged us to distrust commoditized patent medicines and doctors who mystify and create dependence. Someone in our extended family read the exposé of the pharmaceutical industry, *Twenty Million Guinea Pigs,* and it became part of our common culture. I distrusted establishment medicine with a vengeance and rejected most of what I was taught in hygiene classes in school.

School was a problem: I was a good student and loved reading, but knew that schools were an organ of the State set up to mislead us. Their textbooks were "poison" that I had to be protected against. I remember my family teaching me to reject the blatant racism in stories such as *Little Black Sambo.* Some teachers were themselves radicals and members of New York City's Teachers Union. They encouraged political discussion and organized debates on such topics as the Soviet-Finnish War, boycotting Japanese goods because of Japan's invasion of China, or a fourth term for President Roosevelt. On the other hand, my fourth grade teacher complained about me: "He's a very bright boy, but already a communist."

My father taught me that a communist should master bourgeois knowledge and appreciate its achievements but remain skeptical and go beyond it. He carried out part of this program when I was twelve or thirteen, sitting me down on Friday evenings for Bible study from an atheist, materialist perspective. The Bible was an important part of the culture, and our side had to know it at least as well as the believers whom we would meet either as allies or adversaries. A companion piece was Thomas Paine's *The Age of Reason.* Thus armed, I recall cornering a startled classmate in the schoolyard with my aggressive "Do you believe in God?"

We were different. While my friends were in Hebrew school after "regular" school four afternoons a week, I waited in the alley outside so that we could play when they were released. At movie Westerns, I sided with the Indians and always lost. A solemn oath among communist children ended with "On my pioneer's honor, touch red" and us touching something red.

Most of the time I rather enjoyed being different, but my mother now feels my friends and I deprived ourselves of many opportunities through our aloofness and others' rejection. She also feels that I deprived myself of some of the pleasures of childhood and adolescence by being "too serious." I disagree. I never felt that being like everyone else was a virtue, and in the 1950s I was furious with radical parents who sent their kids to religious community centers to "belong."

I always felt alienated from the sexist jokes and behavior that were part of preteen boys' culture. As a young child I was taught that sex was natural, and I didn't understand the humor in sexual jokes. This was often misinterpreted as ignorance about sex itself. At my progressive summer camp, boys and girls changed into swimsuits together twice a day, and to this day nudity is not of itself erotic for me.

The 1930s were an exhilarating but scary time for a communist kid. I was very aware of fascism. Friends of the family were going off to Spain to fight Franco, and my room was the coatroom for meetings in support of the Abraham Lincoln Battalion. I knew about the Nazi concentration camps and anti-Semitic laws and rampages. I met Ruby Bates, a prosecution witness in the Scottsboro case who repented of her perjury and helped expose the rape frame-up of six Black young men. I knew about the fascists in the United States—the German American Bund, the KKK, Father Coughlin, the Silver Shirts, the Black Legion—and lynching and pogroms were part of my nightmares. My father had been threatened by the Christian Front. I expected that fascism would come to the United States and that I would die young; this undermined my interest in a healthy lifestyle.

But there was a new world growing up in Russia, and we were in a way part of it. We sang Russian songs and saw Soviet movies. When I was three or four we went to New Jersey to isolate me from a cousin who was thought to have meningitis. It was the first time I had seen a woman driving a car. I complained, "Ladies don't drive!" but was told in no uncertain terms, "In the Soviet Union they do!" With all the prestige of the revolution behind it, this was the start of my feminist education.

May Day 1936, New York City. Courtesy of the Tamiment Institute Library, New York University, John Albok Collection. Photograph by John Albok.

I had comrades all over the world. Since I expected fascism to come to America, my strongest sense of identification was with the German antifascists—the Thaelman Battalion, volunteers who fought Franco in Spain—and the internal resistance in Germany itself. My boyhood fantasies of heroics were of clandestine organizing culminating in a dramatic revelation of our strength in a strike or uprising or prison break. My romantic fantasies were of woman comrades in science and revolution.

Later, when I was sixteen and my father had just died, I used to imagine I saw him down the block or on a passing subway train. I suppressed my grief by pretending that he hadn't really died, that his death was a deception arranged to hide his being on some secret mission for the Communist International, which was why I couldn't approach him.

It took a touch of arrogance to hold firm in the face of all the propaganda around us—anticommunism, sexist values, racism, praise of competition, personal ambition to "get ahead" or accumulate things. My hatred of competition carried over to sports and games. I enjoyed the outdoors and swimming, biking, and hiking. But I didn't apply myself wholeheartedly to competitive sports and had only limited interest in the fluctuating fortunes of professional teams, except as a Red fan: I was interested in boxing for the Joe Louis/ Max Schmeling championship fight, followed the pitching of Satchell Paige in the Negro National League, and was briefly a Dodger fan when a campaign in the *Daily Worker* led to the hiring of Jackie Robinson, breaching the major leagues' Jim Crow pattern.

In my teens, my friends and I used to gather of an evening to listen to music and play chess. I never became competent at chess because I couldn't get excited about making all that effort just to win over someone else. I concentrated on the music instead, and was guided in my tastes by my older friends. In defiance of Stalin's own tastes, we collectively sneered at Tchaikovsky and enjoyed Stravinsky.

I consciously rejected the notion of "success" and was often embarrassed by praise that seemed to compare me to others. My image of a good life was being a good communist and scientist, sharing with other good communists. Later, when I was elected to the National Academy of Sciences and turned them down because of their complicity in military research during the Vietnam War, some of the supportive mail I received praised me for a "hard decision." It really wasn't hard. The decision was a purely tactical one: was it better politics to join the Academy and raise issues from within (which my friend Richard Lewontin had already tried unsuccessfully before resigning the year before) or to get maximum but short-lived publicity for the antiwar and radical science movements? Other "decisions" in adult life, such as defying the House Un-American Activities Committee, were also of this kind. I was subpoenaed in 1959 when HUAC was conducting investigations into "why we lost Cuba." After sparring for a while with the committee's counsel about particular people, whether I knew Spanish, and my travels, I walked out of the hearing. There had been no soul-searching pacing of the floor the night before trying to decide whether to give them what they wanted. It was simply out of the question. Some principles had long been a part of my being, such as not crossing a picket line, not telling racist jokes, and not giving names to the enemy. The public acts were merely their visible expression.

Having The Truth helped. We had to be, and generally were, better informed than everyone else. I was proud of knowing politics and history and theory, and my family was proud of my precocious knowledge. I studied the transcript of the Moscow purge trials and was convinced of the guilt of the defendants. (I remind myself that I was only nine or ten at the time.) I acquired the skills to wade into political debates with devastating one-liners. Here victory was allowed, not to get ahead of someone but to advance our cause.

In addition to politics I read science. The works of Engels and contemporary Marxist scientists such as J. B. S. Haldane, J. D. Bernal, Christopher Caudwell, Marcel Prenant, and I. V. Oparin got me excited about dialectics. I daydreamed dialectical relationships and doubted classroom science from a Marxist point of view. I wondered what arithmetic would be like if $A \times B$ were not equal to $B \times A$. I loved asymmetry and complexity, threshold effects, contradiction. I got excited about the social origins of scientific theories, was fascinated by "non-Western" science. I thought about the origin of life when this was still considered outside the range of science. I told my indignant science teacher that chemical laws could evolve and that I doubted people from outer space would use the periodic table.

Dialectical thinking, with its emphasis on complexity, context, change, discontinuity, interpenetrations, and contradictions, was and has remained a thing of beauty for me and the guiding theme in my scientific research and my political teaching in Party study groups, popular lectures, and writings. In a peculiar way it also undermined my self-confidence. Although I was a good student and generously praised for it, I attributed my academic achievements not to my own abilities but to having insider knowledge of the universe by having access to Marxism, while my peers were handicapped by bourgeois blinders. I expected that dialectics might bring me easily to the boundaries of knowledge, but I often doubted my own capacity to contribute anything original.

★

My first independent political organizing involved forming "Young Friends of the Abraham Lincoln Battalion" with the other eight- and nine-year-old children of my parents' circle. This movement folded after two or three meetings. We had no material base: we had to depend on our parents for transportation, we had no funds to contribute, and, after learning a few things about Spain and fascism, there was nothing more for us to do.

When I was in seventh grade I read about an organization called American Youth for Democracy, which was being red-baited in the press. I decided it was the organization for me. My father was encouraging, but also told me to bear in mind that a communist organization is not a communist society and that I should not be shocked to find examples of pettiness, greed, opportunism, bossiness, and unkindness. He illustrated these points with episodes from his own life in YPSL, the YCL, and the Party.

This lesson stayed with me. It allowed me to be repelled by the behavior of some communist leaders, to be furious with some of our organizations, embarrassed by oversimplified analyses, and yet not be bitter or disillusioned with our long-term struggle. Later, reading Rosa Luxembourg put it in perspective for me: we are attempting to build the future with the attitudes, beliefs, ambitions of the present. At times this long-term view made me too placid in the face of the unacceptable and slow to turn disapproval or sadness into outrage. But it also freed my commitment from the fluctuating fortunes of the movement. At the present moment of disarray and even despair in the Left—when the call to "reexamine" previous ideas often means their abandonment—the need to replace capitalism with a more humane, cooperative society seems even more urgent, but the path less clear and the victory more remote. My sense of permanent and imperfect struggle encourages me to look for new ways to be a good communist.

To my disappointment, AYD was not a communist organization, although it was led by communists. I met other young leftists there; we had many political questions, which we asked our parents. They referred us to Marxist writings and told us to figure out answers for ourselves. The resulting study groups were the start of our deciding what we, as distinct from our families, really believed and were an exciting counterpoint to the simplistic stuff we got in school.

My friend Gabby played the guitar and sometimes baby-sat for Woody and Marjorie Guthrie. A few of us occasionally went with Gabby to the Guthries' and learned about People's Songs, a group of radical musicians and songwriters who met in Pete Seeger's basement apartment in Greenwich Village. Defying an enormous lack of musical talent, I bought a guitar and joined the "Brighton Sharecroppers" as a songwriter. I had one song published in support of the 1945 General Electric strike ("The C. E. Wilson Song") and a few months later recognized musicological necessity and moved on.

When my friends were going off to college and joining the Party I was still under seventeen, too young to qualify for membership. But I recruited for the Party, participated in its activities and in the internal struggles of the Brooklyn College branch, and waited impatiently to come of age.

Finally, at seventeen I finished high school and entered New York University. The Party was not very visible on the campus, but I tracked it down with a relative's help. I joined in 1947, only to leave seven years later. I didn't stop being a Red, though, and with my wife raised three red diaper babies and am grandparenting (at last count) three red diaper grandchildren. I think the *rebbetzin* of Kremenchug would be pleased with what she started.

Secrets of the *Susan Ann*

Susan Ann Protter

Susan Protter was born in 1939 in New York City. Following completion
of a master's degree in French language and literature and a brief stint as a
high school teacher, she began working in the publishing industry in the
mid-1960s. Since 1971 Protter has operated her own literary agency.

Protter's parents kept their political affiliation a secret and discouraged
their daughter from asking questions. Protter's memoir conveys an unset-
tled sense of a life controlled by something that she could not define.
Heightening her bewilderment was the contradiction between the family's
upper-middle-class lifestyle and the values her parents professed. As an
adult, Protter has maintained an ambivalent connection to left-wing culture and a distance from left politics.

I believe I owe my life to the Communist Party. As I understand it, my parents wanted a large family but conception eluded them and after ten years of
marriage they had not had any children. In January 1939 my father was sent
to upstate New York for six weeks of Party training. After three weeks, my
mother was allowed to visit. I was born the following October.

I was raised in an ostensibly middle-class Jewish family. My father was an
attorney, and my mother a housewife. My father, a great sailor, owned a 43-
foot schooner named after me. On the surface, my childhood was ordinary—
a typical American life. We lived in nice homes, took vacations, and spent
holidays having fun with our large extended family. But it slowly became clear
to me that we lived quite differently from the other families in the neighborhood.

My parents were classic communists; they spent all of their waking hours
at meetings, planning meetings, or discussing meetings. My father was absorbed by issues of apparently momentous importance, such as Henry Wal-

lace's 1948 presidential campaign and producing concerts for Paul Robeson. My mother was always organizing something. Occasionally, she took me to the Teachers Union office or a meeting hall to lick stamps, stuff envelopes, and perform other simple chores that a child could manage.

My parents often shared accounts of their activities with me with enormous enthusiasm. When I was four or five, my father regaled me with stories of strikes by longshoremen and bakers that he, as a lawyer, had played a part in organizing and resolving. We often went to picnics, parties, bazaars, and rallies. We marched in parades under banners proclaiming peace and other noble causes. I found these events rather colorful, although, in truth, I didn't have a clue as to what was going on. But I knew it was all very, very important.

While my parents indoctrinated me with the progressive point of view, they never admitted to being Party members. All I knew was that they were active members of the American Labor Party (ALP). On the occasions that I asked my mother, who often quoted Stalin or Lenin, if she and my father were Party members, she either took the Fifth Amendment or denied it vehemently. I learned to back off. While I was always secure with my parents, I never felt close or connected to them. There seemed to be an invisible wall that kept us apart emotionally.

As an only child, I, perhaps, spent more time with my parents than my friends who had sisters and brothers. I was also very curious and asked a lot of questions, which often went unanswered. I was encouraged to entertain myself and not be nosy. While I was a reasonably creative child and played with my toys and stuffed animals, I was also very lonely. I learned very quickly that there were questions I could not ask, that some subjects were reserved exclusively for adults. I remain today a person who has enormous difficulty asking direct or probing questions. I still feel that I may be treading, somehow, on forbidden ground.

Home was not the only place where there were secrets. Our activities could only be discussed within the family or with special people, people who lived by the same beliefs that my parents knew were right and true, those of Marxism-Leninism. I had to keep secrets from friends, relatives, and teachers. Doing so was enormously alienating and made me feel left out of the real world. When Elizabeth Gurley Flynn came to visit, I was told not to tell anyone. I was brought in to say hello and then sent to my room and instructed not to come out until told to. At the time, it did not seem at all odd. It fit with my sense that everything my parents did was both secret and important.

Indeed, my childhood was surrounded by a sense of importance and purpose. To my parents, only a lack of education prevented others from seeing that Marxist-Leninist principles would come to pass "in our lifetime." I was further assured that this was a progressive, not necessarily communist, point of view. The ideas of Marx and Lenin were socialist and the basis of many different approaches and schools of thought, according to my dad. He, naturally, followed the true course.

My parents firmly believed that the coming revolution would miraculously make all social ills disappear. When I told my father of problems that I had with other kids or in school, rather than try to help me resolve them, he lectured me on how everything would change after the revolution. What I today see as normal childhood fears and desires were usually perceived and subsequently dismissed within the framework of the evils of capitalism.

Politics played a defining role in our lives. People were either progressive and like-minded or they were not, in which case much of what they said could be dismissed as uninformed or, worse, reactionary. I could not watch Kate Smith, Arthur Godfrey, or Red Skelton on television—they were seen by my parents as definitely reactionary.

At Camp Woodland, if your father was in jail it gave you a certain cachet. One summer the son of an important film producer told us that his father was a Democrat. While I liked him and thought he was nice, I was not certain if he actually fit in; from our point of view, Democrats were conservatives.

At Brooklyn Community School, we had no homework, no grades, wore whatever we wanted, and called our teachers by their first names. When I was in the "nines" during the Chinese revolution, our teacher, Alfred, read dispatches to us from the *Daily Worker*; to give us a balanced view, he also read us the *New York Times* so we were aware of the "official American propaganda."

My parents were dedicated to the future, but for me life existed only in the present. I longed to be a Brownie or a Girl Scout and did not understand why my parents perceived them as fascist organizations. Even though my school allowed me to wear whatever I wanted, even shorts, what I really wanted was to wear a school uniform and walk in pairs behind a nun in a habit like the kids who went to Catholic school. These desires of mine made my father berserk.

While I was raised to be proud that I was Jewish, I was also told that we did not believe in god. We did not observe any Jewish holidays. At about age ten, I was sent to learn Yiddish at an after-school program sponsored by the International Workers Order. My parents felt that Yiddish was a vital and useful language, unlike the new Zionist language, Hebrew, which was politically totally unsuitable. I liked the school and enjoyed learning a new alphabet and language. But I brought home a menorah during Hanukkah, and that was the end of that.

By 1951, my father could no longer practice labor law, as the leadership in the unions he worked with had become conservative. He went into business, and in 1953 we moved to Long Island. I remember family friends coming to visit us and poring over a map to show my parents where other progressive families lived. There were not a lot of them in Suffolk County.

It was a difficult time for my family. My mother was seriously injured in an automobile accident and was hospitalized for several months. That she lived is a testament to her strength. When she recovered, she appeared to have lost her driving commitment. "The accident," as it came to be known, changed everything. My mother no longer had any interests outside our home and family. She was an excellent hostess, played cards, and did lots of gardening, but she never became truly friendly with her new acquaintances, the wives of the Jewish professionals in town. She did not seem happy in this new role. I tried to encourage her to become active in the community, as she had been in Brooklyn. She went to one or two meetings of the PTA and said it was more of a social group than an activist organization. I suggested the League of Women Voters, which always got good press in our home, but she seemed totally unmotivated.

My father maintained his Party membership. When he offered to have a political meeting on our boat and to hide Party leaders in our home, my mother put her foot down and told him that it was too dangerous and she did not want him risking jail. He acquiesced, and that marked the end of my parents' active political involvement. Even their reading matter changed when my father dropped his subscription to the *Daily Worker.*

The affluence of our lifestyle conflicted with the lessons I had learned from my parents. In 1954, when my father needed a new car, he bought two Cadillacs, a convertible and a sedan. Horrified and ashamed, I stayed up all night arguing with him and did not want to go to school the following day. His explanation was that he would rather spend his business's money than pay the taxes to the government. I avoided the subject of cars whenever it came up, which was frequently among teenagers in those days. My parents and I had had so many discussions about the merits of having the simple things that one needed and not keeping up with the Joneses that it was impossible for me to accept his point of view; I saw it as a rationalization.

In Huntington, activities revolved around church or synagogue. At thirteen, around the time I began high school, I became very interested in religion, all religions. I found a copy of William James's *The Varieties of Religious Experience* at home and read it avidly. Fascinated by the different beliefs of my schoolmates, I attended church and synagogue with them. My father took poorly to what was probably a normal rebellion for an atheist teenager. He threatened to disown me if I ever devoted my life to religion in any form. We had frequent arguments about god. I felt that I had made great inroads when he asked me to explain what an agnostic was.

In 1956, at the age of sixteen, I entered Syracuse University. I had dreamed of college as an exciting place where I would engage in meaningful discussions and activities as my parents had done before we moved away from New York City. In those days, there was little activism on campus. I began to spend time at the home of the senior chaplain, a Methodist, where a group of students would regularly get together to discuss serious subjects, meet interesting people, and drink tea. I also got to know the Jewish chaplain, a political science professor. I liked him a lot, as he seemed to combine my interests in politics and religion. He encouraged me to come to a meeting of the Student Zionist Organization.

In the Student Zionist Organization, I found the zeal and commitment that I had experienced as a child. I was promptly elected president of our branch. But I realized that I was a fish out of water when I attended a regional conference. I was totally ignorant of the facts when we engaged in debates with mock Arabs, role-playing the different sides. One evening we listened to a recorded presentation of David Ben Gurion's speech on the day of Israel's independence in 1948. Everyone in the room was weeping. I sat there dry-eyed not only because it had no particular meaning to me but because I couldn't understand a word of Hebrew. I resigned the next day. I had been attracted to the fervor, not the goals, of the organization. My mother later explained to me that it was very common in political groups to make the most innocent member president because nobody who knew what was involved wanted the job.

Perhaps because of my disillusionment with Zionism, I never thought about studying religion. I was intrigued, however, by political science. It was immensely interesting to learn the philosophy behind our way of government, something I had never learned at home. But I frequently found myself disagreeing, even becoming angry, with my professors' positions about communism, considering their views to be blatant bourgeois bigotry about the Left. This was particularly true when they spoke about how the Party was directed from Moscow and how members were encouraged to infiltrate other organizations such as the American Labor Party, which they maintained was nothing but a front organization. From my point of view, my parents had been participating members not infiltrators in the ALP. I had no reason to doubt their words. But as time went on and my suspicions grew, it became painfully clear that my professors had painted a more truthful and accurate portrait of the events in my life than my parents ever had.

I was twenty-five when my parents finally admitted that they had been Party members and told me about their activities. In fact, my father had been Party treasurer in Brooklyn and boasted that it was the only time the borough organization was ever solvent. My mother told me that the Party dictum had been not to tell the children because they were young and might talk. In the abstract that makes sense. But I found the reality extremely painful and isolating. I am still hurt and angry about it. My mother's explanation makes me feel that the Party was more important to them than I was.

As an adult, I am aware of the contradictions in my childhood. Despite my parents' political positions, we lived in a comfortable home, I went to private schools and camps, we had a large sailboat, and we lived very well. At the time, I saw nothing unusual in this. My father was able to resolve any confusion I may have felt, no doubt due to his excellent Party training.

I was pleased, if not delighted, when as an adult I heard the expression "red diaper baby" for the first time. Growing up I was an outsider. Now there was a group that included me. When I attended a workshop for red diaper babies, I expected to be right at home. Ironically, when most everyone else spoke about their working-class backgrounds and their continued activism, I once again felt very much the outsider.

The ultimate effect of my early years is that I am rather apolitical and distrustful of politics and politicians. I have, on occasion, become active around particular issues, but I could never be considered an activist. I am a registered Democrat with no deep feeling for the party.

My father died in 1984. To the end, he remained a true believer in Marxism and socialism and very much a Stalinist. My ninety-plus-year-old mother lives on Long Island, where she reads the *New York Times* every day, remains fascinated by current events, and leads a typical suburban life. Her Party involvement is part of the distant past. For me, these memories are the vestiges of an unsettling childhood.

Cookies and Communism

Norah C. Chase

Born in 1942, Norah C. Chase grew up in New York City and New Hampshire. She has taught English at Kingsborough Community College in Brooklyn, New York, since 1968. Chase has a Ph.D. in women's studies and writing; her dissertation, a biography of her grandmother, is entitled "A Woman's Way of Revolution: How Elba Chase Nelson Became a Communist Leader in New England."

Chase has written about the place of "women's work" in movements for social change. Here, she focuses on her grandmother as a supportive figure and role model in describing how a red diaper upbringing influenced the development of her political and professional identities.

One of my earliest memories is of looking up at a stove topped with three-foot-high pots full of food—my mother had loaned her kitchen to a group of strikers. Food and politics have remained closely woven in my mind.

When I was a young child, I began spending my summers on a farm in New Hampshire with my paternal grandmother, Elba Chase Nelson, who headed the Communist Party of New Hampshire for three decades, and her second husband, Charlie Nelson.

A Latvian Jewish immigrant, Elba came to the United States in 1903 when she was about twelve years old. She became a leader in many social reform organizations in Boston: the settlement houses, the YWCA, the Retail Clerks Union, the Women's Trade Union League, and the Socialist Party. In 1912, she married Fred Bates Chase, a native of New Hampshire who could trace his ancestry in America back to 1636. Leader of a machinists' local, Fred also headed the Massachusetts Socialist Party. Because of Fred's ill health, the Chases moved to the backwoods of New Hampshire, where they raised five children. In the early 1930s, Fred ran for public office on the Communist Party ticket. After Fred's untimely death in 1933, Elba became the head of the Party in New Hampshire.

I knew Elba mainly as a nurturing grandmother and the best cook in the world. Whenever my father, her third son, came to visit, she made his favorite chocolate cake. For me, she made cookies—big, perfectly round, and filled with a lemony raisin mixture that was heavenly. Those who knew Elba have wonderful memories of her arguing the political issues of the day or asking you how you were doing and listening carefully to your answer as she rolled out dough or walked back and forth between the wood stove and the dining room table to serve a healthy, delicious meal with food straight from the garden.

My grandmother's hospitality, her cooking, and her other "women's work" (cleaning, child care, community service, and care of the sick)—indeed, all the activities of her daily life—were woven together with her more traditional political activities like the multicolored strands of the braided rugs she made to raise money for the *Daily Worker*. She fed her own children, the children of comrades, adult boarders who were political activists, recuperating comrades sent to her by the Communist Party, left-wing gatherings and fundraisers, and vacationing political leaders. Her boarders paid for rooms and home-cooked meals, and she used this cash to help support her family and its political work. She took food to neighbors in need and cooked pies for local events, thereby establishing herself as a member of the community. And, of course, she sent food to striking workers. She did all this while becoming the first woman in the state to have her name on the ballot for governor, running for the Governor's Council, earning the title "The Most Talked About Woman in New Hampshire," giving speeches, and doing all her regular Party work.

My parents, who had met through the Communist Party, separated when I was a small child. My mother remarried when I was seven. She and my stepfather shared their dedication to the Party and to education. My mother graduated from factory worker to union organizer to CP organizer to secretary at Brooklyn Community School, a progressive private school, and finally to schoolteacher. We lived around the corner from the school in an integrated neighborhood and were surrounded by "our kind of people." As the Red Scare developed in the 1950s, it was very good to be in this supportive environment.

On the farm in New Hampshire, I was also surrounded by people from our world: my family, the boarders, and the folks from Hobo Ranch, a nearby summer colony. I absorbed the values and moral structure of the Left. There was a sense of hope in the future, of purpose in adult political activities, of meaning and joy in the music, and of specialness. There was a commitment to being fair, to helping others, to ending racism, and to nonmaterial values.

In fifth grade I got into trouble for helping a Black classmate; my teacher accused me of doing the work for him. The boy's father was somewhere in the South and had been shot four times in the back; the son didn't know if the father was alive. Since my father was also in the South somewhere, working for the CP to organize Blacks and whites into an integrated union, and I had no idea if he was OK, I must have identified strongly with this classmate.

In sixth grade I had a more sympathetic teacher; I now realize she must have known about me and the five or six other left-wing kids in her class. One was the daughter of James Jackson, editor of the *Daily Worker*, who went into hiding in the early 1950s when the Communist Party ordered him to do so. The FBI followed his daughter to class every day to see if her father would try to make contact. We didn't know how to help, so, in a show of support, we elected her president of our class.

While school was pleasant, I felt an undercurrent of anxiety. I had helped my mother give out leaflets to save the Rosenbergs, who had two sons who were roughly my age. I felt that if it happened to the Rosenberg boys, it could happen to me. My parents could be killed. I could be killed.

The night the Rosenbergs were executed, my mother and I were with my maternal grandparents, Betty and Herman. Everyone was waiting for a last-minute pardon. I recall that the radio was on and then the lights dimmed, although they probably didn't. My Grandfather Herman said, "It served them right." I was absolutely horrified by his callous comment and walked out on the back porch, where I cried hysterically. My grandfather had suddenly become the enemy. It made the horror of the executions much worse. My mother later said that her father was terrified that his daughter's political work might endanger her, so he said that ugly thing out of love. Soon after, my grandparents moved to Florida and ceased to be family in any real sense to me. I never forgave my grandfather for his comment about the Rosenbergs.

By the age of thirteen, I had read a lot of books about the Holocaust and about the persecution of Leftists and African Americans. For years during my childhood I worried about whether or not I could keep silent under torture. In my young mind, right-wingers, McCarthyites, and the Nazis merged into one enemy. The sense that the Nazis could come again tomorrow was then, and remains now, absolutely vivid and terrifying. I don't recall ever talking with adults about these fears. What was talked about was how to answer the door and what to do if the FBI visited. I was not told the last names of people who came to the house for meetings. These early experiences have left me with a recurring terror of the human potential for inhumanity, of the cruelty of people toward other people.

But, much of the time, fear was relegated to the background, and I enjoyed the vibrant culture of the Left. I sang in Earl Robinson's children's chorus; we rehearsed at my school and performed at Carnegie Hall with Pete Seeger, Paul Robeson, and other folk heroes. I lived for those concerts, which reaffirmed my faith in the future and my sense of community. We would yell for Pete to sing "Wimoweh" the way others would soon yell for Elvis Presley. In New Hampshire, after a hot, dusty day of field work, all the kids would pile into the back of my father's truck and head for a swim in the town's crystal-clear pond; on the way we merrily shouted our songs: "We Shall Not Be Moved," "Hold the Fort," and many others.

After seventh and eighth grades at Brooklyn Community, I entered Hunter College High School, a school for "intellectually gifted young ladies." By that time I knew better than to talk openly about my family's politics. It was 1956. Family members had already been questioned by investigating committees. Some had lost their jobs; some had spent time in jail. There was no left-wing political action at Hunter High, but a couple of weeks into my first term, I figured out a way to identify kindred spirits. I announced in homeroom that I was thinking of forming a folk music club and would like to talk to anyone who was interested. One classmate responded. Gingerly we asked each other, "What singers do you like? What songs do you know?" She gave the "right" answers, and we became best friends.

When I got ninety-eight, an unusually high grade for me, on a Russian history test, I was too busy trying to figure out where I had lost the two points to realize that my grade was a dead giveaway of my interest in the Soviet Union and therefore of my politics. While I was still poring over my test, our history teacher explained that he wanted each of us to interview someone at the Soviet Embassy. Without thinking, I raised my hand and asked where it was. He responded, "Miss Chase, you mean to tell me that *you* don't know where the Soviet Embassy is!" I was mortified and worried because I now realized that I had clearly given away my political sympathies. I felt worse when I discovered that everyone else knew the Soviet Embassy was only one block from our school.

My best friend went with me to the embassy, and we had a great time chatting with one of the Russians. We talked mainly about the educational theories of the educator Makarenko; we had devoured his three-volume series *Road to Life* about how homeless boys were well taken care of and educated to contribute to society. I saw it as a Soviet equivalent of *Little Women* or *Jo's Boys*, which I had also loved.

My family was still somewhat politically active, and I continued to see some left-wing friends at parties and concerts on the weekends. All this changed when I was sixteen years old and we moved to the suburbs. About the same time, my father moved from New Hampshire, so the Chase farm was never the same, although I still visited my grandmother Elba. Simultaneously, the full impact of the Khrushchev revelations hit and my mother and stepfather drifted away from the Party. Active politics disappeared from our lives.

In 1959, I was accepted for early admission at a college where a relative taught. There was no question in my mind that if I opened my mouth and said the wrong thing, I could cost him his job, a calamity not even to be imagined! This challenge reinforced childhood concerns about keeping faith and not talking. The question of would-I-talk-under-torture was replaced by the constant worry about slipping and carelessly saying something that would reveal my family's political background.

After college my habit of silence continued. At the University of Minnesota in the early 1960s I was a traditional graduate student; when I returned to the East in the mid-1960s I went to Rutgers and concentrated on a doctoral program in comparative literature. In 1968, I got a full-time job at Kingsborough Community College in the English department, where I am to this day. In the late 1960s and early 1970s, I went on the major antiwar marches and participated in the teach-in at my college after the Jackson State and Kent State student murders. But for more than a decade I told almost no one at work about my family's politics for fear of being red-baited.

It took me ten years to get tenure at Kingsborough Community College. The last two years I had to fight for reappointment; being on the union executive committee turned out to be more problematic for my career than I had envisioned when I agreed to run for office. Throughout my tenure fight, I frequently thought of both my mother's bravery as a young union organizer and my grandmother Elba's enduring strength through many political and personal struggles. In 1978, just after I got tenure and before I could celebrate, a close friend being considered for tenure was red-baited and fired; some members of the administration and of the tenure committees had talked about whether she was a "card-carrying member of the Communist Party or only close to it." In retrospect, my silence all those years appears to have been necessary. If the college had known about my family's political background, I probably would not have won my tenure fight.

Since then I have, for the most part, put aside the old fears and have given talks—even at my own college—about my biography of Elba. Talking or writing about the history and culture of American communism gives me a sense of freedom, wholesomeness, normalcy—and still of fear.

My grandmother Elba represents for me the best in the Old Left. I admire her commitment to caring for people while working to build a better future. For some members of the Party, ideology came first and people a not-so-close second. My father ended a close friendship of twenty years over a political argument. When my mother wanted to remain at home with me, her first-born child, the Party insisted she was urgently needed, so she returned to full-time work. Often people who left the Party or who were thrown out became "untouchables" to those who remained. Elba, on the contrary, valued friendships with people who had different political perspectives and never closed her door to anyone. Even though she was a Party leader, she never placed political line before human relationships. I still miss her very much.

The Weight of Inheritance

Bettina Aptheker

Bettina Aptheker, born in 1944, was raised in Brooklyn, New York, and attended the University of California at Berkeley, where she was involved in the civil rights and antiwar movements. Aptheker is a professor of women's studies at the University of California, Santa Cruz. Her most recent book is *Tapestries of Life* (University of Massachusetts Press, 1989). In this selection from a longer memoir, Aptheker provides insight into the ways issues of gender and sexuality were approached within the CP milieu and how they influenced the coming of age of a lesbian red diaper baby.

Born in Fort Bragg, North Carolina, a war baby. Raised in Brooklyn, New York, the only child of Jewish communists. It is the 1950s.

Of the Jewish daughter it has been written: "To inherit a father's dreams makes you the eldest son. To further his ambitions makes you heir to the throne."

My mother's last name has always been Aptheker. I am told this from when I am very little, because it is so unusual and makes us so special. She and my father are first cousins; their fathers are brothers. Philip, mother's father, was very handsome, tall, thin, with a shock of wavy hair parted down the center, wire-rimmed glasses, and sharp features in the only surviving photograph of him that I have seen. Mother tells me he was a revolutionary with a flair for acting. He fled czarist Russia, came to America, married, was poor, died before my mother was born. He is a romantic figure to me. I think the wildness of my imagination must come from him. Father's father, Benjamin, was short, stout, built like a wrestler, with a soft, fleshy face, kindly looking, and robust, with thick curly hair. He also fled czarist Russia, came to America poor, married, and made a fortune "manufacturing ladies' underwear." He died in a fire in his factory. This happened long before I was born.

My mother's first name is Fay. She is ten years older than my father. She is just shy of her fortieth birthday when I am born. Before she marries she earns her living "in a social work agency." My mother is a dancer who has trained with an associate of the modern dancer Doris Humphries. She is also a fine pianist, a lover of classical music and of the theater. She sings in the Jewish People's Philharmonic Chorus. They give concerts at Town Hall and Carnegie Hall.

I can remember sitting next to my father in the orchestra section of Carnegie. It is in the mid-1950s, long before the hall was renovated. We are in maroon-colored seats with a rough-textured fabric. I am loving the music, so proud of my mother. She is wearing a white silk blouse with ruffles down its center and a long black skirt that drapes in pleats to her ankles. I could always pick out her voice, a pure soprano soaring above the chorus for my ears alone.

My mother is a beautiful woman. Every morning I watch as she comes from her bath in a thin, flowered dressing gown, smelling of soap and talcum powder. Her dark brown hair, almost black in its lushness, extends below her hips. I watch her stand before the half mirror above the dresser. She braids her hair in one long strand, which she then wraps around her head in a shining crown, her ritual coronation. She wears smart tailored blouses and skirts, suits and dresses, picked with exquisite care from the racks of Lord & Taylor or Abraham & Straus. She is stunning in these clothes. Makeup is applied with discretion: lipstick, powder, a bit of rouge, then maybe a dash of perfume, mildly scented. I remember the smell of her freshness, like a spring morning, the breadth of her smile, the expanse of her laughter, the optimism of her energetic thrust out into the world as she left for work.

When I am six, she returns to work full-time; she is employed as a travel agent. By the late 1950s and early 1960s when travel to Eastern Europe and the Soviet Union opens up, she knows all the best places, the best hotels, has special connections about what to see and where to go. She takes people on tours. Travel is a great passion in her life. She leaves my father and me to fend for ourselves, eating hot dogs and hot pastrami sandwiches and ice cream sundaes at Howard Johnson's. "Did you spoil her?" she asks my father upon her return, with a certain Yiddish-sounding intonation that means the question is purely rhetorical. Her salary and commissions support our family.

My father has been blacklisted since 1938 when he was named as a communist before a New York State legislative committee. He is outraged—not because he was named but because the information was false. He didn't join the Communist Party until 1939. He holds a doctorate from Columbia University, whose press published the original edition of his dissertation, *Ameri-can Negro Slave Revolts*, but whose history department will not offer him a job, nor will any other. Mother joined the Communist Party in 1929, only ten years after it was founded.

My parents adore each other, are devoted to each other, wait years to marry each other over the objections of his family: they are cousins, she is older, she is from a lower economic class.

My parents saw in their marriage a perfect union. Two years later on a small card with a pink bow provided by the U.S. army hospital came the printed announcement: "Born to Captain and Mrs. Herbert Aptheker, a daughter, Bettina." "You were so funny looking," Daddy always said, remembering the moment of my birth, his first sight of me, "with black hair and enormous feet, and breathing, breathing, like this." He illustrated, pursing his lips together like a fish, taking in great gulps of air. Mother didn't appreciate his humor. For her I was to be the perfect daughter: immaculate, feminine, exquisitely cultured. And ultimately for father, too, I was to be perfect: a communist essence, like a perfume, pure in my revolutionary devotion. This is out of their love for me. A perfect daughter, a special family.

When I am four my father takes me out to the great green expanse of Prospect Park and begins to teach me how to play baseball. As a student he pitched for Columbia, and for a brief time he'd actually gone into the pros, pitching in the minor leagues. I am learning how to bat. We are using a Spaulding, a kind of pink rubber ball. I hit it. It sails out of the park and bounces off a policeman's head. I can still see my father off in the distance retrieving the ball, explaining to the policeman, waving his arm in my direction. I stand still, raising the bat high above my head in confirmation.

At ten I am in the same park throwing a baseball with Johnny Yormark, who lives in the apartment next to ours on the sixth floor. We are both using our mitts. We are competing, each throwing the ball as high and far as we can. A man watches us. He comes over to me. "Are you a boy or a girl?" he asks.

"A girl," I say, sure of the answer.

"You can't be," he says. "You throw that ball like a boy. Girls can't throw that way. They're missing a bone in their shoulder."

"I'm a girl," I say, still sure of the answer.

At twelve years old, at Higley Hill camp in Vermont, I am the pitcher for the softball team. I prefer to pitch baseball, where you throw an overhand pitch with a smaller ball and have more control. I practice the underhand throw with this larger "soft" ball. I learn how to manipulate my wrist to throw curve balls.

LITTLE LENIN LIBRARY
VOLUME 28

WOMEN
AND
SOCIETY

By V·I·LENIN

INTERNATIONAL PUBLISHERS
381 FOURTH AVENUE · NEW YORK

Courtesy of Linn Shapiro.

The fast pitch is much slower than an overhand delivery, but I work at it. We are playing a team from a nearby camp. I am the only girl on either team. The boys on the opposing team come up to bat first. They laugh at me. In the course of the game I walk a few batters, but no one gets a hit.

Ritually, every morning, I watch my father shave. I am fascinated by this process and practice it on myself in the afternoons after school, imitating each of his actions; however, I am careful not to use a razor blade in the heavy silver-handled holder. Father stands barechested in front of the sink, looking into the mirror on the medicine cabinet above it. He has no hair whatsoever on his chest. He runs the hot water only, and builds a thick lather in his hands using a bar of soap. He smears the lather onto his face, careful to get it between his lips and nose and down under his chin. Once finished, he rinses off his face and dries it with a towel, inspecting the results in the mirror. He uses no aftershave lotion. Then he opens the medicine cabinet, takes out the roll-on deodorant—"my anti-stinko," he tells me. For years I believe this is what everyone calls it.

I remember my father in his thirties, with a broad, full chest, a slim waist, and no hips. He is about 5'8", has very short, curly, almost black hair, hazel eyes, soft, fleshy hands and face, large nose. By his forties the waist and hips fill out making for a straight line, shoulders to thighs, and he wears reading glasses with thick black rims. His hair turns white the summer of my fourteenth birthday as he turns forty-five. I see Mom walking up the path toward me at summer camp, and I wonder who the man is next to her until I see it's my father, newly cropped and white-haired. On closer inspection I see a small trace of black curls at the back of his neck that will remain for years.

My father, Herbert Aptheker, is a historian. His field is African American history. He is always reading or writing, settled at the vast mahogany desk with the lion heads at each of its four corners inherited from his mother. It just fits into the entrance hallway of our Brooklyn apartment. He writes by hand on a yellow pad with large, broad, confident strokes of the pen. Each letter is definitively shaped, every word plainly legible. Occasionally he works at his typewriter, set on a rickety metal table next to the desk. It is a very old model Royal with keys that seem to stick up on springs. He pecks away at it with the index finger of each hand.

The history of African American people is at the center of my earliest memories. The history walks around the living room of my childhood home: W. E. B. Du Bois, Paul Robeson, William L. Patterson, Alphaeus Hunton, Louis Burnham, John O. Killens, Charles White, Doxie Wilkerson. There are women also: Shirley Graham Du Bois, Eslanda Robeson, Dorothy Hunton, Alice Childress, Beah Richards, Louise Thompson Patterson, Dorothy Burnham, Elizabeth Catlett, Yolande Wilkerson. I come to understand that the men are the history. The conversation that counts flows in and around their ideas, their experiences. This is where my father is engaged and where mother listens, without comment, focused, intense. My father lives for this history, writes about it, teaches it. I grow to love the men and women who come to our home, their stories, their robust laughter, the warmth that envelops our living room with such good times.

By eight I am attending my father's lectures, delivered at the Marxist School, located on Broadway near 14th Street in Manhattan. The school opened in the late 1950s after the federal government (literally) padlocked the doors of the Jefferson School, which had been run more or less openly by the Communist Party. I can still recall how I felt in the lecture hall, seated in one of those straight-backed red cushion chairs and smelling the wet, dirty, grimy odor of an old Manhattan building. I am skinny, small; my heart is pounding. I am breathless for an hour in anticipation of father's thundering indignation at the oppression of Black people, hailing the abolitionist movement, John Brown, the slave revolts, Reconstruction, Du Bois, the struggles against lynching and peonage and for education and suffrage. The struggle for Black liberation is central to world history, he passionately proclaims.

During the 1950s the *New York Times* refers to my father as "the Communist Party's leading theoretician." I am about seven when he is called to testify in Washington, D.C., before the McCarthy Senate committee. The hearings are televised. I am at a friend's house. The TV is on. I don't understand anything about the communist "threat" or the purpose of these televised hearings. All I see is my Pop on television. I am very proud. I shout: "Look! My daddy's on television!" There is a terrible silence in the house. My friend's parents shut off the TV. Nobody says anything. Then I go home. Then her parents say I can't play at her house anymore. I don't care. I play baseball with the boys on our block in the empty lot where the subway tracks surface. I retrieve our ball when it goes onto the tracks, picking my way carefully over the "live" third rail. This is the unspoken rule by which I get to play.

Julius and Ethel Rosenberg are executed the summer before my ninth birthday. My mother pulls me onto her lap one evening when she gets home from work. We are in the big green leather chair in the living room. She says, "I have something very important to tell you." Her voice is soft, almost without inflection. I can feel her breath on my cheek. "Your daddy and I are communists. You must never, ever tell anyone. Do you understand?" I remember feeling small. I say I understand. I remember nodding my head. I remember feeling like my eyes are very large.

I am in the bunkhouse at Camp Wyandot, where so many of us children of communist and progressive parents spend our summer. "Progressive" means people who are not actually members of the Communist Party but who have political ideas very close to those of the Party. I am about nine or ten. It is at night. We are all in bed. We are talking. We are comparing parental status, outranking each other. "My parents are communists," someone says. "Mine aren't," someone counters, challenging the virtue of still being a member of something as stupid as the Communist Party. I pipe up. "My parents are communists, too," I say. Then I freeze. I have betrayed the secret. I am terrified. FBI agents are lurking outside our bunkhouse. They have heard me. They will arrest my parents. . . . I fall into an exhausted, terror-filled sleep, the image of my parents dead, executed like the Rosenbergs, riding my dreams for weeks afterward. I never tell a soul I have betrayed the secret. Instead, I pray to be forgiven by a God I know my parents do not believe exists. I am not sure. I think maybe He will help.

In fact, my parents are never arrested. My father never goes underground, as happens to so many of the fathers of the children I know. My father does go to Mexico, however, to find the comrade in the Mexican Party who had betrayed Gus Hall, a Party leader who had fled the country after being convicted under the Smith Act of "conspiring to advocate the overthrow of the government by force and violence." Gus had been sentenced to eight years in a federal prison. He was brought back into the United States without even the pretense of an extradition hearing. My father finds the informer.

For my father, for my mother (but less adamantly), the Party is everything. Glorious, true, righteous, the marrow out of which Black liberation and socialism will finally come. The truth is in absolutes. Loyalty, loyalty to this movement, above all else. "Arise ye prisoners of starvation," my mother sings in a piercing, haunting rendition of the "Internationale." "Avante, Popular!" my father calls, chanting the song of the Italian Popular Front against fascism, without melody and with resolute confidence. It is his version of "Avanti Popolo" with a New Yorker's inflection.

I fall in love with my first woman when I am five: Dorothy Hunton, the wife of my father's colleague, Alphaeus. A warm glow fills my heart. I think she is the most beautiful woman I have ever seen. Then I fall in love with Martha Schlamme, a Jewish folksinger who fled Vienna before the war, then with my third grade teacher, then with a best friend's mother, then with my high school English teacher.

I know to hide these feelings. I know they are wrong. I know I am twisted, deformed in some terrible way. I hide this terrible blemish upon the perfection I am supposed to be. I am consumed with guilt.

When I am in my late twenties an older comrade whom I dearly love confides in me. She tells me that in the early 1950s she had been instructed by the Party leadership to question women in the Party about their sexuality. In particular she was to ask them if they'd ever had a homosexual liaison. If the answer was yes she was instructed to ask them to voluntarily resign from the Party or face expulsion. "Even if it was only once," the comrade says to me. "Even if they had since married." She goes on, explaining: "It was to protect the Party from potential informers. If they were desperate enough to hide their sexual encounters, the FBI could force them into becoming informers." There is a silence into which I say nothing. "I'm so ashamed of myself," she tells me. "It was wrong." Now as I remember this comrade's confession I think that I *must* have known of this as a child. I must have heard these discussions around me, known the consequences of my feelings for women as I reached adolescence: to be made an FBI informer or be expelled from the Party/my family, to be cast out. I have erased my childhood memory of this, the way any child faced with an unfathomable reality erases it.

★

At thirteen I write a short story for our high school magazine. It is called "A Knight in a Brooklyn Morning." It is about a Black boy and a white girl whose respective father and mother leave their neighborhoods in Brooklyn (realistically, then, Bedford-Stuyvesant and Flatbush) and take them each to the zoo at Prospect Park. They meet at the polar bear's cage. The polar bear is there. The little girl loses her red balloon. It drifts over the big iron spikes toward the bear. The little boy climbs the fence, reaches up and over. He saves the balloon.

Of course I see finally in writing this that I was the Black boy, a fictional hero providing my ultimate redemption, signifying the perfection I strove to become.

From Woolworth's to Managua

Tom Berry

Tom Berry grew up in New York City, where he was born in 1944, but has spent most of his adult life on the West Coast. After working as a film editor, carpenter, and social worker, he returned to graduate school and is completing a doctorate in political science. He plans to teach at the community college level.

Berry describes the process of developing an adult political identity distinct from, although not antagonistic to, his red diaper heritage. Reflecting on the differences between his style of activism and that of his parents, Berry has commented, "I've never joined a political party, although I can't say I never was tempted to. There have been times when I felt something was missing in my political life that membership in a party might have provided."

I came of age politically on a sunny Saturday morning in April when I was ten. Making up some excuse to give my parents, I left our lower Manhattan apartment after breakfast. Feeling a sense of adventure, I self-consciously strode through our housing project to the Woolworth's store on 14th Street. As I passed the playgrounds already full of kids, I was mindful of a purpose that set me apart, a different reason for being out early on such a morning.

There was already a picket line when I got to Woolworth's, a sparse circle of protestors in front of the store. Most were carrying placards supporting the struggle to integrate Woolworth's lunch counters in the South. I remember mostly white people, one or two Black people, no other kids. I think I was disappointed the line wasn't longer, my sense of being part of a larger cause somewhat deflated. On the other hand, the small size of the group meant that my arrival made a difference—and also made it harder for me to leave. Once there, I was immediately either "in" or "out." There was no buffer zone of public space from which I could anonymously observe the scene before deciding to join in. I was welcomed into the circle by a middle-aged Black woman, who seemed to be in charge. I was handed a placard, and suddenly I wasn't outside anymore.

While I don't remember much of the rest of that morning, one incident stands out: an elderly white man, his face pinched with anger, stares at me and calls me a "communist." Others on the line quickly counsel me to ignore him, but I find this hard to do. Although I know that in our family and among many of our friends communists are the good guys, I have absorbed enough of the anticommunism of mainstream America to feel hurt and afraid. I know that it is not a good thing to be called a communist by a stranger, especially in a public situation when the word is hurled at me like a curse. Perhaps also I know, secretly, that the accusation is true, that I am a communist, or at least the son of communists, something the others on the picket line can't and shouldn't know.

Looking back from the vantage of adulthood, I wonder about the impact of my parents' post-McCarthy secretiveness on my own political development. Was it to avoid this kind of pain and public embarrassment that they always seemed to be as inconspicuous as possible in their radicalism? I remember my mother saying many times that communists had to distinguish themselves by their ideas, not by how they dressed or behaved in public places, certainly not by their lifestyles. I rebelled against these rules (especially when it came to "dressing up" for demonstrations), but on a deeper psychological level I think I got the message. As an adult I found myself looking at ragged protestors through my parents' more critical eyes.

I left Woolworth's that day feeling both relief and exaltation. When I returned home for lunch, my parents were supportive but puzzled as to why I hadn't told them beforehand. The reason was clear to me: to do so would have been like asking permission, and picketing Woolworth's would have been that much less my own.

Not long before the Woolworth's episode, my family had been involved in an unsuccessful effort to integrate the privately owned but publicly subsidized housing project where we lived. There were no Black or Hispanic tenants among a population of about twenty thousand. Despite the multiethnic complexion of the surrounding neighborhood, my Puerto Rican friend who lived across the street was not free to play on "our" playgrounds. A tenants' committee (led by Party members like my parents) decided to try to force the project management to accept one Black family (themselves communists) as an opening wedge toward integration.

The situation was very tense. The racist backlash was such that the tenants' committee had to provide around-the-clock protection to the Black family.

White committee members took turns staying overnight with them in their apartment, behind a barricaded door. On the playground, the children of committee members were expected to provide companionship and some amount of protection to Dean, the Black couple's only child. I found this very difficult. I was a shy, not very aggressive kid, and the racism of other white kids on the playground was painful to see. Though perhaps not consciously, I think I also resented being put in this position. (Dean and I never became close friends, which isn't surprising given the pressures we both faced.) I found myself in the middle of a wrenching struggle, which, important as it was, I couldn't fully comprehend and which was not of my own choosing. My trip to Woolworth's was probably some kind of personal response to this earlier experience.

In general, my parents didn't force their politics on me or my brother. At the same time, since politics was their life, politics shaped my life, too. Along with many other communists, they took a stand against racism before it was widely acceptable to do so, and they also battled against the knee-jerk "Blacks can do no wrong-ism" of the Party itself. I could see with my child's eyes that these were difficult, emotionally trying battles and that many were lost. I understood that being a communist was not an easy or glamorous career, and I could feel the pain of defeat, whether in seeing Dean's family forced to leave the project or my mother in tears when the Rosenbergs were executed.

Because I was exposed to political struggles that were not my own and because I could see how wrenching they could be, the process of forging my own political identity carried a special urgency. The process started early—perhaps in front of the Woolworth's on 14th Street—but it also took a long time. It wasn't until my late thirties, when I became active in support of the revolutions in Central America, that I fully achieved a political voice of my own. By that time, my father was dead from cancer and my mother had long ago left active politics behind. She was proud of what I was doing ("my son, the public speaker") and didn't question the justice of the cause, but she was fearful that my life might become consumed by politics, to the detriment of family, security, and career. To some degree this caution reflected regret over choices she had made that favored politics over career, regret that colored her real concern for my well-being. She wished I didn't have to go to Nicaragua to see the Sandinista revolution for myself.

During these years between Woolworth's and Nicaragua, I sometimes found myself feeling envious of those I met in various causes whose political identity was forged, of necessity, out of rebellion against their parents' politics. This always seemed to me a simpler, cleaner, and perhaps more "legitimate" coming of age. I think I wasn't yet fully aware or accepting of my own rebellion and so was drawn to that of others. When I finally began to sort these issues out, I could see that the struggle to differentiate my own from my parents' politics was a real and challenging one, not least because I was growing up in a world with different opportunities for political action and different constraints as well. For one thing, with no credible party to guide us, politics was not as completely definitive of our lives as it had been of theirs. We had perhaps more political choices but no up-to-date road map to show the way.

In the course of my growing up, my parents and I shared a certain emotional bond by believing in socialism—my mother and I still do. The injustices of capitalism seem to stir our juices in a special way that is hard to explain. This didn't come from any preaching on my parents' part. Nor, as I discovered when I was old enough to recognize such things, was my parents' communism very ideological. Sure, they looked to the Soviet Union as a model until Khrushchev denounced Stalin, but at least in later years they didn't seem to be engaged in the ideological debates that raged on the Left. Perhaps they had when they were younger. My mother insists their decision to join the Party—which they did together—was based on careful study, not youthful emotion. Perhaps this is one reason my mother's commitment to socialism survived. But I think the emotional component is also key. Having a socialist vision provides psychological and intellectual anchor, and moral compass as well, in a complex and turbulent world.

I started to think about these issues again when I returned to school to get a doctorate in political science. Sitting in graduate seminars, I would be conscious that something was driving me—a special history and an emotional bond connecting me to that history—that I didn't share with others in the room. Around the same time my daughter was born, and I began thinking about what kind of political being I wanted her to become, how my politics would look to her, and how she would relate to my politics. I like to think I will give more attention to my daughter's *feelings* about growing up "political" than my parents knew how to do. I want her to share in the bittersweet energy of "the good fight," whatever shape it might take, and at the same time to give her the space she needs to become her own political person. Somehow, my parents did that for me. They prepared me for making my own political choices, mostly by simply including me in their own. I probably saw and understood more than my parents thought I did, and I have no doubt my daughter will, too.

Cheering for Khrushchev
and Other Childhood Memories

Steven J. Diner

Born and raised in the Bronx, Steven J. Diner attended the High School
of Music and Art in Manhattan. He studied history at the State University
of New York in Binghamton and at the University of Chicago, where he
completed a Ph.D. He is a professor of history and dean of the faculty of
Arts and Sciences at Rutgers University-Newark. He is married to the
daughter of a Labor Zionist, whom his father thought "progressive-
minded" despite her "right-wing" origins.

Diner describes how his political sensibilities evolved from those of his
father, who fervently supported the Soviet Union while voting for Democratic Party candidates and encouraging his children to make the most of
the opportunities offered by a capitalist society.

I don't remember when I first realized that our family was different from most
of the others who inhabited the five-story apartment buildings of our neighborhood in the north Bronx. Different, that is, from most of the other Jewish families, since I knew next to nothing about the Irish and Italian kids who
went to St. Brendan's parochial school, and in any case lived in separate buildings from the Jews. (Protestants were nonexistent.) Superficially we were
pretty much like everyone else: two parents, two children, a two-bedroom
apartment, and a father who took the subway to work downtown. To be sure,
my mother began working around the corner in a small blouse factory when
I was in third grade, leaving work in time to give me lunch when I came home
from school at noon. But working moms, although not the norm, were not
exactly exotic. Most of my friends had families that, unlike us, owned cars,
and had fathers who knew how to drive. But neither the absence of wheels
nor the presence of a working mom distinguished us significantly from our
Jewish neighbors.

My father's idealization of the Soviet Union made us different. Born in Russia in 1905, my father formed his political identity during the Bolshevik Revolution. His mother died when he was a boy, and his father came to America just before the start of World War I. The egalitarian ideology of the revolution inspired my father, and he secured a position from the local Bolshevik committee as manager of an apartment building in the city of Kharkov in the early 1920s. Communication with his father in New York was very difficult during the years of the war, the revolution, and the civil war, but in 1922 my grandfather sent money to bring his four children to America. Not eager to leave the Soviet Union, my father nonetheless acceded to his father's wishes and came to the U.S. with his two sisters. His younger brother refused to leave. In New York, he found work in the garment industry, joined a union, became a member of the International Workers Order, and made close friendships with other Russian Jewish immigrants of similar political persuasion. He married my mother, a Jewish immigrant from Poland, in 1939. My mother was not especially interested in politics, but she had several leftist friends and she was comfortable with, if always a bit cynical about, the pro-communist politics of my father, his sisters, and their friends.

My mother did not view religion as a tool of the capitalists to exploit the workers, but she still had little use for the synagogue and for Jewish ritual observance. It is not surprising, then, that on Rosh Hashana and Yom Kippur we were among the very few Jews in the neighborhood who did not go to *shul*. For this I was profoundly grateful, but I hated those days anyhow because my mother would not let us go out of the house unless we wore a suit and tie. To dress otherwise, she said, employing a logic that I have never fully comprehended, would be an affront to our neighbors.

Most of the boys I grew up with went to Hebrew School at one of the local orthodox synagogues, where they learned to read but not comprehend Hebrew prayers. My brother and I went to the Emma Lazarus Folk *Shule*, which met in the basement of our building my first year then moved around the corner to a room in a commercial building that had previously housed an office of the American Labor Party.

I was perhaps eight years old when I started at Emma Lazarus. We learned a bit of Yiddish and sang Yiddish songs. The one I remember best was written by the great Yiddish poet I. L. Peretz and set to the tune of Beethoven's "Ode to Joy":

Vayse, broyne, shvartse, gele,
Misht di farbn oys tsuzamen,
Ale mentshen zaynen brider,
Fun eye tatn, fun eye mamen.

White, brown, black, and yellow,
Stir and mix these colors together;
All people are brothers,
From the same father, from the same mother.

It would be years before I realized that Beethoven used the German poetry of Schiller and not the Yiddish poetry of I. L. Peretz (written well after Beethoven's death) in the final movement of the Ninth Symphony.

The Emma Lazarus Folk *Shule* observed some of the Jewish holidays—particularly Hanukkah, Purim, Pesach, and Sukkos, I suppose because all of these represented a struggle of the Jewish people against a protofascist oppressor. I have no memory of the teachers ever talking about Yom Kippur or Simchas Torah, the day of atonement and the celebration of the Torah. What I most remember about the *Shule* were the secular parables and political lectures interspersed between Yiddish lessons—stories of great strikes, accounts of the execution of Julius and Ethel Rosenberg, descriptions of the evils of Nazism and fascism. After I spent three years at Emma Lazarus, the school folded, and my mother enrolled me in the Shalom Aleichem Folk *Shule*, a Yiddishist school without any obvious secular political ideology. My father grudgingly accepted my attendance at what he called a "right-wing school." I was upset, however, when the teacher at this new school announced one day to the class that I had previously attended a "communist school." At age ten, I was not yet old enough to know what communist meant, but I knew that it wasn't intended as a compliment.

As time went on, I became increasingly cognizant of my father's pro-Soviet politics. My father would talk how about good things were for workers in the Soviet Union. He pointed with pride to Sputnik and regularly denounced Soviet bashers. I especially remember watching David Susskind's interview of Nikita Khrushchev on television in 1959. Several of my father's friends had come over to watch it with us, and they all cheered whenever they thought Khrushchev scored a point on David Susskind.

My father's sister Mary shared his political sympathies. She used to take me downtown for dinner at the Horn and Hardart cafeteria, followed by a movie. I couldn't figure out why she always took me to Russian-language films. I hated them because I could not yet read well enough to follow the English subtitles. But I soon understood that we went to these movies for the same reason that my father always ordered Russian dressing with his salad.

My parents occasionally spent a summer weekend at a leftist Jewish resort north of New York known as Lakeland. Whereas typical Catskill resorts had lavish food and Borscht Belt comedians, this one featured lectures on the lawn every morning on subjects like "The Crisis of Capitalism." Attached to Lakeland was a children's summer camp, Kinderland, which my brother attended. (He later went to Camp Wo-Chi-Ca—Workers' Children's Camp.) He recalls sitting in the bunk one day when the counselor came running in excitedly, telling the boys, "The North Koreans have invaded South Korea." My brother asked him, "Are the North Koreans the good guys?" The counselor responded, "Of course."

There was lots of historical and political conversation in our house, especially at dinnertime. My father would tell us that strikes were workers' only weapon against merciless bosses and that we should never cross a picket line. When workers complained to Herbert Hoover that they could not find jobs, he told them to sell apples. Franklin Roosevelt (pronounced "Roo-zuh-velt") saved capitalism. Stalin went to great lengths to save millions of Russian Jews from Hitler. The Soviet Union had no choice but to invade Czechoslovakia, to put down a reactionary anticommunist movement and to protect Russia from future German aggression. Dad denounced Republicans regularly, but reserved special venom for three "fascist anti-Semites": John Foster Dulles, Joe McCarthy, and Richard Nixon.

How did I make sense of my father's communist sympathies in the Cold War atmosphere of the 1950s? One might expect a young person caught between such political extremes to experience personal agony, or at least considerable confusion. But in fact I suffered little from the dissonance between school and home. Not that I ignored politics. To the contrary, my father made me deeply conscious of political and social issues at an early age. I think I understood intuitively that for my father the Soviet Union was at once an icon and a metaphor for social justice. I dismissed his religious beliefs as easily as he dismissed those of orthodox Jews and embraced the metaphor.

The truth is that despite his avowed attachment to communism, my father's political sympathies were very ecumenical. Essentially he divided the world into progressives and reactionaries. All those who wanted to bring about greater economic and social justice were "progressives." Although he employed Marxist rhetoric, Dad was a registered Democrat who voted faithfully for Roosevelt, Truman, Stevenson, Kennedy, Johnson, Humphrey, McGovern, and Carter. Unlike true ideological leftists, he did not view "liberals" as the real enemy. He bristled when I criticized the Soviet Union but concluded nonetheless that I was "progressive-minded." Some of his closest friends opened small businesses, but their entrance into the petty bourgeoisie did not diminish their status as fellow leftists. Indeed, he himself contemplated opening a dry-cleaning store.

In the end, my father was very proud of his accomplishments in America and especially of his sons' upward mobility and professional status. Russian communism was his religion, but like those who continue to practice their ancestral religion long after they have ceased to believe, my father mouthed the ritualistic slogans of Russian Marxism but demonstrated his belief in the promise of American opportunity. Capitalist America could be made just, or at least more just, and children of the proletariat need not remain in the proletariat.

Irving Howe put it best. "Like no other group in modern history," he wrote in *World of Our Fathers*, "the immigrant Jewish workers meant to realize the Marxian ideal that the task of the working class is its self-abolition. They can hardly be blamed that things did not occur quite according to plan."

Perhaps I have redefined my father's radicalism to suit my own sensibilities. Like my father, I am fixated on politics. I believe that government should try to achieve greater social equity. A part of me deeply resents inherited class privilege. I usually vote for Democrats and support universal health care, government programs to achieve social and economic opportunity, higher taxes for the wealthy, and abortion rights. So is this the legacy of my father's Jewish radicalism? Would he be pleased that nineteen years after his death at age seventy-four I still consider myself a liberal? I think so, and I think he would still call me "progressive-minded."

Proud to Be Working Class

Roberta Wood

Roberta Wood, born in Baltimore on the Fourth of July, 1949, has been living in Chicago since the mid-1970s. Wood works as an electrical instrument and testing mechanic and is a union activist.

A member of the National Committee of the Communist Party, Wood is among the relatively small number of red diaper babies who have embraced their parents' political affiliation. She describes how a positive view of the contributions and values of the working class has been central to her identity and life choices. Wood's story thus challenges accepted notions of the pervasive pull of the American Dream, especially for the Baby Boom generation.

My parents were my heroes and role models. I wanted to be just like them when I grew up.

My father seemed tall and infinitely strong. He'd throw one kid up on his shoulders, grab one more in each arm, then charge up a hill without losing his breath. He carried the steel mill in his hands not huge but strong, with slag and grit in every layer of callus. My mother had beautiful dark wavy hair and an unshakable air of serenity. We children were enveloped in a world of security in her calm voice and strong smooth hands.

What made me most proud of my folks was the unending procession of co-workers, friends, neighbors, and comrades who came through our house to talk over problems and grievances; to work out organizing strategies; to share wisdom, great spaghetti, and lemon meringue pie.

If you had to grow up in capitalist U.S.A., the best place to do it was in the Communist Party!

Given what else was going on in the '50s for working-class kids, being a red diaper baby was a big plus. The '50s were hardly the idyllic family values utopia decade they are portrayed as, especially for steelworkers' kids, who were privately embarrassed when they compared their homes and families to middle-class "Father Knows Best" perfection. Being ashamed of your relatives with foreign or southern accents, your home with the old wringer washer and the beat-up car on blocks in the yard, and even your own dad, who slept in his underwear instead of pajamas—judging yourself below standard—isolated you from your family and other kids.

As children of communists, we were able to reject the anti-working-class propaganda that made fun of us and our families. We saw the nobility of honest productive work, felt contempt for parasite bosses, took pride in the fight against racism, felt the honor of working-class solidarity. Self-esteem was never a problem. Our parents' love and a class outlook on society gave us a profound sense of confidence and optimism in the future.

My family on my mother's side were Russian Jewish immigrants. My father's family came from midwestern farmers. We had the best of all worlds: we had a chubby grandma named Bubby and spent Friday nights dining on her golden chicken soup and matzoh balls and drinking in the unending praise of what smart, brilliant, gorgeous children we were (also nice). We also had a Christmas tree every year and presents for all holidays. Our family Easter ritual was usually a civil rights march in Washington, D.C.

We sang civil rights songs, union songs, Appalachian folk songs. We felt pride in the achievements of African Americans, Native Americans, and people in countries all over the world. Paul Robeson, Woody Guthrie, Pete Seeger, Leadbelly, the Weavers, Florence Reese, Langston Hughes, the heroic Rosenbergs were all ours.

Part of our culture, too, were the stories of legendary working-class heroes like Charlie Parrish, who taught himself everything about the millwright trade, secretly studying blueprints, and forced the company to give him a job as the first African American millwright at Sparrows Point. In Baltimore, a Jim Crow town, we had the opportunity to see comradeship and respect between African American and white workers and their families.

In the McCarthy era, some parents were afraid a child might repeat a remark in an inappropriate place, so they would limit the dinner table discussion to family matters. Dad had great disdain for those who hushed up when a child entered the room "as if their own kid was going to be a stool pigeon on them." The folks didn't swear much, but one word was so terrible it apparently couldn't be pronounced, only spelled by spitting each letter out through one's teeth with utter contempt. It seemed to be reserved for blast

Courtesy of Judy Kaplan.

furnace superintendents and members of Congress. I wondered to myself why "S.O.B." was such a bad word.

Thirteen steelworkers from Bethlehem Steel, including my father, were called before the House Un-American Activities Committee in 1957. For refusing to "cooperate" (testify), they were summarily fired. All of the men had families, and between them, they had hundreds of years of seniority. I was seven, in the second grade, and my brothers were nine and four.

Those were scary times. Both of my parents were called before HUAC. My Uncle Roy was in jail, serving a sentence under the Smith Act. The HUAC hearings were front-page news in the *Baltimore Sun*. Some kids told us their folks said they could still play with us anyway because "it wasn't the kids' fault what the parents did." Some neighbors became cold and aloof, but others dropped by and made a point to lend a hand with some ongoing home improvement project. One, who laid firebrick in the open hearth, helped put in our new fireplace. Some naive workers and neighbors later told my dad they figured he and my mother would soon be arrested for whatever terrible thing it was they had done. When they weren't, it became clear that Bethlehem management had used HUAC to undermine the union by purging the most militant, antiracist union activists and intimidating the rest of the work force.

By the time I was thirteen and in the eighth grade, a lot of changes had happened to our family. We were living in Riverside, California. Both parents were students, my father on his way to a degree in biochemistry and my mother to a Ph.D. in medical anthropology.

Along with African American and Chicano neighbors, our family was at the center of a school boycott that integrated some of Riverside's schools. A chapter of CORE was formed; at age fourteen, I was secretary. We marched with the farmworkers and boycotted grapes. We helped young carpenters manufacturing mobile homes to organize a union; we picketed for fair housing in nearby cities; we went to peace demonstrations.

In high school I worked on an underground newspaper focused on free speech issues. Our group was multiracial, which was somewhat radical in a town dominated by orange growers and an Air Force base. We looked down on cheerleading, football games, proms, graduation ceremonies, and traditional school activities. We wore black turtlenecks, pierced ears, long hair, sandals, and embroidered peasant blouses. Cramming as many kids as we could get into somebody's old car, we drove anywhere not Riverside—the beach, the mountains, the desert, and to antiwar teach-ins in Los Angeles. I was the only one who didn't have to lie to my parents, but I did anyway. I still don't know why.

I always knew what I wanted to do with my life—be a revolutionary, make the world a better place, fight for socialism. In those days, going to college was assumed and affordable. I wanted to go where the action was—Berkeley.

I arrived at Berkeley in the fall of 1967. The antiwar movement was at full steam. My friends and I went to every demo, picket line, hearing, or whatever that anybody called, and I volunteered for any assignment, no matter how humble.

Like many others, I considered myself a Maoist. It seemed that everyone rejected the "traditional" Communist Party as out-of-date, too conservative, sell out, not militant. "Students will make the revolution." "The working class is bought off." These were some of the prevalent ideas on a campus which, after all, was populated predominantly by upper- and middle-class youth. I started to realize that some of the Sproul Plaza big mouths (including my boyfriend) had only the most superficial understanding of Marxism or philosophy but more than made up for that with arrogance, bombast, and bullying.

I dropped out of school "for a semester" and got a job on the midnight shift at the post office. I formed a close relationship with Bill Taylor, head of the Southern California district of the Communist Party, and his wife, Shirley. Bill had unending patience, perseverance, and good humor; we sat up till three or four in the morning night after night, smoking his Marlboros and arguing about feminism and the class question. Bill was as adamant for full equality for women as any feminist I've ever known. An African American who spoke a bit of Yiddish, he was right at home with all the other *alte kockers* (old farts), as he got a big kick out of calling himself.

I saved up $1,000 and took a charter flight to Europe, hitchhiked from Frankfurt to Dublin, Sicily to Prague. I made my way to the World Congress of Women in Helsinki, Finland, where some Soviet delegates invited me to join a huge women's international delegation touring the Soviet Union. In September 1969, after returning from Europe, I asked to join the Party. In the Soviet Union, I had seen a society in which many problems had been solved. Nurseries and kindergartens, health care, subsidized clothing for children, free vacations, sports and summer camps were available to all. Racism was illegal. International friendship and solidarity were official government policy. What I saw put a lie to the anti-Soviet slanders I had heard from the Berkeley New Left. I had seen that all the really serious people around the world were in their respective communist parties. And it certainly didn't hurt that they were the nicest people, too!

A bright-eyed young person joining the world revolutionary movement at the age of twenty, I was very idealistic—ready to give my life, endure untold hardships and privations, make heroic sacrifices at a moment's notice for the cause of the revolution. More often, the struggle called for attending untold numbers of meetings, battling infuriating mimeograph machines and torn electro-stencils, and getting up way before the crack of dawn to hand out leaflets at plant gates. I liked it all. Some from the New Left put down the Communist Party because included in its membership were so many old and some really old people. I saw it as a big plus. I found myself surrounded by *bubbes* of all nationalities and genders. Exclaiming, "the youth, the youth," they'd pinch your cheeks, ply you with healthy food, and proclaim how brilliant and gorgeous you were. But these veteran comrades had stories and experiences and wisdom that would knock your socks off.

In 1970, I signed up for the Venceremos Brigade, part of an international effort to help the Cubans harvest a record ten million tons of sugar cane. One evening, a few of us *brigadistas* wandered a couple of miles down the road to a neighboring *campamento* (work site). We sat around some old wooden tables late into the night with a group of Cuban tobacco factory workers and their families, who were also volunteer cane cutters. For the first time in years I felt completely at ease with a group of people—they weren't my age, gender, or nationality, only my class. I felt as if I had come home.

Back in LA I began applying for factory jobs. I wanted what I thought of at that time as a real job and to learn a trade. I applied at dozens of industrial enterprises, including Bethlehem Steel. I had come back from Cuba with the strongest right arm west of the Mississippi (I thought), but none of these places would hire me. The guy at the Bethlehem Steel personnel office said the problem was that they didn't have women's bathrooms. I filed an EEOC complaint.

I finally started working as a presser at a garment factory. Next I went to Harvey Aluminum, a part of Martin Marietta. There I was a water tester on an assembly line making plumbing fixtures. We women at Harvey had the dubious distinction of being the lowest paid members of the steelworkers union. On the line you could talk only to the people on either side of you. I was between Donna, a Black woman from Louisiana, and Betty, a white woman from Arkansas, who were best friends. Betty's machine tightened the little bolts that hold the faucet handles on. She liked to brag that all she did at work was screw all day long.

I quit that job to go to work full-time for the Party. I may be one of the few people in history who actually increased my income doing so. I helped to organize the Communist youth organization, the Young Workers Liberation League, in Southern California. In 1974 I met with Party leaders Gus Hall and Henry Winston in New York. They strongly encouraged me to move to the Midwest and get work in the steel industry, where women were beginning to be hired for the first time since World War II. I arrived in Chicago on April 15; nine days later, I was working as a laborer in the Alloy Bar Mill at US Steel's huge South Works plant.

I loved the steel mill. We worked rotating shifts, were often covered in grease and grit, and put up with foremen who were just plain mean. But I was awed by the power and massiveness of the physical operation—imagine liquid steel glowing like the sun and running down troughs from a hole in the side of the blast furnace. It took thousands of workers of every age and nationality with highly developed skills and tools to come up with this product. From the shipping building, I could look across Lake Michigan and see Chicago's skyline topped by the Sears Tower, the world's tallest building, made with structural steel from our mill.

I felt like my life was in the groove I wanted it to be in. I had finally fought my way into an apprenticeship program, was active in the union, and had been elected as the first woman officer of Steelworkers Local 65. I was involved in working-class struggles in South Chicago, in the women's caucus of the union, in putting out a rank-and-file newsletter—and we had an active Communist Party club in our mill.

I met my husband, Scott, one snowy February morning when he was distributing copies of *Labor Today* magazine outside the mill. In the whirlwind romance that followed, we sat up for days and nights talking earnestly. On March 8, International Women's Day, we made the decision to get married, and we were married at the union hall on May 1, 1978—May Day.

I learned one fundamental value as a red diaper baby that has served as an anchor throughout my life: a deep appreciation for workers and the working class, respect for the wisdom and skills of people who create everything that feeds, clothes, and houses us. Dad was always speaking admiringly about someone's skills: So-and-so was a great bricklayer, someone else was a master carpenter, my mom was a skilled medical technician. The grandeur of the work process, fascination with the unique relationship of the working class to science and technology and the future were part of our family's values.

Bill Taylor used to say that bourgeois morality was based on "faith, hope and charity" but the working class needs struggle, unity, and solidarity. In my family, we never felt that we were losing or sacrificing anything to participate in political struggles. We did it for our own good and our own future, not out of pity or feeling sorry for someone else who was "less fortunate." Like my mother, I feel that children cannot be properly raised without being a part of a movement bigger than themselves. The struggle does even more for the individual than the individual does for the struggle.

Without the Party, it would be hard to live in the world the way it is. Belonging to the Party, I feel connected to everyone else in the world, to the past and the future. I can make my own contribution, however small, and still feel part of humanity's greatest undertaking yet.

I am now the parent of three daughters. The mother-child relationship, with its connection to the past and future, the joy, the optimism, and the aggravation, reflects and intensifies the emotions and experiences I have found in the working-class movement and the Party. I hope that my daughters become conscious members of the working class, that they find some degree of satisfaction and serenity, as I have, from being part of the worldwide movement for the liberation of humankind . . . and, of course, that they make me a *bubbe* in due time.

"So Here I Am"

Judith Clark

Born in New York City in 1949, Judith Clark was active in the social movements of the 1960s and 1970s. She has been imprisoned since 1981 at Bedford Hills, New York State's maximum security prison for women, on charges stemming from an armed robbery in which three people were killed. Clark completed studies for her bachelor's degree while in prison, twenty years after being expelled from the University of Chicago for participating in a 1969 sit-in. She then went on to earn a master's degree in psychology.

Clark teaches prenatal and parenting classes at Bedford Hills. She has published several articles about mothers in prison, and her poetry has appeared in the *New Yorker* and other publications. In this memoir, she describes, without self-pity, the political evolution that led to her imprisonment.

There's no question I was a red diaper baby. I was still in diapers when my mother, Ruth, journeyed across two oceans with my two-year-old brother and me to the Soviet Union to join my father in a three-year sojourn. My father, Joe, was a CP organizer from the age of fourteen. In 1949, when I was born, he was a Party leader and writer for the *Daily Worker*. My mother, like many Party women, was a mass organizer, working with settlement houses on the Lower East Side and on the congressional election campaigns of progressive politicians such as Vito Marcantonio. She was also the primary breadwinner of our family.

On a deeper level, my story is about being the child of ex-communists. My mother left the Party soon after we came back from the Soviet Union in 1953, appalled by what she'd seen there and unwilling to reenter what she felt was the dogmatic, stilted, controlling culture of Party life. My father held on for three more years, waging a battle, along with others, to transform the Party; they wanted it to be less tied to the Soviet Union and more defined by U.S. conditions and sensibilities. In 1956, when Khrushchev's revelations of Stalinist crimes did not usher in major changes in the U.S. Party, my father left.

I was six years old. Though my father later insisted that he sat my brother Andy and me down to explain his momentous decision, I have no memory of it. For a long time, I didn't understand what had changed. To the extent that I was aware of politics, I still thought of my family as Red. Being Red meant worrying about the FBI coming around, like they did on my brother's first day of school. It meant knowing about the Rosenbergs and the heroes of the Abraham Lincoln Brigade and knowing that the fight against fascism was far from over. It meant feeling personally responsible that the dozen or so Black children who were bused from Coney Island to my elementary school in Bensonhurst feel welcome, and later being jealous of my brother, who got to go to the 1963 civil rights March on Washington while I was consigned to watching it on TV. It meant the joyful release I felt each summer when we went to Lake Mohegan, where I played with other red diaper kids and sang folk songs.

My parents seemed as wrapped up in the world as ever. When their friends came over to dinner, I sat quietly at the table, sneaking food to the dog, while all the adults talked at once, arguing politics and world affairs—my father's voice rising above all the others until my mother would scream, "Joe! Calm down!"

But I knew something crucial had happened. Papa was around the house more than ever. I sort of knew but didn't understand that he was blacklisted: denied jobs because he had been a Communist. He continued to take my brother and me to Coney Island every Friday to walk along the boardwalk, eat hot dogs at Nathan's, and play skeeball. But I felt bereft when he disappeared into his tiny book-lined den, where he typed furiously and sat brooding, preoccupied with "important things" I could only imagine.

As my father sank into silence, my mother seemed to rise in a whirl of fury and determination. She worked like a demon, advancing from door-to-door interviewer to the top ranks of the market research and public opinion polling field. While my father's mission was to right the wrongs he had perpetrated in defending Stalinism, my mother's was to drag our family into mainstream America.

I felt like something very important had been lost, but I didn't know what. Alone at times in our apartment, I looked for clues. I trod quietly into Papa's den, searching over his desk and through the books on the walls, picking out titles that caught my eye, like *The God That Failed*, trying to understand the words I read. If fascism and McCarthyism were bad and the struggles of labor and for civil rights good, how could my parents give up on all that? I knew they still cared about these issues, but their passions were steeped in anger and regret about the past.

Gradually, I developed my own theories. My parents came to represent two poles of the universe. My father was the Old World of Yiddish stories and songs, Jewish intellectualism, revolutionary history and sacrifice. My mother represented assimilation, "making it," Sweet Sixteens, and department stores. I romanticized Papa's brooding anger, forgave him his preoccupied distance, and lapped up the intimate times we spent together every Sunday, when he drove me from Brooklyn to my music school in Greenwich Village. I took in his sense of fervor and guilt, imbuing it with my own meanings, and became determined to hold on to our traditions and past. By the time I entered my teens, I too had a mission: I would be "the keeper of the flame" in my family.

At fourteen, I joined a citywide school boycott initiated by parents and community leaders, demanding integrated quality education. I remember going to Reverend Milton Galamison's church for a freedom service, feeling overcome with awe when a sea of Black people, dotted with occasional whites, rose together in song. I felt that I'd finally found my way back home. All that I'd lost when my parents left the Party I regained by joining with this new African American culture of resistance and hope.

My mother and I fought over the things that teenage daughters and mothers often battle about: clothes, boyfriends, lifestyles. But for me, these fights were nothing less than a holy war in which I carried the burden of history. Fearing the bite of my mother's angry tongue, I chose guerrilla tactics of avoidance and subterfuge over open confrontation. She bought me pink dresses and wool cardigans; I wore black dungarees and turtlenecks. She moved the family to a better neighborhood with better schools; within six months, I'd found the two other girls in my junior high school who were red diaper kids. She lobbied for me to join the cheerleaders in high school; I cut school to sneak off to the Village with my friends. I rejected the blond sons of doctors she liked and fell in love with a working-class radical, just like Papa.

I was my father's daughter, clinging tenaciously to the world he had forged for me, standing strong in the face of my mother's drive toward the mainstream, trying to breath life into a dream that I needed to believe was still his.

One early morning in my junior year of high school, this uneasy equilibrium was shattered. As a member of Student CORE (Congress of Racial Equality), I was planning to participate in a one-day school boycott in which we all would gather at Boys High in Bedford-Stuyvesant—an all-Black school—to dramatize the inequality of de facto segregation. My father woke me at dawn. He sat uncomfortably at the edge of my bed and told me that he and my mother had decided I could not go because they feared for my safety. I was stunned. How could my father take my mother's side over mine? In my shame and anger at not participating, I finally felt my father's betrayal. I swore that I would take up the path that they had abandoned.

In the years that followed, I leaped into the New Left with a vengeance, always pushing toward the extremes of militancy and ideology. My father's fits of fury and political harangues, which had been directed at others, were increasingly pointed at me. I dodged his bullet words and silently clung to an older image of him and our relationship. Deep inside me, in that place beyond logic and reason, I was still my father's daughter.

A generation has passed. I am the mother of a fourteen-year-old daughter. I have been in prison since 1981, serving a life sentence for charges stemming from an attempted robbery in which three people were killed. Since Joe's death six years ago, my mother has raised my child.

In my fifth year inside, when my daughter was six, I was locked down in punitive segregation for two years, charged with conspiracy to escape. Alone, depressed, sunk into a stillness that seemed like death, I felt one heart calling out to me: my daughter's. Because I wanted to reach out to her, I knew I wanted to live. I would have to be willing to question my life choices and assumptions, to try to understand what drove me. Spinning back through time, I replayed family history and legend. I found myself writing about our years in the Soviet Union. I tried to imagine the trip as my mother might have experienced it. I pictured her sailing off on the *Queen Mary*, away from family, country, and friends, without money or proper documents, with two small children in tow. I imagined how she felt, living in a repressive, foreign land, unable to work, limited in her social contacts and language, taking care of her children while my father was busy with work and political affairs. How cut off and frustrated she must have been, how depressed and angry.

I wrote for hours, and when I emerged back into my own present, I felt a new sympathy for and appreciation of that woman who was my mother. I, too, knew depression, loneliness, and rage. I felt new respect for her courage and her determination to make changes in our lives once we returned. I knew that even in her days in the Party she had been a bit of a subversive, laying claim to her individuality and independence. While recognizing the importance of history and ideas, Ruth chose to live in the here and now, in the give and take of people, work, and change. I felt that I could learn and draw strength from such a woman in my own journey toward understanding and reclamation, for myself and my child.

We sit together in the prison visiting room—my daughter, Grandma, and me—gossiping about my friends and old comrades, who are part of my child's extended family and whom my mother has grown to know and accept. "Did you hear about . . . ?" Ruth throws out tentatively, ever the researcher, wanting to know more. I take up the gambit, sharing some juicy details and history, relaxed enough to open up about my friends. My daughter listens and questions and voices her opinion, delighted to be included in this spicy, adult gabfest about love affairs, marriages, and relationships. Then she pushes into new terrain, asking Grandma, "How about you and Grandpa?" Ruth raises herself up in her chair and proclaims, "We had the perfect marriage." Feeling playful and bold, I tease and prod her, until an impish grin lights up her face and she reveals a secret or two.

I sit, drinking in this easy banter, sweet laughter, and slightly risqué intimacy. I want to preserve this moment so I can recall it later.

Now my daughter and mother are debating the pros and cons of the City Council decision to spend a large sum of money to renovate their local subway station. My daughter argues, "How can they spend all that money on a subway station when there are homeless people all over the neighborhood who need shelter and food and services? It's not fair!"

Grandma rejoins, "What's one got to do with the other? That station is so old and antiquated and its stairway so narrow that I can't use it for fear of getting run over by the rush hour crowd. Did you ever think of what it's like for older people?"

I listen and laugh. It feels so old and familiar. So much our family. But with new voices and visions with each generation. We are Clark women, all of us: survivors and fighters, for our family and in the world.

In My World

Susan Moscou

Susan Moscou was born in Michigan and grew up in New York City. She works as a family nurse practitioner providing primary health care at a shelter for homeless families in the Bronx.

Moscou's story is one of seamless continuity between childhood and adult experiences and values. She grew up in a supportive interracial CP community, continues to surround herself with other red diaper babies and activists, and remains committed to the beliefs that she shares with her parents.

In my world, all the moms were Black and all the dads were Jewish.

My father met my mother when he was a union organizer at an automobile factory in Flint, Michigan, in the late 1940s. My mother was working on the assembly line.

My mother grew up in Flint and gravitated toward progressive politics because she desired an interracial lifestyle. My father, an only child, grew up in the Bronx. Although his parents were not politically active, his Aunt Rose was a member of the Communist Party. My parents were married in 1950, and both sets of parents disapproved. Growing up I had minimal contact with my three living grandparents—my father's parents and my mom's father.

I was born in 1951 in Flint, Michigan; my sisters were born in 1952 and 1955. We lived in Flint until I was five years old, and then we moved to New York City because my mother wanted us to grow up in a diverse community and because my father had been fired from his job and blacklisted after appearing before HUAC in 1955.

We lived in a middle-income housing project in Queens. The project was predominantly white, but many Black families resided there. Across the street was a cooperative apartment complex where my parents quickly found the "political" families, including several interracial couples. These couples and their children became part of the progressive community I would grow up in.

Although we lived in Queens, my neighborhood extended beyond these boundaries as my parents defined a larger community for us. Our community encompassed a rich, culturally diverse society of progressive politics and interracial families. I assumed everyone grew up in this kind of environment. It took me a long time to realize that I had a sheltered upbringing.

In public school, I never felt that my ideas were vastly different from the so-called norm since my political allies from the neighborhood held similar beliefs. We ran for many student government offices, supporting each other in elections.

I remember not standing for the Pledge of Allegiance and feeling OK about this because I understood that I could handle the repercussions of my actions. My parents encouraged my sisters and me to think for ourselves and to stand up for our beliefs. In fact, I think our charge was "Go forth and disrupt." We often clashed with school policies, but our parents always supported us and helped us understand the social and political issues surrounding these conflicts.

My parents felt it was important for my sisters and me to identify ourselves as Black. I have always understood that I was interracial, but when asked about race I identify myself as a Black woman. My parents realized that a racist society would identify my sisters and me as Black because our mother is, so to offset society's negativity about Blackness, we claimed the identity and felt positive about it. My father understood the destructiveness of a race-conscious society and did not view our identification with Blackness as negating him. My parents did two unusual things as an interracial couple: they discussed race and surrounded us with other interracial children. Their ability to face these issues prepared me well to deal with my interracial background.

We lived in the most integrated neighborhood possible for the 1950s. Because my father was white, he never had trouble renting apartments. When Black friends were denied housing in New York City, my father would apply for the same apartments, which would then suddenly become available. Our friends would then move in and have the locks changed.

Religiously, my sisters and I also grew up in a mixed marriage. My father is an atheist, and my mother an agnostic. Although raised as atheists, my sisters and I learned about our cultural heritages and celebrated Christmas, Hanukkah, and Passover.

I grew up in a flurry of political activity and summered at progressive camps that bolstered my family's political philosophy. I remember when my parents refused to send us to public school when radical teachers went on strike demanding integration. Instead, we attended Freedom Schools, where we were taught by the striking teachers and community leaders. Later, many of these teachers became our allies when other students and I continued political activities at school.

My political beliefs were not diminished through junior high, high school, and college. I met people who shared my activism, including other red diaper babies. My interracial and left-wing circles grew and became part of my extended community.

I sometimes wonder if I have romanticized my upbringing. I love and admire my parents' intelligence that led to their understanding of what it meant to be an interracial couple in the '50s and how it would affect their children. I love being interracial, Black, Jewish, and progressive because these things have given me access to a wondrous, vibrant existence in which I am always me and never feel the need to be someone else.

I continue to live in the world that my parents defined and created—a world that passionately confronts inequality and struggles against racism and sexism.

Really Normal

Renee Bell

The youngest author in this anthology, Renee Bell was born in 1974 in Philadelphia, where she was raised in a multigenerational left-wing family. Unlike many of the other contributors, Bell grew up in the CP milieu at a time when the Party had become a small organization with little impact on the larger society. She describes an experience shared among red diaper babies across the generations: trying to live in and reconcile two worlds.

I remember going on demonstrations as a child or to Communist Party conventions and people saying, "Wow, both your parents and grandparents are communists! You're a *real* red diaper baby!" I never understood what the big deal was. Didn't everyone go to demonstrations before they could walk? Didn't everyone have a mother who knew Dr. Martin Luther King and a father who constantly held meetings in the house? Didn't everyone's parents travel to the Soviet Union and grandparents go to Cuba? It didn't seem unusual that my grandfather had spent many years in the Soviet Union and was one of the first prominent African American members of the Communist Party USA. I just thought my family really loved travel and politics!

As I grew older and wiser, I began to understand why it was such a big deal. There aren't many people who believe that the country they live in is capable of change and are willing to fight for that change. The people in my family are willing to struggle for the rest of their lives for social justice, an end to racism, a decent educational system, affordable health care, and the end to nuclear warfare. I was raised to believe that fighting for your convictions is absolutely essential. This did not seem out of the ordinary to me; it seemed very logical.

Neither my parents nor my grandparents pushed me to adopt their views; it was a choice that I made on my own. My parents raised me to trust my own perceptions and ideas no matter what they may be. Granted, I was brought up around meetings, demonstrations, strikes, picket lines, and other signs of struggle, but by the time I reached the age of eleven, I began attending these events because I wanted to. They were fun. I loved the chants, the camaraderie, and the feeling of having the power to change the world. I was not forced to walk with my parents or attend at all. My parents gave me the opportunity, and I chose to take it because I felt it was important and necessary. I saw the things that were happening in this country: layoffs, homelessness, national debt, racism, anti-union movements, and the "Cold War," and I realized that I needed to do something, no matter how small.

Growing up in a communist household opened up many opportunities for me. In 1987, when I was twelve, I went to Cuba with the Young Communist League (YCL) and the Venceremos Brigade to participate in the Jose Martí International Pioneer Camp. The camp was five weeks long, but the experience will stay with me forever. My openness to other cultures, political backgrounds, races, and religions really helped me adjust to Cuba and the hundreds of different people that I met from all over the world. I became particularly attached to the Nicaraguan delegation. These kids, barely in their teens, had already experienced war and death; all that I had experienced were braces and school. I suddenly had a new appreciation for my life and a new anger toward President Reagan. When I got home, one of the first things that I did was to write Reagan a letter about my experiences with the Nicaraguans and my anger at how he could support the Contras. Needless to say, I never received a response. I live with the thought that these people who were such good friends may be dead.

The next summer, I attended Camp Artek in the Soviet Union. At first I was not thrilled about attending (how could I have a magnificent time in the Soviet Union when there was nothing in the world better than Cuba?), but I was very anxious to travel, so I went. Once again, I had a wonderful time meeting people from all over the world. I traveled with over one hundred children from the U.S. We spent a week in Moscow and then four weeks at the camp.

I was visiting the Soviet Union in the middle of the Cold War, which made the trip even more interesting. It was such a beautiful country that it made no sense to me why the U.S. and the U.S.S.R. were at odds. As in Cuba, the people were friendly and happy. Many were fascinated by the U.S. and Americans. I was happy to share my experiences and, in turn, learn about others' lives.

A lesson I learned from being in these two countries is that the U.S. is far behind in its educational system. It was very embarrassing going overseas and not knowing the language when everyone else knew English. Many of the kids knew English, Spanish, and their home language. It was sad when people would ask us about U.S. history and none of the Americans could give an answer, yet people from other countries could answer questions about their country and the United States. A few people in our delegation couldn't even tell you who was president.

I attended Central High School, a public school in the city of Philadelphia. It was very integrated: African American, Asian, Hispanic, white, lower class, middle class, and upper class. As I entered high school, my classmates looked upon me as different because I had had such an interesting childhood. I'd been to Cuba and the Soviet Union and had spent weekends in New York and Washington at demonstrations. It was unheard of for teenagers to participate in politics, let alone go to political events in their spare time. If I told people at school that I had been to New York, they would automatically assume that I was visiting the Empire State Building or doing something they considered exciting. When I told them that I went for a demonstration, their faces went blank because they had no idea what people did at demonstrations. The only thing they knew was what they saw on the news, people at demonstrations starting a fight or getting out of control. I explained what I, and many others, do at demonstrations: walk, chant, and sing. This, unfortunately, was not very exciting to my classmates, so they just shook their heads and moved on to what the next person did for the weekend. This reaction eventually caused me not to share my other political activities and the activities of my parents.

The problem I had growing up as a red diaper baby was trying to explain my viewpoints and my parents' political affiliation without actually telling the truth. Being in the Communist Party is taboo in this country. Though it's prohibited to hold political affiliation against a person in the job market, it's not prohibited to hold it against a friend in high school or college. In my world history class freshman year, the teacher started explaining how the Soviet Union was a dictatorship and no one there was free or allowed to live a decent life. I spoke up about my experiences, and I was essentially laughed at by the teacher. Another incident took place in my physics class. A classmate had heard something on the news the night before about socialized health care in the Soviet Union and started talking about the "fucking communists." It was pretty difficult going through my school years feeling too uncomfortable to tell people what kind of meetings my parents held every week. It was frustrating to be proud of something in my heart but, because of fear of being ostracized, not being able to share that pride with others.

When I turned thirteen years old, I joined the Young Communist League because I wanted to be a part of the struggle to change this country. I was treasurer for a few years and an active member until I went to college. Being in the League was exciting, although, in a way I felt as if I was going against everything that my friends believed in. They spent their weekends shopping or hanging out. I went to YCL meetings every other Sunday. I still hung out on the weekends with my friends, but sometimes I had to be late. I became accustomed to going to demonstrations, handing out literature, and then trying to explain to my classmates when I would see them on the street what I was doing and why. I wouldn't lie about what I was handing out; I would just say that I wasn't sure exactly what the literature was about. I was doing a friend of the family a favor and helping out for the day. My classmates and I were satisfied with this answer.

But this explaining was also nerve-racking and annoying. Sometimes I couldn't remember whom I told and whom I didn't tell about my family's political beliefs. Plus, I didn't understand why I felt the need to hide what the papers I was handing out were about. I just knew that I should tell only very close friends. My parents didn't put the idea of hiding things into my head; they just told me that not everyone accepts our political views. I interpreted that as: keep my mouth shut and, if necessary, lie! Each time I decided that I didn't need to hide anything, family and friends would joke about the FBI and their spying techniques.

I knew the FBI took pictures of us at demonstrations and thought that because I had visited both the Soviet Union and Cuba, the FBI probably had a file on me. I was sure that the letter I had sent to Ronald Reagan discussing U.S. support of the Contras was added to this file that, in my mind, was growing and growing and would never stop. The thought of our phones being tapped and that every time I went to a political event at the Party office in New York the FBI was watching me made me absolutely disgusted and a bit frightened. What was I doing to make the government scared enough of me to actually keep a file on me? It has never been confirmed that I have an FBI file, but the impact of that thought caused me to become cautious about what I believe and with whom I share my beliefs. I credit this paranoia to the media. When I was old enough to join the YCL, the prevailing view of communism was so negative that it is no wonder that a thirteen-year-old became intimidated. Luckily it didn't affect me enough to keep me away from politics. Instead, it gave me the feeling of rebellion and made me want to participate even more.

Today, in my early twenties, I am a graduate student in animal science at Michigan State University. I am no longer active in the YCL, but I now share my experiences and viewpoints without fear of intimidation. Being a student, I am unable to participate in many political events, but because my friends are open-minded and intelligent, I am able to have discussions in which my experiences and thoughts are expressed and often debated with others. I feel that if someone does not accept me simply because of my beliefs, then he or she is not an individual I can be truly comfortable around or develop a friendship with. I no longer feel intimidated by what I believe in or have ideas about.

Glossary

Abraham Lincoln Brigade: Twenty-eight hundred volunteers from the United States fought in the Spanish Civil War (1936–1939) to defend the government of Spain against an uprising led by General Francisco Franco. Although the volunteers served in military units named after Lincoln, Washington, and John Brown, in popular usage all are known as members of the Lincoln Brigade. Almost one-third of the Lincoln Brigade died in Spain. They and their surviving comrades became heroes to the Left, "premature antifascists" who had put their bodies on the line to stop the rise of fascism in Europe.

American Labor Party (ALP): Between 1936 and 1956, the ALP offered voters in New York State a pro-union, antiracist, and mildly socialist electoral alternative. Many CP members were active in the ALP.

Earl Browder (1891–1973): General Secretary of the CP from 1934 to 1945, Browder guided the Party through the Popular Front and World War II. After the war, Browder attempted to preserve the CP's role in mainstream American politics. Most CP members supported Browder's attempts to maintain the Party's visibility; fewer accepted his political views, which muted distinctions between labor and capital and proclaimed a continued unity of interests between the Soviet Union and its capitalist wartime allies. In 1945, Jacques DuClos, head of the French Communist Party, issued a severe critique of Browder's aims, which was widely interpreted as a message from the Soviet party. Browder quickly became a leader without followers: he was removed from his position and expelled from the CP in 1946.

Comintern: The Third (Communist) International formed in 1919 as a counterweight to Allied-German attempts to reshape the international world order after World War I. Intended as an organization of coequal communist parties, the Comintern quickly became a policy arm of the Soviet party. It was dissolved during World War II to allow Western communist parties to function without the stigma of Moscow's control.

Eugene Dennis (1905–1961): Dennis began his CP career in the 1920s as a labor organizer and then moved to Moscow and international work with the Comintern. In 1938, at the Comintern's request, he returned to the U.S. to become part of the

CP's national leadership. Dennis often positioned himself between the opposing political stances taken by Earl Browder and William Z. Foster. Dennis replaced Browder as CP General Secretary in 1946 and then served as Party Chairman from 1959 until his death in 1961.

W. E. B. Du Bois (1868–1963): By the time Dr. Du Bois joined the CP in 1961, he was this country's leading African American intellectual and a sociologist and historian of worldwide renown. His decision to affiliate with the beleaguered Party at the height of the Cold War served to increase the CP's prestige.

Elizabeth Gurley Flynn (1890–1964): After years as an IWW labor organizer and civil liberties activist, Gurley Flynn joined the CP in 1938. A dynamic speaker, skillful organizer, and down-to-earth writer, Gurley Flynn soon became the Party's highest ranking and best known female member.

William Z. Foster (1881–1961): After participating in various wings of the labor movement, Foster joined the fledgling CP in the early 1920s. He became Party Chairman in 1932 and continued in that role until 1957. Foster was known for his revolutionary or "hard line" positions and for his loyalty to the Soviet Union. His authority rivaled that of Browder and Dennis, the two General Secretaries under whom he served and with whom he often disagreed.

House Un-American Activities Committee (HUAC): Designated a permanent committee of the U.S. House of Representatives in 1946, the House Committee on Un-American Activities quickly became known on the Left as the House Un-American Activities Committee for its blatant disregard of First Amendment rights, lack of legislative function, and persecution of left-wing activists and sympathizers. In 1975, after decades of anti-HUAC organizing by the Left and civil libertarians, a reorganization of the House committee structure provided a convenient way to quietly abolish HUAC.

Industrial Workers of the World (IWW): Founded in 1905 as an alternative to the AFL, which organized only skilled workers and created racially segregated locals, the IWW aimed to build "One Big Union" of skilled and unskilled workers regardless of race or gender. Many CP leaders and members had their first political experience in the IWW. The IWW continues to exist today, headquartered in Chicago. Its members are known as Wobblies.

International Labor Defense (ILD): Founded in 1925 by a disparate grouping of left-wing activists, the ILD provided access to lawyers and organized broad support for arrested union and political activists. Sacco and Vanzetti, Tom Mooney, and the Scottsboro defendants were among those whose cases were taken up by the ILD. Eventually, the CP became the major organizational force in the ILD. After World War II, the ILD's functions were taken over by the Civil Rights Congress.

International Workers Order (IWO): Formed in 1930 as a left-wing breakaway from the Socialist Party's Workmen's Circle, the IWO became the nation's only racially and ethnically integrated fraternal association. It offered low-cost insurance and sponsored recreational and cultural activities in which many CP members participated. Although economically viable, the IWO was forced out of business in 1954 after being cited by the U.S. government as a subversive organization.

Tom Mooney (1892–1942): Jailed for twenty-three years on trumped-up charges that he had bombed a Preparedness Day parade during World War I, socialist and California Federation of Labor organizer Mooney became a national and international labor hero. The CP held numerous rallies and raised money to support efforts to "Free Tom Mooney."

Peekskill: This small town in upstate New York was the scene of a violent confrontation during the summer of 1949, when local mobs attacked people who had come to hear Paul Robeson perform in an outdoor concert. The name "Peekskill" became synonymous with post–World War II repression against the Left.

Popular Front: From the mid-1930s through World War II, communist parties worldwide adopted policies known as the Popular, Peoples', or Democratic Front. (Minor political differences marked each variation.) Officially promulgated by the Comintern in 1935, the Popular Front called for united action across classes and between communist parties and noncommunist organizations to oppose fascism and struggle for the maintenance of basic civil liberties and political rights. Achieving socialism no longer stood as the first task of communist parties. In the United States, the CP's many Popular Front undertakings included a prominent role in building the CIO and the American League against War and Fascism, participation in state and local politics, and stimulating interest in an interpretation of U.S. history that emphasized this nation's revolutionary past.

Paul Robeson (1898–1976): The son of a slave, Paul Robeson became an athlete, lawyer, singer, actor, linguist, and political activist. Although he was not a member of the CP, Robeson's political positions often coincided with the Party's, and he unstintingly offered his prodigious talents in support of left-wing causes. As punishment for his views, the federal government deprived Robeson of his passport, thus severely curtailing his ability to earn a living as a performing artist.

Rosenberg Case: Ethel and Julius Rosenberg were arrested in 1950 and charged with conspiracy to commit espionage. Prosecutorial and judicial misconduct characterized their fourteen-day trial and sentencing during the height of the Cold War. The CP initially remained aloof from the case, but by 1951 national and international organizing had begun in earnest and many CP members and their children participated in marches, petitions, and letter-writing campaigns in support of the Rosenbergs and codefendant Morton Sobell. The June 1953 execution of the Rosenbergs holds a place in the collective memory of the American Left parallel to that of the assassination of John F. Kennedy in mainstream popular memory.

Scottsboro Case: In 1931, nine young Black men were arrested and charged with having raped two white women on an Alabama freight train. The CP-led ILD entered the case after the men had been tried and sentenced to death. Using both legal and political strategies, the ILD brought the case to national and international prominence—and brought the CP to the attention of Black Americans. While several of the defendants served lengthy jail terms, none was executed. CP members and their families who took part in actions to save the defendants at times risked their own personal safety or reputations; participation in the case became a marker of political commitment to build a nonracist society.

Senate Internal Security Subcommittee (SISS): Established in late 1950, SISS functioned as the Senate's counterpart to HUAC. SISS conducted hundreds of investigations, looking at, for example, reports of subversion in the Departments of State and Defense; the operations of educational, youth, and civil rights organizations; and campus organizing in the Sixties. SISS was abolished in 1977, two years after the demise of HUAC.

Smith Act Trials: The 1940 Smith Act made it illegal to teach, advocate, or encourage the forcible overthrow of the U.S. government. When members of the Socialist Workers Party were indicted under the law in 1943 for their criticism of U.S. policies during World War II, the CP did not protest. In the 1950s, hundreds of CP members, including national and state Party leaders, were charged, convicted, and jailed under the same legislation, prompting a national campaign by the Party to keep their leaders out of jail and expose the law's unconstitutionality.

Judy Kaplan, a second-generation red diaper baby, grew up on a chicken farm in Bucks County, Pennsylvania. She lives in the Boston area, where she works as a scientific editor.

Linn Shapiro is a Brooklyn-born red diaper baby. As a historian, she focuses on the politics and culture of the American Left. She also develops humanities-based public programming and works on issues related to human rights in Chile.